Italy
TravelBook

Ninth Edition

Written by Sally Roy
Ninth edition verified by Sally Roy
Series Editor: Sheila Hawkins
Project Editor: Bookwork Creative Associates

Published by AAA Publishing, 1000 AAA Drive, Heathrow, Florida 32746.
The *AAA Italy TravelBook* was created and produced for AAA Publishing by AA Media
Limited, Fanum House, Basing View, Basingstoke, Hampshire, RG21 4EA, UK.

Text © AAA Publishing 2013, 9th edition.

Maps © AA Media Limited 2013.
Maps in this title produced from mapping © MAIRDUMONT/Falk Verlag 2013.
Traffic signs © Crown copyright. Reproduced under the terms of the Open
Government Licence.

ISBN: 978-1-59508-517-7

Cover photos
Main cover photo and spine: Gondolier, Venice, Italy, © Neil Farrin / Jon Arnold
Images / SuperStock.
Back cover: View from the 13th-century Villa Rufolo garden towards the Amalfi Coast,
Italy, © SIME / eStock Photo.

Cataloging-in-Publication Data is on file with the Library of Congress.

Color separations by Digital Department AA Publishing.
Printed in China by C & C Offset Printing Co. Ltd.

A04764

Restaurants line the attractive harbor in upscale Portofino, on the Riviera di Levante

Foreword

Are you searching for the real Italy? This book will help you find it. Our selection of the great cities and the best of the towns and the stunning terrain will give you a taste of this beautiful nation's diversity. Explore the monuments of Rome, Italy's capital; enjoy Florence's unsurpassed works of art; and revel in the unique charm of Venice, a city built on water. Dynamic Milan shows you that it offers more than industry and designer-name shopping. The vibrant southern cities of Naples and Palermo contrast intriguingly with the well-ordered northern centers.

Outside the cities you'll discover a varied and welcoming country, its landscape a natural backdrop for urbanity and culture. Northern Italy butts the ragged peaks of the Alps; the glorious Italian Lakes give way to the dramatic scenery of the Dolomites; and the Apennines – Italy's "backbone" – extend almost the entire length of the peninsula. The coasts are home to bustling seaports such as Genoa and sun-and-sand resorts such as Rimini. And the countryside holds some of Europe's prettiest small towns and villages.

The AAA Italy TravelBook's practical information about these places, including tips on getting around and suggestions for where to stay, will help you plan the details of your trip. We've included maps, descriptions of things to see, and ideas for eating, drinking and shopping. Our suggested walks and drives will give you a different perspective on featured areas. Armed with our insider advice, you'll be on your way to getting the most out of enchanting Italy.

Contents

In southern Italy, Matera's *sassi* (cave houses) are a fascinating sight

Key to symbols
⊞ map page number and coordinates
✉ address
☎ telephone number
⊙ opening times
Ⓢ nearest subway/mainline train station
▤ nearest bus/trolley bus/tram/funicular route
⛴ ferry
🍴 restaurant
⚱ admission charge
ℹ information
For conversion charts, see the inside back cover

Introduction to Italy

Whatever you're looking for – heady days in the great outdoors, beaches to laze on, stunning art and culture, stylish cities or picturesque villages – you'll find it in beautiful Italy (*bell' Italia*). Whether it's your first visit or your fiftieth visit, Italy will meet your expectations and have you sighing for more. Its ever-changing scenery, treasure trove of art, history and culture, and warm-heartedly sincere population who understand the value of enjoyment are the staple backcloth to one of the biggest treats of your life. Their forebears gave us literature, the seeds of our civilized democracies…and the Renaissance. More recently their legacy has been a benchmark for uncompromising style and a cuisine that has taken over the kitchens and tables of the world. And La Musica!

A busy street in Ortigia district, Siracusa, Sicily

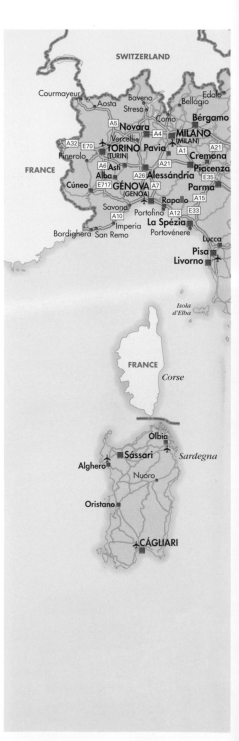

The Shape of the Land

From top to toe, Italy is scenically heart-stopping, with contrasting landscapes of varied beauty. The great Alpine massifs of the north, snow-capped even in summer, give way to mist-laden plains and to a rolling, fertile heartland, the classic landscape of grape and olive, and the dry and desolate beauty of the sun-baked south.

Italy's long coastline snakes around the country, encompassing everything from misty lagoons to pine-clad white cliffs to curving stretches of golden sands, all fringed with azure and turquoise waters. The country is predominantly mountainous, with the northern Alps and Dolomites (Dolomiti) forming a natural barrier with Italy's neighbors.

The long spine of the Apennines (Appennini) runs almost the whole way down the country, in some areas stretching virtually from coast to coast. Throughout Italy, much of this upland area is wooded, with huge tracts of

Above: Marsh gentians growing in the Dolomites
Left: The ferry pulling out of the village of Cannero Riviera, on Lago Maggiore

Sicily and Sardinia to tiny and sometimes uninhabited outcrops.

Climate

Italy's long narrow shape jutting deep into the Mediterranean encourages the perception of a country bathed in perpetual sunshine. However, this couldn't be further from the truth. The orientation of the peninsula and the fact that it is largely mountainous makes for a variety of climatic conditions and temperature differences between the north and south.

Winter brings cold and snow to north and central Italy, but in the south, it's confined to the mountain tops. Sun and showers punctuate spring, until gradually the heat intensifies, the showers dry up and glorious early summer arrives with warm days and cool, restful nights. July and August can usher in stiflingly hot, humid weather and mosquitoes, but the heat is sometimes broken by thunderstorms, accompanied by huge hailstones. This is the time to head for the coast or the

natural forest and great stands of beech, oak and chestnut, which once played a vital part in the economy. The northern plains of the Po river valley are immensely fertile and intensively farmed, as is the rolling, serene countryside of central Italy.

Farther south, there are more mountains. Here the land is harsher, the country less fertile, the climate truly southern Mediterranean. Italy's coastal waters are dotted with islands, ranging in size from true land masses such as

Sunflowers add an eye-catching splash of extra sunshine to fertile countryside

mountains, where the sea is cooling, and the air is fresh and clear.

September heralds a mini-spring, with fresh growth and a flush of fall flowers. In October temperatures drop, more rain falls, and chilling fog descends upon the plains and valleys. By November, in the north, the first snow starts to fall.

The State of the Nation

Italy has a long history, but it's only been a united country since 1870, making it far younger than the United States. The country has been a republic since 1946; the 20 regions enjoy a large degree of self-government, with some, such as Sicily and Sardinia, being semi-autonomous.

Since World War II, Italy has lurched politically through more than 50 governments. The great scandals of the 1980s and 1990s, when the real depths of corruption came into the open, still cause repercussions at every level. Surprisingly, this turmoil had little effect on the economy, which was once one of the most successful in Europe. It's sometimes easy to forget how much has been achieved in just 50 years, as Italy has moved from being a peasant-based,

largely agricultural country to one of the world's leading industrial nations. Early entry into the European Union aided economic development.

There is a very real economic and cultural division in the country. The north is richer, more advanced and more successful than the arid and impoverished south, from which the majority of American Italians emigrated. For the north, foreign markets are closer, the climate is better for agriculture and energy sources, and raw materials are near at hand. Vast sums have been poured into the south during recent years, but the gap remains, with southerners still traveling north to look for work, and northerners still resenting what they see as a drain on their hard work and effort.

Towns and Villages

Italy's history and culture have left a superb legacy. Towns and villages are packed with fine churches, civic buildings and works of art. Every settlement, no matter how large or

Opposite: Looking out over the rooftops of Lucca from the Torre Guinigi

small, retains its central piazza, with churches and municipal buildings grouped around it. Italians have a strong tradition of living in villages and towns. Even in rural areas, the tradition has been to go out from the village to work in the fields. Nevertheless, there's a huge – and historically rooted – gulf between the urban and rural populations, with many farmers still working the land in traditional ways.

The middle class was a late arrival in Italy, only emerging in the decades after World War II and, despite the economic downturn, it continues to grow, though, as throughout Europe, unemployment is rising and disposable incomes shrinking. Earlier affluence led to industrial zones and dismal apartment complexes on the outskirts of countless towns.

The People

Italy's complex history, more a story of a collection of separate states than the history of a nation, has left an indelible mark. Italian statesman Camillo Cavour's famous statement after the 1870 unification, "We have made Italy, now we must make Italians," still holds true. There is no such thing as "an Italian." Ask an Italian where he's from and the answer will never be "from Italy." Italians see themselves as primarily Roman, Sicilian, Tuscan, and so on. Everything about them stems from their native region and its history. So the work-driven Milanese fail to understand the turbulent Neapolitans, and the rational and conservative Tuscans have little in common with the abrasive Romans.

It is precisely these differences that give Italy its appealing diversity, which was strengthened until well into the 20th century by the huge number of regional dialects. With widespread literacy and the growth of television, the Italian language has come to prominence. Modern Italian derives from Tuscan, a medieval dialect used by Dante and Petrarch and based on Latin.

It's a beautiful, elegant, musical and expressive language, which is a joy to listen to even if you don't understand it.

Italian Style

Figuring out what makes Italians tick can only add to the pleasure of your trip to this passionate country. You're bound to have your own ideas on what is typical – peasant farmer, Latin lover, pasta-cooking *mamma* – but beware of stereotypes. For every one that conforms, there's another that proves to be the exception. But a few points may hold true. Italians are incredibly sociable animals who abhor solitude and are happiest doing what everyone else is doing and having fun.

Bella figura – looking good – means a lot, whether it applies to clothes, cars

Women and children parading at the festival of Sant Efisio, which takes place May 1 in Cágliari, Sardinia

or homes. Italians have an innate sense of style and are expert at putting themselves together to the best advantage. Their outlook on life is balanced, with an aptitude for hard work going hand-in-hand with natural spontaneity and a sensuous enjoyment of life's pleasures. Natural kindliness is tempered with a certain detachment; many seemingly deep emotions are fairly superficial. As you travel around, you'll observe these characteristics in everyday Italian life. The tradition of the evening *passeggiata*, when everyone's out strolling on the streets in their fashionable clothes, combines many of these elements; here is the *bella figura*, the chance to be with other people doing the same thing, enjoying one of life's simple pleasures. Watch Italian TV, and you'll see how many truly dreadful game shows there are. The content may be bad, but they're perfect for showing off.

Italians mean well and want to be well thought of; they'll go out of their way to solve small problems, and outbursts of anger are quickly over and forgotten. They make a good deal of noise, but voices are rarely ill-tempered or harsh.

Family Life

Family values are still important – to see them in action, have lunch in any restaurant on a Sunday to observe the 20-strong family groups catching up on the news. Despite having one of the lowest national birth rates in the world, family ties are still very close, with the mother's role being of paramount importance. It's said that the reason behind Italian men's supposedly constant philandering is a desperate search for a woman who will live up to the perfections of *mamma*.

Many parents provide lavishly for their children, who reward them by living at home well into their 30s, then expecting *mamma* and *babbo* to provide the first marital home. Such largesse makes you look good – *bella figura* in action. There's genuine thoughtfulness in the treatment of the very young and very old. Italy is still a country where people value the experiences of older adults. There are few other countries where the coolest teenage boy will go out of his way to admire a baby. Transparent and uncomplicated on many levels, Italians are fundamentally lovable people.

Pleasures and Pastimes

Italians enjoy all the same things that people in developed countries worldwide appreciate, though often with a distinctly Italian twist. Talking, eating and drinking – activities that allow for maximum attention to appearance and involve a group of people – are high on the list. Shopping is very popular, as everyone likes to have the newest styles. Italian men are real "peacocks," and you'll notice that men's stores often outnumber women's stores in the most fashionable areas of town. Both sexes visit their hair stylists regularly; it's an ideal opportunity for more talk.

On the whole, Italians are not big on the great outdoors. Skiing, hiking and sailing are as much about showing off designer outfits as exercising. The top two sports in Italy are soccer and cycling, with the Sunday sports schedules devoted to these two. Following the Italian national soccer team's ignominious exit from the 2010 FIFA World Cup, it went on to achieve a place in the final of the Euro 2012 tournament, which was won by Spain.

Despite 97 percent of the population being baptized Catholic, only about 10 percent attend church regularly, with the figures among young people falling disproportionately. Movies, music and nightclubs attract this age group.

With their innate sense of style, Italians stage excellent exhibitions of every type, so keep an eye open for one that might be of interest.

Passion for Food

Food is a major Italian pleasure. Cooking is immensely varied, with each region, province, town and village having its own specialties and recipes.

Right: Designer shopping in Florence
Below: Italy is renowned for its cooked meats and cheeses, which are on sale everywhere

The town of Orvieto looks out over a fertile landscape from its commanding hilltop position

Dishes are simple and rely on the superb quality of ingredients. Frozen food is available, but menus are still dictated by the seasons, with a rich procession of dishes punctuating the calendar. This makes for great variety, especially if your trip covers several regions. One of Italy's pleasures is the arrival of the "first" – the first Sicilian citrus in the fall, the first *cavolo nero* (black cabbage) from Tuscany and the first raspberries from the cool north.

If you're shopping for food, look for the label *nostrano* on fruit and vegetables, proudly proclaiming they are grown locally. Different regions serve up different types of food, and each thinks its own is best. Northerners fill up on *polenta* (cornmeal) and rice, while southerners couldn't imagine life without the daily mound of pasta. Tuscans eat beans and plain meat. Sicilians love pepper, chili and unusual sweet-and-sour Arab-influenced flavor combinations. Rich cheese and cream appear in mountain recipes, truffles in those from Piedmont (Piemonte) and Umbria. Vegetable sauces, not meat, dominate the *cucina povera* (poor cuisine) of the south. Enjoy it all and

emulate the Italians, who think nothing about taking a drive out to the coast to dine on fish or lobster. Why plan your trip solely around great pictures and historic towns when you could plan it around white truffles, artichokes and red wine?

La Musica

It is generally acknowledged that Italy has always been at the forefront of the development of music but it is not generally known that it was the birthplace of opera. Other countries have since joined the bandwagon to match, and sometimes even better, the Italians. But it was a musician called Claudio Monteverdi (1567–1643) who wrote the first opera, L'Orfeo, in 1607, and his treatment of the legend of Orpheus and the Underworld is still performed regularly. The Italians went wild about it, and to this day have reveled in this form of entertainment. Unlike other Western countries, where classical music is sometimes seen as the exclusive domain of sophisticates, in Italy music and opera are for everyone.

Monteverdi was born in Cremona (see pages 42–43), which became another important milestone in the history of music, as the home of the

The bustling Rialto Bridge in Venice is lined with shops and thronged with visitors

master violin maker Antonio Stradivari (1644–1773), whose Latinized name Stradivarius, or simply "Strad," has become a byword for excellence in violins. Stradivari's life and work are celebrated in Cremona's Museo Stradivariano (see pages 42–43).

Getting Around

Traveling in Italy is relatively easy. The excellent *autostrada* (toll road) network covers the whole country, with the option of driving on good highways if you're not pressed for time and prefer to take a more scenic route. Side roads, particularly in the mountains, can be twisting and steep, and country roads are not always well surfaced. In winter, make cold-weather preparations to your vehicle if you are going to travel in the mountainous regions of the country.

If you're using public transportation, the train system is cheap, punctual and efficient. All towns have a railroad station, but cross-country routes can be slow and complicated. It makes sense to stick to more direct InterCity or Eurostar (ES) services when traveling by train. If you want to get off the beaten track, you'll find even the tiniest places are served by buses.

Driving will be different from back home, but once you're accustomed to the style, you should have no problems. Bear in mind that the speed limits are higher than in the United States, and that Italians tend to drive fast and aggressively but safely.

All major cities have an airport, with frequent flights between cities. Hotel standards vary throughout the country, but all hotels are inspected annually by regional authorities, and, whatever the price range, will be spotlessly clean. Air-conditioning is becoming more widespread but is by no means universal. Buildings can be stifling during summer. By law, heating in some hotels and public places is not turned on until November 1.

Tourism is a major industry here, so English is widely spoken in hotels and

Wooden signs near the Pantheon, Rome

restaurants in principal tourist areas, though hardly at all off the beaten path. Tourist offices and the information they provide vary hugely, ranging from excellent, with up-to-the-minute books and maps in English, to very poor. Do try to speak a few words of Italian; the effect it has is well worth the effort, and it will add a whole new dimension to your visit. Above all, be flexible. Don't be surprised to find transportation schedules that mysteriously change, museums closed when they should be open and major attractions shrouded in scaffolding overnight – this is Italy.

Before You Go

Planning and researching your trip should be fun. There's a wealth of literature on every aspect of Italian life, and you'll get more from your vacation if you do a bit of homework. Think about what you'd like to see and do, try out a few recipes, watch a few movies. Contact tourist boards in the areas you'll be visiting for information on attractions and sights. For some cities, perhaps Rome, think about planning what you want to see in the amount of time you have; planning ahead can ensure that you get the most from your trip.

The Internet

Much information is available on the internet, but the quality of data varies, and some sites are only in Italian. However, it's fun to browse before you go, and the following are informative sites:

■ Official Italian State Tourist Board www.enit.it
■ New York office of the Italian State Tourist Board www.italiantourism.com
■ General information www.travel.it; www.emmeti.it; or www.initaly.com

You can access each region's tourism website by going to www.italia.it and clicking on the regional links at the bottom of the home page.

Timeline

3000–1800 BC	First traces of migratory tribes appear in the peninsula.
700–300 BC	Etruscan federation, centered in present-day Tuscany and Lazio, exists alongside emerging Roman republic.
509 BC	Roman republic established; Etruscan power diminishes.
264–146 BC	Punic Wars against Carthage; Rome emerges as master of the Mediterranean.
AD **200–400**	Decline of the Roman Empire.
550–770	Peninsula fragmented, with different areas under Byzantine, Papal, Lombard and Frankish influence.
800	Charlemagne crowned Holy Roman Emperor. Northern Italy is torn between Pope and emperor for the next 400 years.
circa 1000	Norman invasions in south; Palermo becomes capital of Norman kingdom.
1300–1400	Emergence of the city-states in the north; prosperity is founded on trade and commerce. First stirrings of the Renaissance era.
1442	South unified under Spain and remains in Spanish hands until the 18th century.
1494	French invade the north.
1500–1048	Peninsula is again fragmented under foreign domination.
1848–61	Struggle for unification, led by Giuseppe Mazzini, Camillo Cavour and Giuseppe Garibaldi, with brief republic established in 1848; kingdom of Italy proclaimed in 1861.
1870	Unification completed by the annexation of Rome.
1915–18	Italy sides with Allies during World War I.

The impressive ruins of the arena and arcades inside Rome's famous Colosseum

1921–25	Rise of Benito Mussolini amid postwar social and economic chaos. Mussolini comes to power as dictator.
1929	Mussolini signs Concordat with Vatican, which establishes the Vatican as an autonomous church-state within Italy.
1940	Italy enters World War II on the Axis side.
1943	Fall of Mussolini and armistice with Allies; Germany reinstates him as head of a puppet republic. Allies invade from the south and struggle north.
1944	Rome is liberated.
1945	Mussolini shot and killed near Milan.
1946	The Italian Republic is established.
1957	Treaty of Rome; Italy becomes founding member of the European Community.
1960–85	Period of social and political confusion, inflation and terrorism. Despite this, the population prospers.
1985	Economy steadies, although political confusion and scandal continue. Corruption is rife, but Italy flourishes while a desire for political and institutional reform grows.
1990s	Government drive, led by Giuliano Amato, against the Mafia following the murders of anti-Mafia judges Giovanni Falcone and Paolo Borsellino.
1992–96	Tangentopoli crisis; thousands of political figures are implicated and arrested for bribery and corruption. Public swings against established political parties.
1997	Giulio Andreotti, former prime minister, brought to trial for alleged Mafia connections.
2001	Silvio Berlusconi, prime minister in 1994, is re-elected in May.
2002	The euro becomes the official currency of Italy.
2006	Turin hosts the 2006 Winter Olympic Games.
2008	Media magnate Silvio Berlusconi is elected prime minister for the third time at the age of 71.
2009	An earthquake in Abruzzo devastates the city of L'Aquila and the surrounding countryside.
2011	Europe-wide economic downturn threatened Italy's fiscal stability. Silvio Berlusconi steps down in a welter of scandal and is replaced as prime minister by unelected Mario Monti, an economist and technocrat.

The Normans in Sicily

In AD 827, the Arabs invaded and conquered the island of Sicily, heralding a period of economic growth and political stability. To help maintain their power, the Arabs used mercenaries, frequently Normans from France, who were quick to realize Sicily's rich potential. In 1061, Norman knight Roger de Hauteville became the first Count of Sicily, when he seized Messina, and by 1072, Palermo had become the capital of the Norman Kingdom of Sicily. The kingdom lasted little more than a century, but in that time five kings left a legacy of incomparable art and architecture, while at the same time excelling in administration, religious tolerance and justice. Roger I and his son, Roger II, were among Europe's most successful medieval monarchs, expanding their kingdom to include southern Italy, Malta and parts of north Africa. They were followed by William I, William II and William III; the last was ousted by the Hohenstauffen emperor, Henry VI. The Normans' artistic influence can be seen all over Sicily and the south, while their genetic legacy lingers in redheaded and blonde Sicilians, with straight Norman noses and blue eyes. Even echoes of their language survive in the dialects of remote villages.

Survival Guide

■ Inevitably, Italy's star attractions in Rome, Venice, Florence and other major centers become packed during the summer, as do many coastal resorts. Italians, too, are on vacation. Sightseeing can be exhausting in the heat, and big-city restaurants and shops are often closed while their owners take a break. It makes sense to visit in the spring, late fall or winter, when it's quieter and cooler. May and September are the most popular months in terms of international visitors.

■ One of the chief pleasures of Italy is the *passeggiata* (early evening parade), when the streets are crowded with strolling and chatting locals. It occurs the length and breadth of Italy, in big cities and tiny villages, so be prepared for the streets to become packed for a couple of hours beginning at 6. By 8:30, they'll be deserted.

■ Remember that opening hours, particularly for tourist offices, do fluctuate in Italy. Schedules often depend on the tourist flow; if in doubt, phone before planning your day. Much of Italy closes down from around 12:30 p.m. until 4:30 or 5 while people eat lunch and have a siesta. You'll enjoy your sightseeing more if you do as the locals do and take a midday rest; shops stay open until 8 or 9 in towns and later at beach resorts.

■ Generally, museums and art galleries throughout Italy are closed on Mondays. So if you intend to visit several towns or cities, plan to do your traveling on that day so you don't waste valuable time.

■ Italians spend a great deal of time and effort on their appearance, always showering and changing their outfits for the evening *passeggiata*. They will appreciate it if tourists also make the effort, so try to dress appropriately. Beachwear is not acceptable city wear

in Italy, and you will not be allowed into churches if too much arm or leg skin is showing – this is considered quite disrespectful.

■ Mealtimes are different from those in the United States; it is unusual to eat dinner before 7:30 or 8; lunch starts at 12:30. Some restaurants offer fixed-price menus, but you may want to choose some of the local specialties. Vegetarianism is considered odd, but there are plenty of pasta and side dishes that are suitable for non-meat eaters. Check with the waiter on the ingredients; Italians sometimes think salami, prosciutto and meat stock don't count as meat. Children are welcome in many restaurants.

■ Italians enjoy wine, which they drink at all meals, but the concept of the cocktail hour is alien, as they generally associate alcohol with food. For this reason, if you order a pre-dinner drink in a bar it will always be served with potato chips, nuts or canapés. In Italy, inebriation in public is a serious social taboo.

■ Bars are much more than the name suggests; open from dawn until midnight or later, they offer coffee, tea, soda, snacks, sandwiches and pastries as well as alcohol. They are brightly lit, immaculately clean and efficiently run for speedy service. Italians rarely sit down in bars, and you will be charged extra if you do, as the situation then involves waiter service. All bars have public telephones, restrooms and newspapers, useful for weather maps on the back pages. Smoking is banned in bars, cafés, restaurants and also in many other public places.

■ One of the joys of Italy is shopping in the little local stores, with their wonderful personal service, and at the colorful street markets. Italy has very few department stores except in the cities, and even these bear little resemblance to what you're used to back home. There also are very few shopping malls. Shop and market prices are fixed.

■ If you buy goods to take home, remember to inquire about tax-free shopping. Many stores and outlets offer this, particularly those catering to tourists. If a purchase is a gift, tell the sales person. It will usually be beautifully and artistically wrapped and ribboned.

■ In summer, be sure to drink enough water. With very high temperatures, dry heat and little or poor air-conditioning, it's important to keep your fluid levels high. Caffeinated and alcoholic beverages will further dehydrate you. Drinks in Italy are rarely served with ice; Italians think too much ice is bad for the stomach.

■ Facilities for people with disabilities are improving, but are still not as good as those you would find back home. If you need help, contact local tourist offices.

Night-time in the Campo dei Fiori in Rome, where locals take their evening *passeggiata* (promenade)

Italy

Opposite: A view of the countryside, with San Gimignano and its famous towers in the distance

The Northwest and Emilia-Romagna

Opposite: An Alpine farmstead in Ballino, north of Lago di Garda

The Northwest and Emilia-Romagna

The huge swath of the northwest and Emilia-Romagna sweeps from coast to coast across the top of Italy, a region packed with major cities, historic towns and pretty villages. Its fine landscape encompasses the Alps, sparkling lakes, stunning coastal scenery and the intensive agriculture of the great Po river valley. Prosperous and forward-looking, the entire area gives a taste of the true diversity of modern Italy, where the past has shaped the present against the background of a traditional way of life, and tourism is only a segment of the whole picture.

The Shape of the Land

Much of the northwest is either hilly or mountainous, with the major exception of the Po river valley, a huge, flat and intensively cultivated plain that stretches almost two-thirds of the way across Italy from west of Milan to the Adriatic. The Po valley lies in Lombardy and Emilia-Romagna, Italy's two richest regions.

Lombardy (Lombardia) also boasts the Italian Lakes, celebrated for centuries for their great natural beauty and entrancing mix of water, mountains, woodlands and charming villages. Emilia-Romagna is mainly flat, its fertile farmland giving way to a long stretch of sandy coast on the Adriatic, a favorite destination for families from all over Europe.

In the west lie the regions of Piedmont, (Piemonte) Valle d'Aosta and Liguria, where you'll find some of Italy's most beautiful coastline and mountain scenery. Piedmont is bordered on three sides by the Alps; to the west and south the Maritime Alps straddle the border

with France, and to the north is the Monte Bianco massif. The Western Alps continue south through the Valle d'Aosta and Piedmont. Aosta has deep-cut valleys, rushing torrents and soaring peaks. It has also true areas of wilderness. Liguria, too, has mountains, which run behind the coast from the French border to the region north of Tuscany. The shelter they provide has created a microclimate, where subtropical vegetation flourishes and cold weather is rare.

The Past

The history of this part of Italy is, as all over the country, one of fragmentation until the 19th-century process of unification. During the Middle Ages, the developing cities were largely

independent, Milan being particularly important, while the Renaissance saw ruling families establish influential courts at their power bases in cities such as Mantua and Ferrara. On the west coast, Genoa was one of Europe's great maritime republics, while in Emilia-Romagna, Bologna became home to one of the Continent's oldest and most prestigious universities.

After the French invasions at the end of the 15th century, political power lay for centuries in the hands of outsiders; at various times the Spanish, the French and the Austrians all held Milan, Turin and other major centers. The House of Savoy, which ruled Piedmont, came to be a firm backer of the cause of unification; Victor Emanuel II of Savoy became the first king of a united Italy,

and Turin was the capital for a short time. This background has produced the common Italian tendency to make local rather than regional or national loyalties the strongest. People are passionately proud of their city, town or village, but not necessarily of Italy as a whole.

Modern Prosperity

The northwest, while scenically beautiful, is also work-driven and extremely prosperous, with a much faster pace of life than that in central or southern Italy. Milan is a major industrial and technological center, and has more in common with northern Europe than southern Italy. Turin is a major automobile manufacturing city, the home of motor giants Fiat and

View over Stresa and Lago Maggiore, with the resort of Pallanza in the distance

Lancia. Italy's industrial revolution began in Genoa, which is still Italy's largest port, while Bologna's present-day wealth comes mostly from its computer-associated industries.

Many of the lesser towns, too, have solidly based and thriving industries. Agriculture is still of major importance, with rice, corn and tobacco thriving in the fertile Po river valley, and extensive vineyards in the hillier areas.

Development has brought much new construction in its wake, and you'll find this part of Italy pretty built-up, with many lovely old towns suddenly surrounded by ugly, modern industrial zones and stretches of new housing. The region has rarely been poor or isolated, and this long-established sense of security is evident in the open friendliness and politeness of most of the people.

Exploring the Region

If you're interested in a combination of great scenery, vibrant cities and historic towns, head for the northwest's western section, where there's the bonus of a beautiful coastline. From the foothills of Piedmont there's easy access into the Alpine valleys, and you can hike or drive in clear mountain air surrounded by spectacular views. Lombardy, in the center, has a bit of everything, from the frenetic pace of Milan to the delights of lovely old Bergamo and the violin town of Cremona, while the beauties of lakes Maggiore, Lugano and Como lie within easy reach to the north.

Farther east, in Emilia-Romagna, the flat plains are liberally sprinkled with such historic towns as Ravenna and Ferrara, all packed with artistic treasures. Independent travel is easy in this thoroughly modern region, which has an excellent infrastructure and good roads. A rental car makes sense for your explorations, but if you're spending time in Milan, Turin or Bologna, arrange to pick up your car either before or after your visit; driving and parking can be difficult in each of these cities. It is possible to explore using public transportation, an option that works well if you're concentrating on towns. If you're planning to spend time in the mountains, however, a rental car gives you the chance to explore the area as you please.

When To Go

Spring, early summer and fall, before or after the hordes of European vacationers, are the best times to come. Summer in the Alps is lovely, but you'll be sharing the mountains and hotels with what will seem like half of Europe. September and October, with the spectacular fall foliage at its best, are

Sunflowers are grown for oil throughout Italy

the perfect months. Winter is charming and ideal for skiing enthusiasts. However, the winter season can be long and harsh in the mountains, city pollution is often at its worst, and the plains can be shrouded for days in penetratingly cold mist and fog. The best area to escape to is the western coastal strip, however, the delightful villages here are primarily summer resorts, and winter facilities for visitors are few.

Milan

Noisy, dynamic Milan (Milano) is like no other Italian city. One of the driving forces behind northern Italy's booming economy, it lacks the easy-going charm and relaxed pace you find elsewhere. The atmosphere has far more in common with the countries north of the Alps than with the Italian peninsula.

Seeing the City

Milan is well-endowed with museums, churches and galleries. In addition to the big sights, there are smaller museums and historic churches, large parks and fantastic shopping. Don't neglect areas such as Navigli and Ticinese to the south; these are arty and attractive districts with interesting shops, good bars, clubs and restaurants. They provide fine antidotes to the frenetic city center. Pick up a copy of monthly MilanoMese from the tourist office; it's packed with general information and listings that will help you make the most of your stay.

Getting Around

Milan is a sprawling city, its main streets radiating from the Piazza del Duomo. Most of what you'll want to see lies in a relatively small central area, and you should be able to walk for much of the time. Streets can be packed, so take the subway to a central point near several main sights, then proceed on foot. Or take a city tour; these run daily Tuesday through Sunday, last about three hours and have an English commentary.

Eating

Milan restaurants can be very expensive. But there are more fast-food eateries than in any other Italian city, and plenty of good, moderately priced places. Milan has its own specialties; the best known is probably *cotoletta alla milanese* (similar to wiener schnitzel) and *risotto alla milanese*, a simple, delicious risotto.

Carbohydrates may also come in the form of *polenta*, a type of cornmeal-based porridge. Wine lists in restaurants are often extensive.

Shopping

Fashion and design are Milanese obsessions. Head for the Golden Quadrangle (Quadrilatero d'Oro) where high-fashion boutiques line the streets, and the customers are as eye-catching as the shops. Other expensive shops are in the Galleria Vittorio Emanuele II, while nearby La Rinascente, on the Piazza del Duomo, is a slightly cheaper alternative – a major department store that's a Milan institution. For interesting smaller shops and antiques, head for the Navigli district where there are also discount stores selling designer clothes.

Entertainment

Opera fans will want to attend a performance at Milan's famous opera house, La Scala. There are other places to enjoy classical music around the city, as well as live theater and movies in English. Milan is known as Italy's hippest nightlife center, with a plethora of every type of club as well as jazz and rock concerts.

Parks and Gardens

When it's time to get away from the shops and find a bit of peace, Milan has several parks and gardens where you can do just that. In the old town you can rest up in the Parco Sempione or stretch out on the grass in the Giardini Pubblici (public gardens), or sit by the lake at the Villa Reale gardens.

Essential Information

Tourist Information
Piazza Castello 1 (corner of Via Beltrami)
☎ 02 7740 4343; www.visitamilano.it
Stazione Centrale ☎ 02 7740 4318
City guides bookable through tourist office or contact Travel (☎ 02 7200 1304) who offer tours with English-speaking guides

Urban Transportation
Milan's public transportation (☎ toll-free in Italy 800 808181; www.atm-mi.it) offers a combination of trams, buses and subway. The subway is the most useful, and consists of four lines, the red (MM1), the green (MM2), the yellow (MM3) and the blue Passante Ferroviario, which converge at four main hub stations. Pick up a map at the information offices at the Duomo or Stazione Centrale subway stations. Tickets are valid throughout the different systems; buy them at bars,

tobacco shops or subway stations, singly or in books of 10; 24- and 48-hour tourist tickets also are available; a separate luggage ticket must be purchased for each item. Tickets are valid for 75 minutes and may be used for one subway ride plus unlimited tram and bus rides. Taxis are available throughout the city, or ☎ 02 4040 (Taxi Blu), 02 8585 (Radio Taxi) or 02 6969 (Yellow Taxi).

Airport Information
Milan has two airports: Linate (☎ 02 232323; www.seamilano.eu), 4 miles east of the city center, and Malpensa (☎ 02 232323; www.seamilano.eu), 31 miles northwest. Each handles domestic and international flights, and has a regular bus service to Milan. Bergamo Orio al Serio airport (☎ 035 326 323; www.orioaeroporto.it) is 32 miles northeast of the city center.

Climate – average highs and lows for the month

Jan.	Feb.	Mar.	Apr.	May	Jun.	Jul.	Aug.	Sep.	Oct.	Nov.	Dec.
6°C	8°C	13°C	16°C	21°C	25°C	28°C	27°C	24°C	18°C	11°C	7°C
43°F	46°F	55°F	61°F	70°F	77°F	82°F	81°F	75°F	64°F	52°F	45°F
-4°C	-2°C	-1°C	4°C	10°C	13°C	15°C	15°C	12°C	6°C	0°C	-4°C
26°F	27°F	34°F	40°F	50°F	55°F	59°F	59°F	54°F	43°F	32°F	25°F

Milan Sights

Key to symbols

➕ map coordinates refer to the Milan map on page 32 💷 admission charge: $$$ more than €7, $$ €4–€7, $ less than €4

See page 5 for complete key to symbols

Castello Sforzesco

The Castello Sforzesco (Sforza Castle) is one of Milan's most striking landmarks. The first castle was built by the then-ruling family, the Viscontis, destroyed in 1447 by rebels, and rebuilt by the Visconti successors, the Sforzas. It became one of Europe's most glittering courts, powerful and cultured – Leonardo da Vinci was among the artists patronized by the family. Milan fell to the French in 1499, and the castle was used as barracks until the late 19th century. Today it houses a series of museums, among them the Museo d'Arte Antica (Ancient Art Museum), where you can see Michelangelo's last unfinished *Pietà Rondanini*, and the Pinacoteca del Castello (Castle Art Gallery). The most striking painting here is the bizarre *Primavera* by

The glass-domed Galleria Vittorio Emanuele II

Arcimboldo, a portrait of a woman entirely composed of flowers – 16th-century surrealism at its best.

➕ A3 ✉ Piazza Castello 📷 Castle: 02 8846 3700; Museums: 02 8846 3703; www.milanocastello.it ⏰ Castle: daily 7–7, Apr.–Oct.; 7–6, rest of year. Museums: Tue.–Sun. 9–5:30 🚇 M1 Cairoli, M2 Lanza 💷 Castle free; Museums $

Duomo

The Duomo (Cathedral) is Italy's biggest Gothic building and the third largest church in Europe (after St. Peter's in Rome and Seville Cathedral). Work started in 1386 and finished in 1813. The best way to appreciate the complexity of the spires, sculptures and turrets is by strolling around the roof – with the bonus of city views. Inside, dim light filters in through stained-glass windows to illuminate the soaring marble columns and the crucifix suspended above the high altar, which contains the cathedral's most precious relic, a nail allegedly from Christ's cross.

➕ B2 ✉ Piazza del Duomo 📷 02 7202 3375; www.duomomilano.it ⏰ Duomo: daily 7–7. Museo del Duomo: closed for restoration. Crypt: 9–noon and 2:30–6. Baptistery: 9:30–5:15. Roof: 9 a.m.–10 p.m., late Mar.–late Oct.; 9–4:45, late Oct.–early Feb.; 9–5:45, early Feb.–late Mar. Treasury: Mon.–Fri. 9–1 and 2–6, Sat. 9:30–1:30 and 2–5, Sun. 1:30–4. Yearly closing: Jan. 1st and 6th, Holy Thu., Good Fri., Holy Sat., Easter, Jun. 24th, Aug. 15th, Sep. 8th, Nov. 1st, Mon. and Tue. before Christmas Day, Dec. 25th and 26th 🚇 M1, M3 Duomo 🍴 Bistrot Duomo nearby 💷 Rooftop visits: by stairs $$, by elevator $$$; Treasury $; Baptistery $. For automated ticket system check www.ticketone.it

Galleria Vittorio Emanuele II

An opulent, 19th-century covered shopping gallery, the lofty cruciform structure was designed in 1865 by Giuseppe Mengoni, who was killed in a fall from the roof before the gallery opened. It is constantly busy with shoppers heading for the popular – and very expensive – restaurants and cafés.

➕ B2 ✉ Galleria Vittorio Emanuele II 🍴 Savini, see page 201 🚇 M1, M3 Duomo

Pinacoteca di Brera

Milan's most prestigious art gallery, the Accademia Brera (Brera Academy), houses a huge collection, so concentrate on the highlights or your own interests. The gallery's emphasis is on Italian painting, with the core dating from the Renaissance. Admire the perspective of Mantegna's *Cristo Morto* – a foreshortened view of Christ's dead body from the pierced soles of his feet. It's a fine contrast to the almost contemporary *St. Mark Preaching* by Gentile Bellini, filled with turbaned men and eastern animals. Venetian art is represented by Veronese's *Supper in the House of Simon* and Carpaccio's *Presentation of the Virgin*. The Florentine Piero della Francesca is represented by the Brera's most outstanding work, the austere, balanced and compelling *Madonna with Child, Angels, Saints and Federico da Montefeltro*, all grays and subdued tones with shafts of intense color.

➕ B3 ✉ Via Brera 28 ☎ 02 7226 3264; www.brera.beniculturali.it ⏰ Tue.–Sun. 8:30–7:15 🚇 M2 Lanza, M3 Montenapoleone 💷 $$; $$$ during special exhibitions

Sant'Ambrogio

The lovely Sant'Ambrogio church, founded in the fourth century, is dedicated to St. Ambrose, the city's patron saint. Today's superb Romanesque basilica, reached through the colonnaded quadrangle, dates from the 11th century. The glittering apse mosaics are contemporary, as is the pulpit, carved with ferocious wild animals. St. Ambrose's remains lie buried in the crypt; his fifth-century portrait is in the chapel near the sacristy. There is a small museum in the church.

➕ A2 ✉ Piazza Sant'Ambrogio 15 ☎ 02 8645 0895; www.basilicasantambrogio.it ⏰ Mon.–Sat. 10–noon and 2:30–6, Sun. 3–5 🚇 M2 Sant'Ambrogio

Santa Maria delle Grazie

The refectory (dining hall) attached to the church of Santa Maria delle Grazie draws visitors to see Leonardo da Vinci's masterpiece, *The Last Supper*. Painted between 1495 and 1497, this breathtaking composition captures the moment when Christ announces he will be betrayed by one of his disciples. Despite restorations, the fresco is in a fragile state, its colors faded and much of its detail lost. This is chiefly due to da Vinci's technique; he scorned wet-plaster methods and applied oil and tempera to dry plaster. Within five years the work had started to deteriorate. Matters were not helped by primitive restoration attempts and whitewashing. Most of the building around it was destroyed by a 1943 bomb during World War II.

➕ A2 ✉ Piazza Santa Maria delle Grazie 2 ⏰ Tue.–Sun. 8:15–7 (last admission is 15 minutes before closing). Reservations by phone or online (www.vivaticket.it) are required at least 24 hours in advance (☎ 02 9280 0360; www.grazieop.it). Guided tours in English Tue.–Sun. 9:30 and 3:30 🚇 M1, M2 Cadorna 🚊 Tram 18, 24 💷 $$$ (reduction when purchasing combined ticket with Brera on www.milan-museum.com/booking)

La Scala

From the Galleria Vittorio Emanuele II you emerge on the Piazza della Scala, site of La Scala, Milan's world-famous opera house. First opened in 1778, it has been extensively restored. A museum of opera memorabilia is next door to La Scala (admission includes entry to the auditorium if no rehearsals are taking place). From here, Via Manzoni, one of Milan's most fashionable streets, runs toward the high-class shopping area known as the Quadrilatero d'Oro. It's the site of the Museo Poldi-Pezzoli, a glorious collection of major art works, jewels and sacred jewelry.

➕ B3 ✉ Piazza della Scala ☎ Opera bookings: 02 860 775; www.teatroallascala.org 🚇 M1, M3 Duomo 🍴 Savini, see page 201
Museo Teatrale alla Scala ✉ Piazza della Scala-Largo Ghiringhelli ☎ 02 8879 2473; www.teatroallascala.org ⏰ Daily 9–12:30 and 1:30–5:30; check website 💷 $$
Museo Poldi-Pezzoli ➕ B2 ✉ Via Alessandro Manzoni 12 ☎ 02 794 889; www.museopoldipezzoli.it ⏰ Wed.–Mon. 10–6 🚇 M3 Montenapoleone 💷 $$$

Walk
The Ticinese District

Refer to route marked on city map on page 32

This walk leads you away from the most frequented sights and through the city to the Ticinese district – by day a peaceful area, by night bustling with nightlife.

Take Via Torino out of Piazza del Duomo. At Piazza Santa Maria Beltrade, cross Via Torino and take Via delle Asole on the right to Piazza San Sepolcro.
Behind the church on the piazza, you'll find the Pinacoteca e Biblioteca Ambrosiana (Ambrosian Library and Art Gallery). Commissioned in 1607 by Cardinal Borromeo, this was one of Europe's first public libraries and contains more than 35,000 manuscripts, among them a copy of Virgil once belonging to Petrarch and the Atlantic Codex, a collection of notebooks and drawings by Leonardo da Vinci. The art gallery, too, has some real treasures; look for a cartoon by Raphael for the

School of Athens in the Vatican, and Caravaggio's tactile *Basket of Fruit*, the first Italian still life.

Take Via Zecca Vecchia, turn right onto Via San Maurilio, then left on Via Santa Marta. Follow Via Circo and Via Lanzone to Piazza Sant'Ambrogio, with its wonderful ninth-century church (see page 35). Leave Piazza Sant'Ambrogio on Via San Vittore, then branch left onto Via Olona and left again down Via Edmondo de Amicis. This leads to Corso di Porta Ticinese, and the entrance to the Basilica di San Lorenzo.
This is one of Milan's most important early churches, a central-plan basilica surrounded by three small octagonal chapels. Look for the row of columns outside; these are some of the few reminders of Roman Milan.

Turn right down the Corso di Porta Ticinese to the Piazza Sant'Eustorgio. After visiting thio 12th- to 15th-century church, explore the canal-side areas of Ticinese and Navigli.
The canals and the basin known as the Darsena were part of Milan's port system from the 15th century up to the 1950s. The Corso di Porta Ticinese is packed with offbeat shops, and the surrounding streets are the scene of secondhand and antiques markets on the last Sunday of the month. This is one of Milan's most desirable residential areas, and has some of the city's best restaurants.

The flamboyant facade of Milan's huge cathedral dominates one of the city's busiest squares

A Day in Milan

Most Milanese have daily schedules similar to those of people in the United States and northern Europe – but with an Italian twist. The day starts early, with many workers commuting into the bustling city from the network of suburban subway stations. Many others drive, and the daily struggle to park lends a certain excitement to the day. As all over Italy, breakfast is often eaten in a bar; the time taken by the busy Milanese to drink a cup of coffee and eat a pastry is around five minutes maximum.

The Working Day
Office employees have the same schedules as those in London, Paris or New York. There is no stop for a long lunch and a siesta. People even eat at their desks – which is largely unheard of in the rest of Italy. If people go out for lunch, it will be a quick sandwich from a bar or fast-food counter, unless they are entertaining clients. Most offices work until 6 or 7 p.m.

The Family Day
Many married Milanese women work outside the home; this is a city where equal rights really mean something, and women often hold down key positions. But there are still plenty of homemakers; wives and mothers who spend their mornings cleaning, shopping and preparing a traditional lunch to welcome the kids home from school at 2:30. Italian children have mounds of homework, and mothers often supervise them before chauffeuring the kids to sports events and other extracurricular activities. Dinner is around 8 or 9 p.m. Sunday lunch is the big family event.

The Sybaritic Day
There are many seriously rich people in Milan. They are the patrons of the fashionable art galleries, the exhibitions and the auctions. Women will spend hours at the hairdresser, and shopping is pursued with an obsessive attention to the finest details of personal appearance. Domestic help is common, so wealthy women need not worry about household chores.

The Evening
Milan has a wonderful nightlife, with great restaurants, bars and clubs, and a huge range of cultural events. Young people party during the week, but Friday and Saturday evenings are the traditional nights out.

Outside Italy's world-renowned opera house, La Scala

Regional Sights

> **Key to symbols**
> ➕ map coordinates refer to the region map on
> pages 28–29 💷 admission charge: $$$ more
> than €7, $$ €4–€7, $ less than €4
> See page 5 for complete key to symbols

Alba

Alba is home to two of Italy's most splendid culinary treats: Barolo wine, and truffles, the world's most expensive food. Head for the Via Vittorio Emanuele, Alba's main street. Wonderful shops burst with local products – wine, truffles, cheese, cakes, cookies and mounds of aromatic fungi in the fall. The area's famous white truffles (*tartufi bianci*) are in season during November and December.

Wine is everywhere, and many of the surrounding hilltop villages such as Barolo, Grinzane di Cavour and Annunziata have wineries offering tastings and *vendita diretta* (direct sale). The reds are mainly made from the Nebbiolo grape; the range of flavor and depth is dictated by the soil conditions in the Alba area.

➕ B2
Tourist information 📧 Piazza Risorgimento 2
☎ 0173 35 833, www.langhcrooro.it 🕐 Mon –Fri.
9–6:30, Sat.–Sun. 10–6:30, Apr.–Sep.; Mon.–Fri.
9–6:30, Sat.–Sun. 9–8, Oct. to mid-Nov.; Mon.–Fri. 9–6,
Sat.–Sun. 9:30–6, mid-Nov. to Mar.

Aosta

Heading into Italy through the Alps from France, the scenic Valle d'Aosta leads to Piedmont. This is border country, with Alpine meadows and a chain of castles, where names are both French and Italian and the population is at home with both languages. Aosta, the capital of the region, is a historic town with a wonderfully spacious central piazza and attractive streets. Founded

Snowcapped mountains form the perfect backdrop for Aosta's stone spires

by the Romans in AD 25 as a border camp, it makes an ideal base for exploring the Gran Paradiso (see pages 46–47) and the Mont Blanc areas. The Porta Pretoria dates from Roman times when it was the town's main gateway; there are other Roman remains in the shape of the Arco di Augusto (Augustus' Arch) and the Teatro Romano (Roman Theater). The Cattedrale (Cathedral) has a fine Gothic interior; look for the presbytery floor mosaics and the carved choir stalls. Sant'Orso is another fine church, with 10th-century frescoes hidden up near the roof and a tiny Romanesque cloister.

➕ A3
Tourist information 📧 Piazza Porta Pretoria 3
☎ 0165 236 627; www.regione.vda.it 🕐 Daily 9–8,
mid-Jun. to Sep.; Mon.–Sat. 9–6:30, rest of year
Teatro Romano 📧 Off Via Porta Pretoria 🕐 Daily
9–8, Apr.–Aug.; 9–7, early Mar. and Sep.; 9–6, Feb.
and Oct.; 9–5:30, Nov.–Jan. 💷 Free
Cattedrale 📧 Piazza Giovanni XXIII ☎ 0165 40 251
🕐 Mon.–Sat. 6:30–noon and 2–7:30, Sun. 7–noon and
2–8, Easter–early Sep.; Mon.–Sat. 6:30–noon and 3–7,
Sun. 7–noon and 3–7, rest of year (Museum Sat. and
Sun. 3–5:30, Sep.–Jun.) 💷 Free; Museum $; guided
tour of roof frescoes $$
Sant'Orso 📧 Via Sant'Anselmo ☎ 0165 262 026
🕐 Daily 9:30–12:30 and 2–6, Mar.–Sep.; Mon.–Sat.
10–12:30 and 1:30–5:30, Sun. 10–12:30 and 1:30–6:30,
rest of year; closed during religious services 💷 Free

A peaceful, cobbled street in Arcumeggia, east of Lago Maggiore, renowned for its open-air gallery

Bergamo's lovely Cappella Colleoni, in the heart of the old town

Asti

Asti's "bubbly," Asti Spumante, is enjoyed all over Europe and beyond, and this town is the capital of Italy's sparkling wine industry.

In medieval times it rivaled Milan in importance; today it's a low-key and sedate town with fine towers, churches and palaces along or near the Corso Vittorio Alfieri. The 14th-century Duomo (Cathedral) has a checkered red-and-white facade, but the church of San Pietro in Consavia, with its little 12th-century circular baptistery, is far more alluring. San Secondo, behind Asti's pretty arcaded main Piazza Vittorio Alfieri, was founded in the second century; nothing that old remains, but the delicate crypt dates from the sixth century. Asti bursts into life in September, when its annual Palio is held. This bareback horse race around the Campo del Palio is similar to Siena's, although far less known.

➕ B2

Tourist information ✉ Piazza Vittorio Alfieri 33

☎ 0141 353 034/530 357; www.astiturismo.it or www.terredasti.it ⓒ Mon.–Sat. 9–1 and 2:30–6:30, Sun. 9–1, Apr.–Oct.; Mon.–Sat. 9–1 and 2–6, Sun. 9–1, rest of year ⓘ Palio is held on the third Sun. in Sep.; details from the tourist office

San Pietro in Consavia ✉ Corso Vittorio Alfieri 2 ☎ 0141 353 072 ⓒ Sat. and Sun. 4–7 Ⓦ Baptistery $ or joint ticket with museum $

San Secondo ✉ Off Piazza Vittorio Alfieri ☎ 0141 530 066 ⓒ Mon.–Sat. 7–noon and 3:30–7, Sun. 3:30–7 Ⓦ $

Bergamo

Lovely Bergamo, clinging to the hills above the plain of Lombardy, is divided into two distinct parts, Bergamo Bassa and Bergamo Alta, linked by a funicular railway. Head straight for Bergamo Alta, a beautiful old hill town with gated walls and architectural and artistic delights. The Venetians ruled Bergamo for over 350 years until 1796, leaving a legacy of beautiful buildings and their lion symbol adorning walls and fountains everywhere. The old town centers around the Piazza Vecchia, dominated by the medieval Palazzo dell Ragione (Palace of Reason), a Venetian-Gothic structure. Next to it looms the Torre Civica (Civic Tower); its ancient bell still chimes a 180-peal curfew nightly at 10 p.m. Nearby on the Piazza del Duomo are the Duomo (Cathedral) and Santa Maria Maggiore, a Romanesque church with a gilded baroque interior. Flanking this is the Cappella Colleoni (Colleoni Chapel), designed for Bartolomeo Colleoni, a Venetian mercenary. For views of the town, walk up the hill to the old military stronghold of the Cittadella. Leave time to visit the Accademia Carrara, one of northern Italy's least-known yet most important art galleries. The collection is outstanding, with luminous portraits by Botticelli, soulful virgins by Bellini, and Venetian canal scenes by Canaletto and Guardi. It's under restoration and some of its major works are on display at the Palazzo della Ragione, Piazza Vecchia (tel: 035 399 677 for more information).

+ C3

Tourist information ✉ Via Gombito 13 (Città alta) ☎ 035 242 226; www.turismo.bergamo.it or www.bergamoguide.it ⏱ Daily 9–12:30 and 2–5:30 ✉ Viale Papa Giovanni XXIII 27, Urban Center (Città bassa) ☎ 035 210 204 ⏱ Mon.–Fri. 9–12:30 and 2–5:30

Torre Civica ✉ Piazza Vecchia ☎ 035 247 119 ⏱ Tue.–Sun. 9:30–7 (also Sat. 7 p.m.–9:30 p.m.), Mar.–Oct.; Sat.–Sun. 9:30–4:30, rest of year. Hours may vary 🎫 $

Santa Maria Maggiore ✉ Piazza del Duomo ☎ 035 223 327 ⏱ Daily 9–12:30 and 2:30–6, Apr.–Oct.; Mon.–Fri. 9–12:30 and 2:30–5, Sat. 9–12:30 and 2–6, Sun. 9–12:45 and 3–6, rest of year (closed during services)

Cappella Colleoni ✉ Piazza del Duomo ☎ 0352 210 061 ⏱ Daily 9–12:30 and 2–6:30, Mar.–Oct.; daily 9–12:30 and 2–4:30, rest of year 🎫 Free

Accademia Carrara ✉ Piazza Giacomo Carrara 82 ☎ 035 270 413; www.accademiacarrara.bergamo.it ⏱ Tue.–Fri. and Sun. 10–9, Sat. 10 a.m.–11 p.m., Jun.–Sep.; Tue.–Fri. 9:30–5:30, Sat.–Sun. 10–6, rest of year 🎫 $$

Bologna

Bologna is the capital of Emilia-Romagna. It's an old-brick city known for its wealth, left-wing politics, ancient university and cuisine. Surrounded by sprawling housing and industrial suburbs, the inner historic core is compact, a series of stunning porticoed streets radiating from two main squares, Piazza Maggiore and Piazza del Nettuno. The latter is named after the Neptune Fountain, sculpted by native-born Giambologna in 1556. It's the focal point of the square and its medieval civic buildings, including the Palazzo Comunale and the Palazzo Re Enzo. The nearby Piazza Maggiore is dominated by the church of San Petronio. It houses lovely paintings and an astronomical clock where a shaft of sunlight striking a brass meridian line tells the time.

Bologna's other attractions cluster near the main squares. Head first to the university district, taking in Via Clavatura, with its mouthwatering food shops and market stalls, en route. The

oldest university structure is the Archiginnasio, built in 1565 when the university itself was already several hundred years old. In this quarter, too, you'll find the Due Torri (Two Towers), the only survivors of the many towers that stood in the city in the Middle Ages. You can climb the Torre degli Asinelli to get a good overview of the city.

South from the Archiginnasio stands San Domenico, built in 1251 to house the relics of St. Dominic. These are enclosed in the Arca di San Domenico, a 15th-century sculpture with figures by Pisano and the young Michelangelo.

The Pinacoteca Nazionale (National Art Gallery) has excellent paintings, while the Museo Civico Archeologico (Archeological Museum) features Roman and Etruscan antiquities. For something different, visit the Museo delle Cere Anatomiche, a bizarre and highly idiosyncratic collection of anatomical waxworks used in medical demonstrations at the university until the 19th century. Leave time for wandering the city's arcaded streets and squares, sitting in cafés, window-shopping and enjoying a meal.

+ D1

Tourist information ✉ Palazzo del Podestà, Piazza Maggiore 1/e ☎ 051 239 660; www.bolognawelcome. com ⏱ Daily 9–7 🎫 Note that entry to all state-owned museums in Bologna is free

San Petronio ✉ Piazza Maggiore ☎ 051 231 415 ⏱ Daily 7:45–1:15 and 3–6:30 🎫 Free

Torre degli Asinelli ✉ Piazza di Porta Ravegnana ⏱ Daily 9–6, May–Sep.; 9–5, rest of year 🎫 $

San Domenico ✉ Piazza San Domenico ☎ 051 640 0411 ⏱ Mon.–Fri. 9:30–12:30 and 3:30–6:30, Sat.–Sun. 9:30–12:30 and 3:30–5:30 🎫 Free

Pinacoteca Nazionale ✉ Via delle Belle Arti 56 ☎ 051 420 9411; www.pinacotecabologna. beniculturali.it ⏱ Tue.–Sat. 9–7, Sun. 1:30–7 🎫 $$

Museo Civico Archeologico ✉ Via dell'Archiginnasio 2 ☎ 051 275 7211 ⏱ Tue.–Fri. 9–3, Sat.–Sun. 10–6:30 🎫 $$; free first Sat. of month from 3 p.m.

Museo delle Cere Anatomiche ✉ Via Irnerio 48 ☎ 051 209 1556/1533; www.museocereanatomiche.it ⏱ Mon.–Thu. 9–12:30 and 2–4:30, Fri. 9–12:30 🎫 Free

The Northwest and Emilia-Romagna

Cinque Terre

A string of idyllic coastal villages, crouching beneath precipitous hills running straight into the sea, stretches along the coast of Liguria just north of the port of La Spezia. These are the Cinque Terre, the Five Lands, one of the most alluring clusters of seaside settlements anywhere in the peninsula.

Each village is little more than a picturesque jumble of colorful houses assembled around a tiny fishing harbor – although today the fishing boats share space with expensive and gleaming yachts and pleasure craft. Stony paths, crisscrossing through woods, mountains and coastlines, used to be the only link between the villages. The surrounding steep cliffs, carpeted with flowers in springtime, and planted with olives and grapes, plunge into the crystal-clear sea.

For centuries, the easiest route between the villages was by sea, and you can still take a boat trip; it's a wonderful way to admire the scenery. The railroad arrived in the 19th century and links all the villages; trains run frequently and it's only a few minutes between stops. From north to south, Monterosso is the biggest village, with a good-size beach and accommodations. South lies Vernazza, a huddle of houses with a tiny beach, and then Corniglia, the smallest of the five. Manarola is the pick of the bunch, the quintessential Mediterranean charmer, with a sliver of beach, pretty houses and a busy little harbor. Riomaggiore, the farthest south, is a little larger with an allure all its own.

All the villages have a clutch of romantic waterfront restaurants where you can sample the local white wine produced from the vines clinging to the hills behind.

This coast is the perfect place to relax for a few days, but it's very popular with visitors in summer, so be sure to reserve ahead. You could base yourself in Levanto, a small coastal town lying just to the north. It has a laid-back holiday atmosphere and plenty of accommodations. You can explore the Cinque Terre from there; it's only a few minutes away by train.

Levanto ✛ C1

Tourist information ✉ Via Fegina 38, Monterosso (for the five villages) ☎ 0187 817 506; www.cinqueterre.it or www.parconazionale5terre.it ⏰ Mon.–Sat. 10–1 and 2–6:30, Sun. 10–1

Cremona

Stradivari and his violins draw visitors to Cremona, a prosperous provincial town that once was the home of the great violin maker. Here, in 1566, Andrea Amati established the world's first violin-making workshop, passing his secrets to his son Nicolo and his pupils, Stradivari and Guarneri. There are still more than 80 violin makers and an internationally famous school of violin-making in Cremona. The Piazza del Comune marks the town's center; it's surrounded by the Loggia dei Militi and Palazzo del Comune. You can climb the 13th-century Romanesque Torrazzo in the plaza's northeast corner for great views before visiting the Duomo (Cathedral). Music lovers should first head upstairs in the Palazzo del Comune, where some of Cremona's most treasured violins are kept.

Time also is well spent in the Museo Stradivariano, a museum devoted to violin-making. Before you leave town,

Vernazza, one of the Cinque Terre coastal villages, was founded by the Romans in a sheltered cove

buy some of Cremona's famous *mostarda di frutta*, a deliciously piquant, mustard-enhanced, candied-fruit condiment.

✚ C2

Tourist information ✉ Piazza del Comune 5 ☎ 0372 406 391; www.turismocremona.it ⊙ Mon.–Sat. 9:30–1 and 2–5 (also Sun. and festivals 9:30–1, Jul.–Aug.)

Palazzo del Comune ✉ Piazza del Comune 8 ☎ 0372 407 033 ⊙ Tue.–Sat. 9–6, Sun. 10–6; (Mon. 9–6, Apr.–Jun. and Sep.–Oct.) ✋ $$ ⛽ Guided tours only (in Italian). Short performances using violins from the collection at an extra charge. Reservations required in advance

Museo Stradivariano ✉ Via Ugolani Dati 4 ☎ 0372 407 770 ⊙ Tue.–Sat. 9–6, Sun. 10–6 ✋ $$ (combined ticket with Pinacoteca and Palazzo del Comune)

Ferrara

Ferrara was once a major player on the Renaissance political scene; its court one of the most dynamic in Europe. The rulers were the d'Este family, whose palaces and monuments scatter the city and whose members married into Italy's most powerful ruling families. It was d'Este money that paid for the artistic treasures you see today. Their seat of power was the Castello d'Estense, a bulky, late 14th-century structure worth visiting for the decorated apartments and spooky dungeons. Another d'Este

palace, the Palazzo Schifanoia, has delightful frescoes by Cosimo Tura in the Sala dei Mesi (Room of the Months).

Try to visit the Palazzo Diamanti, the home of the Pinacoteca Nazionale (Art Gallery) and the Duomo (Cathedral), which has a magnificent facade and a museum full of treasures. It is a pleasure to wander the narrow medieval streets around Via delle Volte, which provide a rich contrast to the restrained elegance of the Renaissance palaces.

✚ D2

Tourist information ✉ Castello d'Estense (in the courtyard) ☎ 0532 299 303 or 0532 209 370; www.ferraraterreacqua.it or www.artecultura.fe.it ⊙ Mon.–Sat. 9–1 and 2–5, Sun. 9:30–1 and 2–5

Castello d'Estense ✉ Largo Castello 1 ☎ 0532 299 233; www.castelloestense.it ⊙ Daily 9:30–5:30 (last admission 4:45 p.m.), Mar.–May; Tue.–Sun. 9:30–5:30, rest of year ✋ $$$

Palazzo Schifanoia ✉ Via Scandiana 23 ☎ 0532 244 949 ⊙ Tue.–Sun. 9:30–6 ✋ $$ (combined ticket with Museo della Cattedrale)

Pinacoteca Nazionale ✉ Palazzo Diamanti, Corso Ercole 1 d'Este 21 ☎ 0532 205 844; www.pinacoteca ferrara.it ⊙ Tue.–Sat. 9–2 (also Thu. 2–7), Sun. 9–1 (longer hours during exhibitions) ✋ $$

Duomo and Museo della Cattedrale ✉ Piazza della Cattedrale ☎ Duomo: 0532 207 449; Museum 0532 244 949 ⊙ Duomo: Mon.–Sat. 7:30–noon and 3–6:30, Sun. 7:30–12:30 and 3:30–7:30. Museum: Tue.–Sun. 9–1 and 3–6 ✋ Duomo free; Museum $$

Genova

Genova's (Genoa) greatest days were the Middle Ages, when the city was one of Italy's five maritime republics and had territories stretching from Syria to North Africa. Christopher Columbus was born here. Italy's industrial revolution, based on steel and shipbuilding, began in Genoa, and despite the decline of its industry and docks, it's still the country's main maritime city. The port is the nucleus of the city and is backed by an eclectic quarter of medieval streets.

This confusing city will require perseverance as it sprawls over the coastal hills, with different levels linked by elevators and cog railroads. Don't miss a stroll down Via Garibaldi, an imposing stretch of 16th-century Renaissance palaces. Two now house galleries, the Palazzo Bianco, which displays Italian, Genoese and European masterpieces from the 15th to 18th centuries, including the sensuous *Mars and Venus* by Rubens, and the Palazzo Rosso with its sumptuous interior.

South from here is Genoa's cathedral, San Lorenzo. Up the street lies Piazza Matteotti, the medieval heart of the city. The huge striped building is the Palazzo Ducale, the last in a line of buildings erected for Genoa's ruling Doges from 1384 to 1515.

Streets lead down to the revitalized waterfront, where you can visit the aquarium, take in the fascinating Galata Museo del Mare, the biggest maritime museum in the Mediterranean, housed in the former arsenal buildings, or enter a cabin to ascend architect Renzo Piano's breathtaking crane-like structure, Grande Bigo, with its fabulous port and city views.

✛ B1

Tourist information ✉ Via Garibaldi 12r ☎ 010 557 2903/751; www.turismoinliguria.it ⊕ Daily 9–6:30

Palazzo Bianco ✉ Via Garibaldi 11 ☎ 010 557 2193; www.museidigenova.it ⊕ Tue.–Fri. 9–7, Sat.–Sun. 10–7 🎟 $$$ (combined ticket with Palazzo Rosso)

Palazzo Rosso ✉ Via Garibaldi 18 ☎ 010 557 4972; www.museidigenova.it ⊕ Tue.–Fri. 9–7, Sat.–Sun. 10–7 🎟 $$$

Cattedrale di San Lorenzo ✉ Piazza San Lorenzo ☎ 010 247 1831 ⊕ Daily 7–7. Guided tours Mon.–Sat. 9–11 and 3–5;30, Museum: Mon.–Sat. 9–12 and 3–6 🎟 Free; Museum $$

Aquarium ✉ Ponte Spinola ☎ 010 234 5666 or 010 234 5678; www.acquariodigenova.it ⊕ Mon.–Fri. 9:30–7:30, Sat.–Sun. 9:30–8:30, Jan.–Feb. and Nov.–Dec.; Mon.–Fri. 9–7:30, Sat.–Sun. 8:45–8:30, Mar.–Jun. and Sep.–Oct.; daily 8:30 a.m.–10 p.m., Jul.–Aug.; Easter daily 8:45 a.m.–10 p.m. 🎟 $$$

Galata Museo del Mare ✉ Calata del Mare 1 ☎ 010 234 5655; www.galatamuseodelmare.it ⊕ Tue.–Sun. 10–7:30, Mar.–Oct.; Tue.–Fri. 10–6, Sat.–Sun. 10–7:30, rest of year 🎟 $$$

Colorful houses line the harbor of the great and historic port of Genova

View across Lago di Garda, Italy's largest lake, toward the popular town of Garda

Lago di Garda

The largest of all the Italian Lakes, Lago di Garda (Lake Garda) is a popular year-round destination for visitors from all over Europe and farther afield. The southern end is fringed by gentle hills; the central area is lush with olives, grapes and citrus; and the north is squeezed by craggy mountains.

Northern Riva del Garda is the liveliest resort; it's packed throughout the season. Head down the lake's west side to escape the crowds, perhaps detouring onto the scenic backroads in the hills behind Limone sul Garda before a stop at elegant Gardone Riviera. Heading along the lake's south side you'll come to Sirmione, where there is a beautifully situated castle. To the northeast lies Punta di San Vigilio, with its cypress-filled gardens and white beaches. Farther on, pleasing Malcesine gives access via cable car to the summit of Monte Baldo. In the mountains, there's superb hiking amid carpets of wildflowers. If you've got kids, head for Gardaland, Italy's biggest theme park.

✚ D2

Riva del Garda tourist information ✉ Piazza Donatori di Sangue 1 ☎ 0456 270 384; www.visitgarda.com ⊕ Daily 9–7, May–Sep.; 9–6, rest of year

Gardone Riviera tourist information ✉ Corso Repubblica 8 ☎ 0365 20 347; www.visitgarda.com ⊕ Mon.–Sat. 9–12:30 and 3:30–6:30, Sun. 9–12:30, Jul.–Aug.; Mon.–Sat. 9–12:30 and 3–6, rest of year

Sirmione tourist information ✉ Viale Marconi 2 ☎ 030 916 114; www.visitgarda.com ⊕ Daily 9–12:30 and 3:30–6, Apr.–Oct.; Mon.–Fri. 9–12:30 and 3–6, rest of year

Malcesine tourist information ✉ Via Capitanato del Porto 6–8 ☎ 045 740 0044; www.malcesinepiu.it ⊕ Mon.–Sat. 9–1 and 3–7 (also Sun. 9–1, May–Oct.)

Monte Baldo Cable Car ☎ 045 740 0206; www.funiviamalcesine.com and www.funiviedelbaldo.it ⊕ Every half hour daily 8–7, Apr.–early Sep.; 8–6, early Sep.–early Oct. and Mar.; 8–4:45, early Oct.–Feb. 🎫 $$$ ℹ Expect long lines in summer

Gardaland ✉ Località Ronchi ☎ 045 644 9777; www.gardaland.it ⊕ Daily 10 a.m.–11 p.m., mid-Jun. to mid-Sep.; daily 10–6, Apr. to mid-Jun. and mid- to end Sep.; Sat.–Sun. 10–6, Oct. and Dec.; daily 10–6 Christmas and first week in Jan. Closed Jan.–Mar. 🎫 $$$

Lago Maggiore

When exploring Lago Maggiore (Lake Maggiore) be selective, as some parts are marred by factories and industry. Stresa is an elegant lakeside town; from here you can take a boat to the Isole Borromee (Borromean Islands), an archipelago famed for the baroque gardens on the Isola Bella. Ferries run on to Isola dei Pescatori (Fishermen's Island). Back on the western shore, garden lovers shouldn't miss the gardens at Villa Taranto, created in the 1930s. Cannobio is a charming village that combines a lakeside position with a tangle of stepped alleys.

✚ B3

Stresa tourist information ✉ Piazza Marconi 16 ☎ 0323 30 150; www.illagomaggiore.com ⊕ Daily 10–12:30 and 3–6:30, mid-Mar. to Oct., Mon.–Fri. 10–12:30 and 3–6:30, Sat. 10–12:30, rest of year

Isola Bella tourist information ☎ 0323 30 556 and 0331 931 300; www.borromeoturismo.it ⊕ Daily 9–5:30, mid-Mar. to mid-Oct.

Villa Taranto ✉ Via Vittorio Veneto 111, Pallanza ☎ 0323 556 667; 0323 404 555 (ticket office); www.villataranto.it ⊕ Daily 8:30–6:30, late Mar.–Sep.; 8:30–5, Oct. 🎫 $$$

Mantova

You'll have to penetrate some pretty grim outskirts to reach Mantova's (Mantua's) stunning medieval core, circled by three tranquil lakes, but it's well worth it. The Gonzaga family, another of the great Renaissance dynasties, built the astounding Palazzo Ducale, a huge complex with 500 rooms that was once the largest palace in Europe. A tour here includes the Camera degli Sposi, a room that contains masterful, intimate and tender frescoes by the 15th-century artist Mantegna, showing the Marquis Ludovico Gonzaga with his family and much-loved dog.

Across town lies the family's summer residence, the Palazzo Te, one of the finest Mannerist ensembles anywhere, frescoed throughout by Giulio Romano. This palazzo is a must-see, from the portraits of the Gonzagas' favorite horses to the excesses of the topsy-turvy world of the Sala dei Giganti (Room of the Giants). Elsewhere in town, take a look at Alberti's facade for the church of Sant'Andrea before spending time in the cobbled central Piazza dell'Erbe.

➕ D2

Tourist information ✉ Piazza Andrea Mantegna 6 ☎ 0376 432 432; www.turismo.mantova.it ◷ Daily 9–6, Apr.–Sep.; 9–5, rest of year

Palazzo Ducale ✉ Piazza Sordello 40 ☎ 0376 224 832 or 0376 352 100; www.mantovaducale.it ◷ Tue.–Sun. 8:15–7:15 🎫 $$ ℹ Audio guides available ($)

Palazzo Te ✉ Viale Te 13 ☎ 0376 323 266; www.palazzote.it ◷ Tue.–Sun. 9–6, Mon. 1–6 🎫 $$$

Sant'Andrea ✉ Piazza Mantegna ☎ 0376 328 504 ◷ Daily 8–1 and 3–6 🎫 Free

Modena

Modena is a quintessential northern town – quietly prosperous, its medieval core a delight, its industrial outskirts thriving. Ferrari and Maserati build their cars nearby, and its most famous contemporary citizen was the great tenor Luciano Pavarotti. The historic center is a ring of tight medieval streets around the Piazza Grande. The town's main artistic sight is the 12th-century Duomo (Cathedral), a Romanesque masterpiece with a lurching campanile, the Torre Ghirlandina. The west facade, its portal supported by lions, and the south side have impressive stone relief work, while the serene and lofty interior has more fine wall sculpture.

Modena's museums are housed in the Palazzo dei Musei, a short walk from the cathedral along Via Emilia. The best of these is the Galleria Estense, a pleasing collection amassed by the d'Este family, who left Ferrara (see page 43) for Modena in 1598.

➕ D2

Tourist information ✉ Via Scudari 8 ☎ 059 203 2660 www.comune.modena.it ◷ Mon. 3–6, Tue.–Sat. 9–1 and 3–6, Sun. 9–12:30

Duomo ✉ Corso Duomo ☎ 059 216 078; www.duomodimodena.it ◷ Daily 7–12:30 and 3:30–7 🎫 Free

Galleria Estense ✉ Piazzale Sant'Agostino 5 (off Via Emilia) ☎ 059 439 5711; www.museimodenesi.it ◷ Tue.–Sun. 9:30–7 🎫 $; combined ticket $$

Parco Nazionale del Gran Paradiso

The Parco Nazionale del Gran Paradiso (Gran Paradiso National Park) is a spectacular reserve around the Gran Paradiso massif. It was once a royal hunting area for the Savoys; in 1920 they bequeathed it to the state to become Italy's first national park. The variety of scenery ranges from glaciers and snowy mountains to forests and meadows.

The little town of Cogne makes a good base for great walks, while the high tops are served by cable car. Nearby, at Valnontey, you'll find the Giardino Alpino Paradisia, at its best in June when there are splendid spreads of native Alpine flora. But for the true experience, take to the hills to see chamois, ibex and birds in their natural environment.

➕ A3

Cogne tourist information ✉ Via Bourgeois 34 ☎ 0165 74040; www.regione.vda.it or www.parks.it ◷ Daily 9–7, Jul. to mid-Sep.; 9–1 and 3–6, rest of year

Giardino Alpino Paradisia ✉ Above Valnontey ☎ 0165 74147 🕐 Daily 10–6:30, mid-Jun. to mid-Sep.; 10–5:30, early Jun. and late Sep. (closes for 2 hours each day at lunchtime in May) 🖐 $

Parma

There's much more to Parma than *prosciutto* (Parma ham) and *parmigiano* (parmesan cheese), as you'll soon discover on arrival in this affluent provincial town. Most sights lie east of the Parma river, although music lovers might want to visit Casa Natale di Toscanini (the conductor Toscanini's birthplace) and take a relaxing stroll in the lovely 18th-century gardens of the Parco Ducale across the river. In the old center you'll discover the beautiful 11th-century Lombard-Romanesque Duomo (Cathedral); the interior has works by both Corregio and Parmigianino. The cathedral's 12th-century baptistery, four stories of sculpted pink marble, deserves more than a cursory glance before you head

for the massive Palazzo della Pilotta. Built as a Farnese palace in the 16th century and restored after World War II, it houses the Galleria Nazionale, with a collection of massive Renaissance paintings. Parma also is noted for opera – the Teatro Regio has a reputation that rivals Milan's La Scala.

➕ C2

Tourist information ✉ Via Melloni 1/a ☎ 0521 218 889; www.turismo.parma.it 🕐 Mon. 9–1 and 3–7, Tue.–Sat. 9–7, Sun. 9–1

Casa Natale di Toscanini ✉ Borgo Tanzi 13 ☎ 0521 285 499; www.museotoscanini.it 🕐 Wed.–Sat. 9–1 and 2–6, Sun. 2–6 🖐 $

Duomo and Baptistery ✉ Piazza del Duomo ☎ 0521 235 886 or 0521 235 886 🕐 Duomo: daily 9–12:30 and 3–7. Baptistery: daily 9–12:30 and 3–6:45 🖐 Baptistery $$

Galleria Nazionale ✉ Palazzo della Pilotta 15 ☎ 0521 233 309; www.gallerianazionaleparma.it 🕐 Tue.–Sun. 8:30–1:30 🖐 $$

Teatro Regio ✉ Via Garibaldi 16a ☎ 0521 039 399; www.teatroregioparma.org ℹ Reserve in advance for good seats at the opera.

Delightful old houses reflected in the canal in the beautiful historic city of Mantova

Drive
Mountains and Lakes

Duration: 3.5 to 4 hours

This drive takes you around Lago di Como (Lake Como), the most beautiful of the Italian Lakes.

The route is straightforward, although for some stretches you'll have the option to take either the older, more scenic route along the lakeshore, or the faster route higher up the slopes and through numerous tunnels.

En route you'll have a chance to explore some of the lakeside towns and villages, enjoy some breathtakingly lovely gardens, take steamers up or down the lake, or spend time at one of the beaches along the water's edge. Lake Como's proximity to Milan means huge crowds are the norm on weekends and in July and August, so bear this in mind when planning your trip.

The drive starts in Como, the main town at the lake's southern end.

Como's main industry is silk manufacturing, and the revamped old town center has plenty of outlets where you can buy locally made scarves and fabrics. The town's locale is lovely, but it's always crowded with visitors and the industrial outskirts don't add to its charm, so don't linger – although the cathedral is certainly worth more than just a cursory glance.

Take the SS340 up the west shore of the lake, heading for Argegno.

On the way you'll pass Cernobbio, a pleasant lakeside village that is the starting point for the Via dei Monti Lariani, an 80-mile hiking trail through the mountains. Argegno is a medley of old houses with wooden eaves, steep and narrow streets, and an appealing array of lakeside cafés. Boats run from here to the Isola Comacina, Como's only island, a wild little place that's home to a small colony of artists.

Continue along the SS340 to Tremezzo.

Look for signs to Mezzegra; the Villa Belmonte there was the scene, in 1944, of the execution of Mussolini and his mistress Clara Petacci by partisan leader Walter Audisio.

Elegant Tremezzo has a distinctly fin-de-siècle air. It's worth stopping here to visit the Villa Carlotta, a lavish neoclassic pink-and-white villa built by a Prussian princess and now filled with 18th-century statuary. Its main attractions are the gardens, 14 acres of beautifully tended grounds renowned for camellias and azaleas.

Continue along the lake, passing through bustling and lively Menaggio, with its delightful harbor, to Gravedona, an old lakeside town. At the northern tip of the lake, cross the River Mera, then head down the east fork on the SS36. If time is short, you have the option of taking this higher, faster road or sticking to the old scenic route along the water's edge. Both roads are extremely busy on weekends.

This scenic drive around Lago di Como takes you through the delightful town of Menaggio

Varenna makes a good stop-off along this shore, a pretty place with two more outstanding gardens, Villa Cipressi and the Villa Monastero. South from here you'll be heading down Como's east fork, a fjord-like stretch with granite ridges rising behind the water.

At Lecco pick up the SS583 to Bellagio.

Bellagio has to be one of northern Italy's loveliest towns. Its pretty oleander-planted waterfront, cobbled streets and gracious hotels and villas make it a great place for a stopover.

From Bellagio take the other branch of the SS583, which runs south along the lake's eastern shore back to Como.

Como tourist information
✉ Piazza Cavour 17 ☎ 031 269 712; www.lakecomo.it ⏰ Mon.–Sat. 9–1 and 2:30–6, Sun. 9:30–1,

Jun.–Aug.; Mon.–Sat. 9–1 and 2:30–6, rest of year
Bellagio tourist information ✉ Piazza Mazzini ☎ 031 950 204; www.bellagiolakecomo.com ⏰ Mon.–Sat. 9–noon and 3–6, Sun. 9–noon, Apr.–Oct.; Mon.–Tue. and Thu.–Sat. 9–noon and 3–6, Wed. and Sun. 9–noon, rest of year

Pavia

Only half an hour by train from Milan, Pavia makes a pleasant excursion. It's one of those enjoyable northern towns where you can take a leisurely stroll through narrow streets past towers and piazzas. Its zenith was more than a thousand years ago when it was capital of the kingdom of the Lombards; two major churches, San Pietro in Ciel d'Oro and San Michele, both date from the 11th to 12th centuries.

There's a 14th-century fortress, the Castello Visconteo, which houses the local museum, and a big central square adjacent to the cathedral. Interesting enough, but for a real treat drive the 6 miles to the Certosa di Pavia (Carthusian Monastery), one of Europe's most impressive monasteries. It was built for the Milan Viscontis in the 15th century as a mausoleum and is rich in Renaissance and baroque art. You can tour the church, cloisters and refectory, then stop off and purchase some chartreuse (locally made liqueur) at the monastery shop, still made by the Carthusian monks who live here.

🚩 C2

Tourist information ✉ Palazzo del Broletto, Piazza della Vittoria ☎ 0382 597 001; www.provincia.pv.it ⏰ Mon.–Fri. 9–1 and 2–5, Sat.–Sun. 10–6

Castello Visconteo and Museo Civico ✉ Viale XI Febbraio 35 ☎ 0382 33 853; www.museicivici.pavia.it ⏰ Tue.–Sun. 9–1:30, Jul.–Aug. and Dec.–Jan.; Tue.–Sun. 10–5:50, Sep.–Nov. and Feb.–Jun. 📒 $$

Certosa di Pavia ✉ Certosa di Pavia ☎ 0382 925 613 ⏰ Guided visits only, daily 9–11:30 and 2:30–4:30, Nov.–Feb.; 9:30–11:30 and 2:30–5, Mar. and Oct.; 9:30–11:30 and 2:30–5:30, Apr. and Sep.; 9:30–11:30 and 2:30–6, Jun.–Aug. Contact the Pavia tourist office for further details 📒 Donation

Piacenza

If you enjoy low-key, prosperous small towns, Piacenza, near the Lombardy border, merits a stop. The Roman town marked the end of the Via Emilia, one of the big consular roads, and Piacenza's street plan still adheres to the old Roman grid pattern.

The main square, Piazza dei Cavalli, gets its name from the splendid bronze equestrian statues on either side – they're the work of a pupil of Giambologna and were cast in the 17th century.

The redbrick Palazzo del Comune dates from 1280, the same period as the nearby church of San Francesco. The cathedral is a grand Lombard Romanesque structure dating from the 1220s, much altered over the centuries – the interior is particularly lovely. Piacenza's Musei di Palazzo Farnese (Civic Museum) houses the odd bronze known as the *fegato di Piacenza* (Piacenza liver). This liver-shaped object, covered with inscriptions, dates from Etruscan times and was used to divine the future. The museum building itself was built in the 16th century.

🚩 C2

Tourist information ✉ Cortile Palazzo Gotico ☎ 0523 492 223; www.turismo.provincia.piacenza.it ⏰ Mon.–Sat. 9:30–6, Sun. 9:30–1

Musei di Palazzo Farnese ✉ Piazza della Cittadella 29 ☎ 0523 492 658 ⏰ Tue.–Thu. 9–1, Fri.–Sun. 9–1 and 3–6 📒 $$

Ravenna

The finest Byzantine mosaics in the world (other than Istanbul's) are found in Ravenna, an appealing small town near the Adriatic coast. In AD 402, the Emperor Honorius moved the capital of the rapidly declining Roman Empire to Ravenna, an easily defensible marshland town near the important Roman port of Classis. Until it fell to the Goths in AD 476, it was the imperial capital and continued to thrive under first barbarian and then Byzantine rule.

We owe the wondrous sixth-century churches and their mosaics to the last Romans and the Byzantine rulers, notably Theodoric and Justinian. San Vitale, a typical Byzantine-style basilica richly decorated with glowing mosaics, was begun in AD 525. The mosaics show biblical scenes, while the walls portray the Emperor Justinian and his wife,

Inside the plain exterior of Ravenna's Basilica di San Vitale are some fine Byzantine mosaics

Theodora, an influential figure who had been a prostitute and circus performer. In the basilica grounds is the tiny and jewel-like Mausoleo di Galla Placidia (Tomb of Galla Placidia), whose interior walls glitter with lustrous blue-and-gold mosaics. Nearby there's Ravenna's Museo Nazionale (National Museum), which is worth a quick look. From there head across town to Sant'Apollinare Nuovo, another mosaic-rich sixth-century church. The mosaics here run along each side of the nave, with stately processions of martyrs bearing gifts for Christ and the Blessed Virgin.

On the way to Sant'Apollinare you'll pass through the Piazza del Popolo. En route is Dante's Tomb, a small 18th-century building housing the poet's remains; he died in Ravenna in 1321 after being exiled from his native Florence. The church of Sant'Apollinare in Classe, Ravenna's other Byzantine masterpiece, is just outside the city. Perhaps the most evocative of all Ravenna's churches, its interior is spacious and beautifully proportioned, with glittering gold mosaics.

🚹 E1

Tourist information ✉ Via Salara 8/12 ☎ 0544 35 404; www.turismo.ravenna.it 🕐 Mon.–Sat. 8:30–7, Sun. 10–6, Apr.–Sep., Mon.–Sat. 8:30–6, Sun. 10–4, rest of year

Basilica di San Vitale ✉ Via Benedetto Fiandrini ☎ 0544 541 688 🕐 Daily 9–7, Apr.–Sep.; 9–5, rest of year 🎫 $$$ (combined ticket allows access to Sant' Apollinare Nuovo, Neonian Baptistry and Mausoleum of Galla Placidia)

Mausoleo di Galla Placidia ✉ Via Benedetto Fiandrini ☎ 0544 541 688 🕐 Daily 9–7, Apr.–Sep.; 9–5:30, rest of year 🎫 $$$ (combined ticket with San Vitale)

Museo Nazionale ✉ Via Benedetto Fiandrini ☎ 0544 543 711 🕐 Tue.–Sun. 8:30–7:30 🎫 $$

Sant'Apollinare Nuovo ✉ Via Roma ☎ 0544 541 688 🕐 Daily 9–7, Apr.–Sep.; 9:30–5:30, Oct. and Mar.; 10–5, Nov.–Feb. 🎫 $$$ (combined ticket)

Tomba di Dante ✉ Via D Alighieri 9 ☎ 0544 33 662 🕐 Daily 10–4 🎫 Free

Sant'Apollinare in Classe ✉ Via Romea Sud ☎ 0544 473 569 🕐 Mon.–Sat. 8:30–7:30, Sun. 1–7:30 🎫 $

Rimini

Big, brash and glitzy, with miles of sandy beaches and baking summer sun, Rimini is the archetypal seaside town, a combination of family resort and a buzzing center for the best of European nightclubs. It can be noisy and sleazy, but it's never dull. If you're looking for an Italian taste of the European club scene, this is the place to come. The downside is Rimini's reputation for an active prostitution scene involving all lifestyles.

Rimini, with its satellite resorts, stretches for 12 miles along the coast. The other face of Rimini can be seen inland; here you'll find the Old Town.

Pretty houses in Portofino, one of the Riviera di Levante's most expensive towns

The high spot is the Tempio Malatestiana, designed by the famous Renaissance architect Alberti in 1450 to honor Rimini's ruler, Sigismondo Malatesta. It's an interesting and pleasing building, with an interior housing a Giotto crucifix and a fresco portrait of Sigismondo by Piero della Francesca.

🕀 E1

Tourist information ✉ Piazzale Cesare Battisti 1 ☎ 054 151 331; www.riminiturismo.it ⊕ Mon.–Sat. 8–7:30, Sun. 9–noon, mid-May to mid-Sep.; Mon.–Sat. 9–4, rest of year 🚍 Blue Line bus runs nightly (11 p.m. –4 or 5 a.m.) during the summer between Rimini's clubs **Tempio Malatestiano** ✉ Via IV Novembre 35 ☎ 0541 51 130 ⊕ Mon.–Sat. 8:30–12:30 and 3:30–7, Sun. 9–1 and 3:30–7 🎟 Free

Riviera di Levante

The stretch of coast southeast of Genoa (see page 44) is known as the Riviera di Levante, a chain of fishing villages and resorts backed by mountains and cliffs. The finest section is the Cinque

Terre (see page 42), but if you're looking for an alternative there are several choices.

Down the coast from Genoa is Camogli; its steep streets are lined with colorful houses clustered around a tiny harbor. Rapallo, built in gentle Edwardian times, it's a pleasing mix of elegance and fun, with a lively cultural season in summer. Picturesque Portofino to the south is synonymous with sophisticated dolce vita, a classy and exclusive resort frequented by the rich and famous, with prices to match. For much the same type of village and atmosphere, but less expense, head down the coast to Portovenere, just south of the Cinque Terre. You can explore the coast from here, or take a trip to the lovely island of Palmaria.

🕀 B1

Camogli tourist information ✉ Via XX Settembre 33/r ☎ 0185 771 066; www.turismoinliguria.it ⊕ Mon.– Sat. 9–12:30 and 3:30–6, Sun. 9–1

Rapallo tourist information ✉ Lungomare Vittorio Veneto 7 ☎ 0185 230 346; www.turismoinliguria.it ⊕ Mon.–Sat. 9:30–12:30 and 3–7:30, Sun. 9:30–12:30 and 4:40–7:30, mid-Apr. to Oct.; Mon.–Sat. 9:30–12:30 and 2:30–5:30, rest of year

Portofino tourist information ✉ Via Roma 35 ☎ 0185 269 024; www.turismoinliguria.it ⊕ Daily 10–1 and 2–7, Apr.–Sep.; Tue.–Sun. 10:30–1:30 and 2:30–5:30, Oct.; Tue.–Sun. 10–1 and 1:30–4:30, rest of year

Portovenere tourist information ✉ Piazza Bastreri 7 ☎ 0187 790 691; www.portovenere.it ⊕ Mon.–Sat. 10–noon and 3–7, Sun. 9–noon, Apr.–Sep.

Torino

Capital of Piedmont, Italy's second-richest region, Torino (Turin), on the banks of the Po river, is an industrial city with an elegant baroque center. Its still-discernible French flavor arrived with the ruling house of Savoy in 1574; three centuries later the house teamed up with the Risorgimento's liberal politician, Camillo Cavour, to lend credibility to the unification movement.

In 1860 Turin was the first capital of Italy, and 10 years later its Savoy monarch, Vittorio Emanuele II, became king of the united country. During the 20th century Turin was the headquarters of Fiat, whose owners, the immensely powerful Agnelli family, remain an undisputed force throughout Italy.

The elegant Via Roma bisects the city-center grid plan, and most of what you'll want to see is around here. First stop should be Turin's two main museums, the superb Museo Egizio (Egyptian Museum), the only museum outside Egypt solely dedicated to Egyptian art and culture, and the Galleria Sabauda (Sabauda Gallery), housed in the same building. The Sabauda's artistic base is the Savoy private collections, particularly strong on Dutch and Flemish schools, although you should not miss Pollaiuolo's wonderful Tobias and the Angel, a taut and colorful 15th-century masterpiece.

Nearby, visit the Museo Nazionale del Risorgimento, devoted to Turin's role in unification, with a fascinating section on Garibaldi. Piazza Castello is home to the incredibly opulent Palazzo Reale (Royal Palace), the more restrained Palazzo Madama and the Armeria Reale (Royal Armory), one of the world's great museums of arms and armor.

Off Piazza Castello is the Duomo (Cathedral); its best-known treasure is the Holy Shroud (Sindone). This length of linen contains what many Christians believe to be the imprint of the face and body of Christ. Many people contend the shroud was used to wrap Jesus' body after the crucifixion. Be sure to visit the excellent Museo del Cinema, housed in the Mole Antonelliana, which in the 19th century was one of the world's tallest buildings.

Farther afield is Parco del Valentino, where you can visit the Borgo Medievale, an attractive synthesis of Piedmont's best medieval buildings, constructed in 1884. Continuing along the river, you will find the reopened Museo dell'Automobile (Automobile Museum).

⊕ A2

Tourist information ⊠ Piazza Castello Via Garibaldi ☎ 011 535 181; www.turismotorino.org ⓘ Daily 9–7

Museo Egizio ⊠ Via Accademia delle Scienze 6 ☎ 011 561 7776; www.museoegizio.org ⓘ Tue.–Sat. 8:30–7:30 🎟 $$$

Galleria Sabauda ⊠ Via Accademia delle Scienze 6 ☎ 011 564 1749 ⓘ Tue.–Sun. 8:30–7:30 🎟 $$

Museo Nazionale del Risorgimento ⊠ Via Accademia delle Scienze 5 ☎ 011 562 1147 ⓘ Tue.–Sun. 9–7

Armeria Reale ⊠ Piazza Castello 191 ☎ 011 543 889 ⓘ Tue.–Sun. 8:30–7:30 🎟 $$$

Duomo ⊠ Via XX Settembre ☎ 011 4636 1540 ⓘ Daily 7–12:30 and 3–7 🎟 Free

Museo del Cinema ⊠ Via Montebello 20 ☎ 011 813 8560; www.museonazionaledelcinema.it ⓘ Tue.–Fri. 9–8, Sat. 9 a.m.–11 p.m., Sun. 9–8 🎟 $$$

Borgo Medievale ⊠ Parco del Valentino, Viale Virgilio 107 ☎ 011 443 1701/02; www.borgomedievaletorino. it ⓘ Borgo: daily 9–8, Apr.–Sep.; 9–7, rest of year. Castle: Tue.–Sun. 10–6 🎟 Borgo free; Castle $$

Museo dell'Automobile ⊠ Corso Unità d'Italia 40 ☎ 011 677 666/7/8; www.museoauto.it ⓘ Mon. 10–2, Tue.–Thu. and Sun. 2–7, Fri.–Sat. 10–9 🎟 $$$

Portovenere's waterfront, with its tall pastel-painted houses and cobbled streets

A Taste of the North

In the prosperous regions of northern Italy, you'll find some of the country's best cooking. It features a rich cuisine based on fresh ingredients of superb quality and a range of local specialties. Many of these are either imported or imitated in the United States, but make a point of sampling them on their home ground, where cheese is made from unpasteurized milk, and hams, wild mushrooms and wine have had to travel only a few miles from their point of origin. You'll taste the difference.

Valle d'Aosta and Piedmont

These regions display close links with France, and there are French tones in the local food. Butter, cream and cheese are freely used, and you should try *fonduta,* a melted cheese dish similar to fondue. Piedmont's prize food is the white truffle, in season in the fall from the hills around Alba (see page 39). With an intensity of flavor impossible to describe, this is one extravagance you should indulge in for a once-in-a-lifetime experience. Wild mushrooms are less expensive and another culinary treat; the best variety is *porcini* (or ceps), a meaty-textured and robustly flavored woodland giant often served grilled. The full-bodied wines from the region, such as the fabulous Barolo and Barbaresco, could have been invented as an accompaniment. They go equally well with roasted sweet chestnuts. Much sparkling wine is made in Asti (see page 40), while worldwide favorite vermouths are made near Turin and Barolo. The vines that produce the prized Nebbiolo grapes used in Barolo wines are grown in the Langhe hills, southwest of Turin. The Museo del Barolo (www. wimubarolo.it), which opened in 2010 in the Castello Falletti in Barolo, is dedicated to one of the world's most famous wines.

Lombardy

Piedmont's neighbor, Lombardy, has its own gifts. This is a region where the staple is either rice or *polenta*, as well as pasta. *Polenta* is cornmeal,

which can be served hot (wet *polenta*) or cooled, cut into slices, then grilled or fried. This versatile staple food of the north goes well with richly flavored ingredients such as cheese, mushrooms and pungent meats. Rice (mainly the firm and plump-grained *arborio,* ideal for risotto) is grown in the Ticino area. The classic risotto is the *risotto alla Milanese,* which uses veal juices, saffron, butter, white wine, onions and Parmesan. Milan was the birthplace of *osso buco,* a slow-cooked dish of veal shanks.

Lombardy, one of Italy's biggest cheese-making regions, is the home of *gorgonzola, mascarpone* and *Bel Paese.* If you've enjoyed a vanilla-scented *panettone* cake at Christmas, remember that this also originates in Milan.

Liguria
With Liguria's long shoreline, fish is inevitably a treat, and is found on menus everywhere. The most wonderful local ingredient has to be basil, and you may be lucky enough to see – and smell – a whole field of this heavenly herb as you travel in Liguria. It's used to make the ubiquitous *pesto* and many other dishes. The aroma is complemented by wines from the Cinque Terre (see page 42). Dry and clean-tasting, the wines have a light and flinty bouquet that goes well with the local *focaccia.*

Emilia-Romagna
Across the country in Emilia-Romagna there's more rich, smooth cooking. Many Italians freely admit that you eat better here than almost anywhere else in Italy (except their own region, of course). Parma is in this region and is the home of *prosciutto di Parma* (Parma ham) and *parmigiano* (parmesan cheese). Most local products live up to these two culinary superstars, in quality and flavor. Balsamic vinegar is produced in the region; buy a precious bottle to bring life to your cooking, as just a few drops will go a long way. Pasta, usually made with eggs and stuffed with meat, cheese and herb combinations, is enjoyed here.

Above left to right: *Pesto alla genovese* (basil pesto); Italian cheeses

The Northeast

Opposite: The Grand Canal, lined with superb buildings, is Venice's main highway

The Northeast

Many visitors to Italy's northeast never discover the immense variety of this diverse region, bordered by Switzerland, Austria and Slovenia. Made up of the Veneto, Trentino-Alto Adige and Friuli-Venezia Giulia, the area contains some of Europe's finest mountain scenery, prime agricultural country and a clutch of the country's most alluring towns, including Padova (Padua), Verona and Vicenza. Add to this the economic prosperity brought by the region's industry and a long tradition of farming and wine-making, and the attractions of this tucked-away corner of Italy become clear.

Shaping of the Northeast

The region of the Veneto forms this area's core; this was the heartland of independent Venice, the mainland territories ruled by the Venetian Republic from the 14th to the 18th centuries. Historically settled and prosperous, the Veneto is very much a part of mainstream Italy.

North of the Veneto, the situation changes in Trentino-Alto Adige, a multicultured hybrid of a region made up of Italian-speaking, mainly rural Trentino, and the German-speaking Alto Adige, also known as Südtirol (or South Tyrol). The Alto Adige was ceded to Italy at the end of World War I, having previously been part of the Austro-Hungarian Empire. Ethnic differences here have caused tension and an undercurrent of terrorism over

the years, but a large measure of autonomy has, on the whole, kept the lid on nationalist ambitions.

Friuli-Venezia Giulia borders Austria and Slovenia. This area has quite a mixture of cultures, languages and allegiances. It straddles the hazy bridge between the Mediterranean world and that of Teutonic and Slavic central Europe. Becoming part of Italy after World War I, its final border disputes with the then Yugoslavia were not settled until the 1970s.

The Northeast Today

Although industrialization has marred some of the region's scenic beauty, it has also brought prosperity. The flat coastal plains are scattered with light industry and modern housing. The vast industrial complex around Marghera is best avoided, however. But agriculture is still vital, with arable farming in the lowlands and extensive wine-producing areas in the lower hills.

Tourism is important throughout this region; apart from Venice itself, Verona and Padua draw the crowds, while the mountain splendor of the Dolomites lures skiing and hiking enthusiasts year-round.

On the whole, vacationers here are Italian, and outside Venice you won't encounter the vast numbers of visitors found in other regions. You'll notice more than a touch of Teutonic efficiency in some parts, while the general affluence is striking. Well-dressed people, chic shops and expensive cars catch the eye. There's a good balance between traditional ways and the 21st century, making this corner a real Italian mircocosm.

European Influences

Throughout the Veneto, people are polite, friendly, efficient and hard-working, but without the relentless drive of their neighbors nearer Milan. Like all Italians, they live life to the fullest in a less dramatic and passionate way than

so evident farther south. Accustomed to dealing with international visitors, they know what people expect in the way of facilities.

In the service industries, you'll find English widely spoken. In the main towns and cities the siesta is not as important, which means longer hours for museums and churches.

In Trentino-Alto Adige, you'll immediately notice the Teutonic influences. Trentino is mostly Italian speaking, but Alto Adige is bilingual, with German the dominant language in many places. Teutonic order reigns and mixes delightfully with typical Italian pleasures. Cuisine pays homage to its northern roots, with dumplings and sauerkraut, wiener schnitzel and apple strudel often on the menu.

View of the Basilica di San Marco, in Venice, from the Campanile

Scenic grandeur surrounds many of the upland villages in Italy's Dolomite Mountains

Similar culinary links exist in Friuli-Venezia Giulia, but here the accent is middle European with a strong café culture, cream cakes, goulash and more dumplings. Friuli-Venezia is more ethnically jumbled, comprising a mix of Italian, Slavic and middle European cultures. You'll see evidence of this in the bilingual street signs throughout the region; the dialect here is friulano.

Appreciating the Northeast

Venice is one of the world's most enticing cities, but there's much more to the area. If you make the trip this far north, take time to explore. You should see Verona, as beautiful now as when

Shakespeare set Romeo and Juliet there, while Vicenza, with its tight-knit center and Palladian architecture, should also be high on your list. Padua, although less immediately appealing, has unrivaled artistic treasures. These three can be tackled individually as day trips from Venice, but each deserves an overnight stay to be appreciated fully.

In Trentino-Alto Adige, Bolzano and Merano have great charm, but the real attraction is the Dolomites. These magnificent mountains can be enjoyed by rail or car, but to appreciate them at their best you should try to fit in some skiing or hiking. Farther east, the scenery of Friuli-Venezia Giulia offers

immense variety, from the Alps and the limestone plateau known as the Carso to alluvial plains and stretches of varied coastline.

Trieste has an atmosphere all of its own, while the charms of Cividale dei Friuli and Aquileia are on a par with much better-known areas. Getting around is easy, with good roads, public transportation and plenty of accommodations. To get the most out of a Dolomite trip, rent a car (if you're a nervous driver, however, avoid the dramatic mountain roads).

When To Go

If you enjoy winter sports, you could combine an action-packed skiing trip with a cultural visit to Venice; December and January, when the city is virtually empty of tourists, are the best times to visit. The weather then can be sparklingly clear and bitterly cold or romantically mist-shrouded. If seeing Venice in sunshine is your preference, wait until late spring; May and June are the optimum months for a sunny visit. This also is a splendid time for going to the mountains, when the snows are retreating and the Alpine meadows are coming alive with wildflowers. It's best to avoid the cities during the peak summer months (July and August), when the large crowds and the oppressive heat can make sightseeing rather an unpleasant experience.

Venice

Venice (Venezia) never fails to enchant. Familiar from a thousand pictures, the magical blend of stone and water, with all of its accompanying sounds and scents, will be a highlight of your Italian experience. It may be crowded and expensive, crumbling and shabby, but this treasure-packed city will win your heart. It's a dream waiting to come true.

Picturesque Surroundings

If money is no object, the optimum place to stay is one of the luxury hotels along the Grand Canal, but there are many other options, often in quieter but just as picturesque surroundings.

The *sestieri* (city areas) of Dorsoduro, San Marco, Castello and San Polo are perhaps the nicest parts. Avoid the area around the railroad station where it is less pleasant, although there are plenty of accommodations here for late arrivals. Don't stay in Mestre, a polluted industrial sprawl across the causeway.

Take time daily to work out your itinerary; Venice can be slow to move around in, and shortcuts through the maze of streets will save valuable time. You'll be doing a huge amount of walking as you negotiate the bridges; come prepared with comfortable, well broken-in shoes. Main through-city routes are designated by yellow signs

above head height. The tourist office publishes a bilingual monthly guide to Venice, *Un Ospite di Venezia* (Venetian Guest), which has everything you'll need to know to make the most of your trip.
Try to allow three to four days at least to see Venice; there are enough sights to keep you busy for months. Start by getting a feel for the place before venturing into the crowded visitor areas. A good way to ease yourself in is by taking a *vaporetto* boat; numbers 1 or 2 down the Grand Canal or routes 41, 42, 51 or 52 around the the city are all good bets. Take a boat trip to some of the lagoon islands; public transportation is more fun than a tour. Or simply wander around.

Gondolas
The elegant gondola is a shallow-draft vessel propelled by a single oarsman standing at the back of the boat. Their shape and depth make them ideal for penetrating even the narrowest and shallowest canals. A ride in a shiny-black gondola is an essential experience for many visitors, however, they are very expensive and normally follow a set route.

Dining Out
Typical Venetian starters include delicate plates of mixed seafood and *sarde in saor*, sardines cooked with vinegar, and pasta dishes range from *spaghetti alle vongole* (with clams) to various rice dishes. Venetians eat a lot of fish but some can be expensive, and you often pay for the weight of your portion. Liver and onions (*fegato alla veneziana*) is another local dish.
Tiramisù, now found everywhere, is a Venetian dessert. Made from coffee-soaked sponge cake and sweetened *mascarpone* cheese, its name means "pick-me-up." Most wine comes from the Veneto region on the mainland; wines to look for include Soave, Valpolicella, Bardolino and the excellent Bianco di Custoza. Be sure to try a glass of dry sparkling *prosecco* as an aperitif; mixed with fresh peach juice, it becomes a Bellini. An essential city experience is relaxing over a drink at Florian or Quadri, Venice's most stylish cafés, situated on either side of bustling Piazza San Marco.

Venetian Craftware
The main stores are clustered along the Calle dei Fabbri, the Frezzeria and the so-called Merceria, a network of streets connecting Piazza San Marco with the Rialto. Here the best of the Murano glass manufacturers have their showrooms. Artisan shops selling imaginative craftware are found in the oddest corners, while another temptation comes

in the shape of stunning silk and velvet fabrics, and beautiful lace from Burano. Marbled paper and exotic papier-mâché masks make good souvenirs and you can even buy a gondolier's shirt or hat.

Entertainment

Carnival, when thousands of people wearing costumes and elaborate masks parade through the streets, lasts for 10 days before the start of Lent. The main summer festival is the feast of *La Sensa*, when the mayor and his entourage sail out in the state barge and enact a symbolic marriage to the waters. This is followed in July by the *Festa del Redentore*, a festival of thanksgiving for deliverance from a plague. A pontoon bridge is built across the Giudecca canal to the Redentore church, and the feast culminates in a spectacular fireworks display. During the *Regata Storica* in September, there are races of decorated craft manned by crews in period dress. Year-round entertainment includes classical concerts, theater, soccer games and the casino. *Un Ospite di Venezia* has full listings of what's going on.

Essential Information

Tourist Information

San Marco 71/f ☎ 041 529 8711 (for all tourist offices); www.hellovenezia.com
Aeroporto Marco Polo
Palazzina del Santi, Giardini ex Reali
Stazione Santa Lucia and Piazzale Roma
Viale Santa Maria Elisabetta 6/a, Lido di Venezia (Jun.–Sep. only)

Urban Transportation

If you arrive by car, you must leave it in one of the parking lots on the outskirts. Venice's public transportation system is operated by ACTV (☎ 041 2424; www.actv.it) and uses two types of boats, *vaporetti* (bigger and slower) and *motoscafi* (smaller and faster). All boats are numbered and follow set routes that frequently change. *Vaporetti* leave from docks that are clearly marked with the service numbers. As the same numbers sometimes go in two directions, ascertain which way you're heading before boarding. Tickets can be bought at the dock or at shops showing the ACTV sticker. Save money by buying an hourly, 24- or 72-hour pass, or a 7-day ticket. All tickets must be validated at the machine on the dock before boarding. ACTV publishes two booklets, one showing routes, the other timetables. Water taxis are fast and expensive. They can be hailed, but it is easier to phone (☎ 041 522 2303; www.motoscafivenezia.it). Gondolas are a fun way to travel but are very expensive. The seven *traghetti* (ferries) crossing the Grand Canal at various points are also useful. Pay as you board.

Airport Information

Venice's Marco Polo Airport (☎ 041 260 9260; www.veniceairport.it), on the northern edge of the lagoon, handles domestic and international flights. For city connections, take a bus or taxi from outside the terminal to Piazzale Roma, then connect with your hotel by *vaporetto*. Buy tickets from the office inside the terminal before boarding. Alilaguna (☎ 041 240 1701; www.alilaguna.it) runs a boat service from the airport to the city center. It leaves from outside the terminal. The Blu (blue) and Arancio (orange) services run directly to San Marco. The fastest way to the city is by water taxi from outside the terminal (around 20 minutes).

Climate – average highs and lows for the month

Jan.	Feb.	Mar.	Apr.	May	Jun.	Jul.	Aug.	Sep.	Oct.	Nov.	Dec.
5°C	8°C	12°C	17°C	21°C	24°C	27°C	26°C	23°C	18°C	12°C	8°C
41°F	46°F	54°F	63°F	70°F	75°F	81°F	79°F	73°F	64°F	54°F	46°F
0°C	2°C	5°C	9°C	13°C	17°C	19°C	18°C	16°C	12°C	7°C	3°C
32°F	36°F	41°F	48°F	55°F	63°F	66°F	64°F	61°F	54°F	45°F	37°F

Venice Sights

> **Key to symbols**
> ➕ map coordinates refer to the Venice map on pages 62–63   🚤 nearest boat or ferry stop
> 💷 admission charge: $$$ more than €7,
> $$ €4–€7, $ less than €4
> See page 5 for complete key to symbols

Basilica di San Marco

Venice's cathedral, the Basilica di San Marco (St. Mark's Basilica), was built in 1094 on the site of the ninth-century basilica that reputedly houses the body of St. Mark, Venice's patron saint. Its profusion of domes and sculptures, mosaics and marbles, and a superb fusion of Byzantine, Islamic and Western art and architecture, make it one of Europe's most exotic cathedrals. Allow time to study the mosaics above the marble floors, and to admire the Romanesque carvings around the main door. Don't miss the gold altar panel, the Pala d'Oro, encrusted with jewels and precious enamels, or the four gilded bronze horses possibly dating from the fourth century BC and stolen by the Venetians from Constantinople in 1204.
➕ D2   ✉ Piazza San Marco 1   ☎ 041 270 8311; www.basilicasanmarco.it 🕐 Mon.–Sat. 9:45–5:30, Sun. 2–4, Easter–Oct.; Mon.–Sat. 9:45–4:30, Sun. 2–5, rest of year   🚤 1, 41, 42, 51, 52, 2 (San Zaccaria)
💷 Free; Pala d'Oro $

Ca' d'Oro

The beautiful 15th-century Venetian-Gothic Ca' d'Oro (Golden House) got its name from the gilding that once covered its elaborate waterfront facade. Behind the facade it houses a small art gallery set around the central portego and inner courtyard. Showpieces include Andrea Mantegna's *Saint Sebastian* and Vivarini's polyptych of The Passion. There also are lesser works by Titian, Giorgione and Tintoretto, and some lovely sculpture fragments, bronzes and tapestries.
➕ C3   ✉ Calle di Ca' d'Oro 3932, off Strada Nova
☎ 041 520 0345; www.polomuseale.venezia.

beniculturali.it 🕐 Mon. 8:15–2, Tue.–Sun. 8:15–7:15
🚤 1 (Ca' d'Oro)   💷 $$$

Campanile

Venice's original campanile was reputedly built in AD 902; this graceful edifice collapsed in July 1902, killing no one and leaving St. Mark's untouched. The Venetians vowed to rebuild it, *"Dov'era e com'era"* – "Where it was and like it was" – and 10 years later a perfect replica was complete. It's worth the elevator ride to the top for superb views of the city and as far away as the Alps. Take a look at the instruments that record temperature, tides, wind, moon phases and much more.
➕ D2   ✉ Piazza San Marco   ☎ 041 522 4064
🕐 Daily 9–7, Easter–Jun.; 9–9, Jul.–Sep.; 9:30–4:15, rest of year; closed 3 weeks in Jan.   🚤 1, 2, 41, 42, 51, 52, N (San Marco)   💷 $$$

Canal Grande

The Canal Grande (Grand Canal), an enchanting stretch of water crossed by four bridges and lined with a magical parade of palaces, divides Venice. By day it's traversed by *vaporetti*, tugboats and gondolas and photographed by hordes of visitors. The morning light imbues it with magic, while darkness adds its own enchantment. For the trip of a lifetime, take a number 1 or 2 boat from the train station, sit back and enjoy.
➕ A3–B3–C3–C2–B2–B1–C1   🚤 1, 2, N

Enjoy the sights by taking a trip on the Grand Canal

Collezione Peggy Guggenheim

An 18th-century palace on the Grand Canal is home to the modern art collection amassed by American millionaire Peggy Guggenheim. There are exciting works by Magritte and Picasso, while Jackson Pollock and Joseph Cornell represent American artists. The lovely garden is the perfect backdrop for Marino Marini's disturbing *Angel of the Citadel* and some striking sculpture by Henry Moore.

✚ C1 ✉ Palazzo Venier dei Leoni, Calle San Cristoforo, Dorsoduro 704 ☎ 041 240 5411; www.guggenheim-venice.it ⊙ Wed.–Mon. 10–6 🚤 1 (Salute), 2 (Accademia) 🎫 $$$

Gallerie dell'Accademia

The Gallerie dell'Accademia (Academy Gallery) is Venice's greatest art gallery, a true must-see. Arranged chronologically, the gallery's 24 rooms will introduce you to some spectacular

Looking down the Scala d'Oro (Golden Stairway) inside the Palazzo Ducale

works including Bellini's luminescent *Virgins*, Giorgione's enigmatic *Tempest* and the dizzying perspective of Tintoretto's *Translation of the Body of St. Mark.* Don't miss Veronese's sumptuous *Feast in the House of Levi* or the two lively and colorful narrative painting cycles by Carpaccio and other artists, the *Miracle of the True Cross* and the *Life of St. Ursula.* There's also one work by Canaletto.

✚ B1 ✉ Campo della Carità 1050 ☎ 041 522 2247; reservations 041 520 0345; www.polomuseale.venezia. beniculturali.it ⊙ Tue.–Sun. 8:15–7:15, Mon. 8:15–2 🚤 1 (Accademia) 🎫 $$ ℹ An audio guide of the gallery's highlights is available in English

Palazzo Ducale

Tackle the huge Gothic complex of the Palazzo Ducale (Ducal Palace) when you're fresh, for this is triumphalism on the grandest scale. Each reception and council room outdoes the one before in size, scale and splendor. The palace was the seat of Venetian government, where the Doge lived and held state, the council met, ambassadors were received and prisoners incarcerated.

The present building dates largely from the 15th century, with alterations made after two 16th-century fires. Follow the marked route through the building. It leads through lavish rooms culminating in the Sala del Maggior Consiglio (Great Council Chamber), dominated by Tintoretto's *Paradiso*, the world's largest painting. Don't miss the prison building, reached by crossing over the famous Bridge of Sighs, which spans a canal to the right of the Palazzo's facade.

✚ D2 ✉ Piazzetta San Marco 30124 ☎ 041 271 5911; www.visitmuve.it ⊙ Daily 9–7 (last admission 6 p.m.), Apr.–Oct.; 8:30–5:30 (last admission 4 p.m.), rest of year. Guided tours morning only 🚤 1, 41, 42, 51, 52, 2 (San Zaccaria) 🎫 $$$ ℹ An audio guide in English is available from the front desk

Piazza San Marco

Napoleon called the Piazza San Marco (St. Mark's Square) "Europe's largest drawing room," and this wonderful open

Revel in the sights and sounds of Venice as you cross the Rialto bridge at night

space is crowded around the clock. It's Venice's only piazza – the others are all officially campi – and is lined with a harmonious mélange of fine buildings and arcades. The 15th-century Torre dell'Orologio (Clock Tower), with its gilt-and-blue zodiac clock, leads into the Merceria, an elegant shopping street that connects to the Rialto. Near the water, on the piazzetta, you'll see two columns topped by St. Mark's lion and St. Theodore's crocodile, both ancient symbols of the city.

✚ D2 ✉ Piazza San Marco 🚤 1, 2 (San Marco) or 1, 41, 42, 51, 52, 2 (San Zaccaria)

Punta della Dogana

The Punta della Dogana (Customs' House Point) is home to the buildings that once housed the warehouses of Venice's customs house, designed by Giuseppe Benoni and built between 1677 and 1682.

In 2007 François Pinhault, the millionaire collector, leased the buildings, which had been neglected for years, and spent €20 million on their restoration and conversion into a contemporary art space. Inspired by traditional architecture, the interior fuses the old brick and stone with steel, glass and concrete. This superb synthesis of old and new by the Japanese minimalist architect Tadao Ando is a fitting backdrop for an exciting, contemporary space, showcasing cutting-edge, 21st-century art. Pinhault's own taste dictates the themes for the annual exhibitions, which feature works from his own collection as well as specially commissioned pieces.

✚ C1 ✉ Campo di Salute, Dorsoduro 2 ☎ 041 523 1680; www.palazzograssi.it ⏰ Daily 10–7 🚤 1 (Salute), 2 (Accademia) 💷 $$$

Rialto

During the Middle Ages, the Rialto was Europe's financial and banking center, a sort of medieval Wall Street, where fortunes were made and lost. The Grand Canal is spanned here by a shop-lined bridge, which you should cross to wander in Venice's main market, one of the city's best sights. Stalls are bright with fruit and vegetables or glistening with fish and shellfish, while the surrounding streets are edged with enticing food stores and lined all the way along with cheerful souvenir stands.

✚ C2 ✉ Rialto 🍴 Trattoria alla Madonna, see page 204 🚤 1, 2 (Rialto)

San Giorgio Maggiore

The architect Andrea Palladio bequeathed two great churches to Venice, the Redentore and San Giorgio Maggiore (St. George the Great).

The harmonious structure of San Giorgio adds the finishing touch to the view of St. Mark's Basin; you can take a boat to get there. The church's graceful lines perfectly embody Palladio's strict neoclassic tenets, while the stunning view from the campanile has to be one of Venice's best.

➕ D1 ✉ Campo San Giorgio, Isola San Giorgio ☎ 041 522 7827 🕒 Daily 9:30–12:30 and 2:30–6, May–Sep.; 9:30–12:30 and 2:30–4:30, rest of year 🚤 2 (San Giorgio) 💺 Free; elevator to campanile $

Santa Maria della Salute

The great domed church of Santa Maria della Salute (Our Lady of Health and Salvation) dominates the entrance to the Grand Canal. It was constructed in 1630 in thanksgiving for Venice's deliverance from the plague, in which 45,000 people died, a third of the city's population. Every November on the feast of *La Salute*, Venetians cross a temporary pontoon bridge to give thanks for their deliverance more than 350 years ago. Not only is it one of the city's outstanding landmark buildings, the church's impressive interior contains fine paintings and sculpture, including works by Titian and Tintoretto.

➕ C1 ✉ Campo della Salute 1 ☎ 041 522 5558 🕒 Daily 9–noon and 3–5:30 🚤 1 (Salute) 💺 Free

Santa Maria Gloriosa dei Frari

Both Titian and the composer Monteverdi are interred in this Franciscan Gothic church. Built around 1250, Santa Maria Gloriosa dei Frari (Glorious Virgin Mary of the Brothers) contains two superb Titians – the great *Assumption*, prominently hung over the high altar, and his *Madonna of Ca' Pesaro*. Best of all, though, is Giovanni Bellini's luminous *Madonna and Child with Saints*. Considered one of the world's greatest paintings, you'll find it tucked away in the sacristy.

➕ B2 ✉ Campo dei Frari ☎ 041 275 0462; www.basilicadeifrari.it (Italian only) 🕒 Mon.–Sat. 9–6, Sun. 1–6 🚤 1 (San Tomà), 2 💺 $ or $$ with multi-church "Chorus Pass" ticket

Santi Giovanni e Paolo

Venice's largest church, also known as San Zanipolo, is dedicated to St. John and St. Paul and was built by the Dominicans in the 14th century. It's a massive and imposing Gothic structure that is the resting place of more than 25 doges. The monuments on their tombs represent the best of Venetian medieval sculpture.

Inside, don't miss Giovanni Bellini's polyptych of *St. Vincent Ferrer*. Outside, the great equestrian statue of mercenary Bartolomeo Colleoni by Verocchio is among the city's sculptural treasures.

➕ D3 ✉ Campo SS Giovanni e Paolo ☎ 041 523 7510; www.basilicasantigiovanniepaolo.it 🕒 Mon.– Sat. 9–6, Sun. noon–6; closed Sun. during services 🚤 51, 52 (Ospedale) 41, 42 (Fondamenta Nove) 💺 $

Scuola di San Giórgio degli Schiavoni

From 1502 to 1508, Carpaccio painted the modest headquarters of Venice's Slavic (Schiavoni) community with a series of paintings, including scenes from the lives of Dalmatia's patron saints, St. George, St. Tryphon and St. Jerome. The highlights are *St. George Slaying the Dragon* and *St. Augustine in His Study*.

➕ E2 ✉ Calle dei Furlani 3259/A ☎ 041 522 8828 🕒 Mon. 2:45–6, Tue.–Sat. 9:15–1 and 2:45–6, Sun. 9:15–1 🚤 1, 52, 2 (San Zaccaria) 💺 $$

Scuola Grande di San Rocco

In 1564 Tintoretto won a competition to decorate the walls of the headquarters of the wealthy confraternity of St. Roche. He spent the next 23 years working on this stupendous cycle of wall paintings and ceiling panels. There are more than 50 in all, each illustrating scenes from the Old and New testaments.

Start your tour upstairs in the Sala dell'Albergo, which spotlights the magnificent and revolutionary *Crucifixion*, then move into the upper hall before viewing the 1587 ground-floor paintings, which include the *Annunciation* and the *Flight into Egypt*.

➕ B2 ✉ Campo San Rocco 3052 ☎ 041 523 4864; www.scuolagrandesanrocco.it 🕒 Daily 9:30–5:30 🚤 1, 2 San Tomà 💺 $$ 🛈 English audio guide available for rent

Walk
Quiet Streets and Small Canals

Refer to route marked on city map on page 62

This walk runs through the Dorsoduro and San Polo quarters. You'll walk a lot during your stay, and some of your most serendipitous discoveries will be made en route.

Start on the Fondamenta delle Zattere alongside the water. Head right, turn right before the first bridge and walk along the Rio di San Trovaso. Cross the first bridge, turn left and pass San Trovaso church.
As you walk along Rio di San Trovaso, look for the gondola yard, or *squero*, on the other side of the canal. It was established in the 17th century and there are always gondolas under construction. The church of San Trovaso was built between 1584 and 1657. The cool and spacious interior has two fine paintings by Tintoretto, the *Temptation of St. Anthony* and the *Last Supper*.
Keep bearing right until you come to another canal, the Rio Ognissanti. Walk beside it, crossing one canal and passing five bridges on your left. Cross another canal, then walk straight ahead down Calle Chiesa to a wider canal. Turn right. Keep the canal on your left and pass two bridges. When you come to another canal in front of you, turn right, keeping the water on your left once more. Continue straight along the Fondamenta del Soccorso beside the canal until you come to the Campo dei Carmini.
The Scuola Grande dei Carmini stands on one side of the square. Its upstairs hall has an exuberant ceiling by Giambattista Tiepolo. The panels show a scene from the order's history, *Simon Stock Receiving the Scapular*.
Veer left through the square and walk into Campo Santa Margherita.

One of the most appealing of all Venetian squares, Campo Santa Margherita has a genuine neighborhood feel. There are always fruit and vegetable stalls set up, and local stores and bars predominate. It's a good place to pause for a drink or ice cream at one of the many tempting bars and cafés.
Go straight ahead through the long square and down the narrow street at the far end, Calle della Chiesa. Cross the bridge over the wide Rio di Ca' Foscari into Campo San Pantalon. Bear right across the square, past the church, and turn left down Calle San Pantalon.
San Pantalòn (San Pantaleone) was a healer. The church ceiling is decorated with 60 panels depicting his life. The artist Fumiani never saw his work completed; he fell off a scaffold at the end of his labors. Of more artistic merit is *San Pantaleone Healing a Boy*, the last work completed by Veronese.
Cross the next street, turn right and then immediately left down another narrow street ending at a bridge over a canal, Rio della Frescada. Turn left, then directly right past the front of the Scuola Grande di San Rocco (see page 68). After visiting the Scuola, exit and turn left, then right down the Salizzada San Rocco and skirt around the church of Santa Maria Gloriosa dei Frari (see page 68) into the Campo dei Frari. From here, follow the yellow signs which will lead you back to the Rialto district.

Squero di San Trovaso, a gondola repair yard

Islands in the Lagoon

There's more to the Venetian lagoon than just the city. This fragile, landlocked sea is scattered with islands, some thriving and historic communities, others remote and peaceful. Try to explore a few; they fall into groups, and you could spend a marvelous day away from the crowds.

Graves and Glass

San Michele and Murano are very different. San Michele is the site of the city's main cemetery. Murano is home to Europe's oldest glass-making industry. It might seem odd to visit a cemetery, but stop for half an hour on your way to Murano at this unique burial ground. Among the well-tended graves and monuments bright with flowers are the last resting places of Ezra Pound, Sergei Diaghilev and Igor Stravinsky.

Murano makes a good contrast. Glass has been made here since 1291, when the furnaces were moved away from the city as a fire precaution. Venetian craftsmen were Europe's most skillful glass-blowers. Today these skills are very much in place, and there are large numbers of workshops where you can see glass being blown. Sadly, most of the design is horrendous, although there are some treasures. The Museo Vetrario (Glass Museum) has a huge collection. Murano's main church is Santi Maria e Donato, a superb 12th-century structure with a wonderful colonnade and equally fine mosaics and marble walkways within.

Four Islands to the North

You'll need a whole day to do justice to the four islands lying across the lagoon to the north of the city – Burano, Mazzorbo, Torcello and San Francesco del Deserto. Burano, all brightly painted houses, leaning campaniles, narrow canals and sun-splashed piazzas, is still a fishing community. It's historically noted for the exquisite lace made by the women of the island; the industry has practically died out, but you can admire local work in the Museo del Merletto (Lace-making Museum).

A bridge links Burano to Mazzorbo, with its canalside houses. It's a lovely place to pause, and you'll feel a sense of history here. Venice's age-old feel is at its strongest in timeless Torcello, just across the water. This island, with its overgrown canals and green fields, is one of the most evocative and magical places in Italy. Once the most important island in the lagoon, Torcello was pushed off history's map and left to gentle decay by 12th-century silt and malaria. Today, only the basilica of Santa Maria Assunta and the church of Santa Fosca are reminders of its heyday. Santa Maria was first built in the seventh century; the pulpit dates from this time, but the rest of the church is 11th century. High above the altar, the

apse mosaic shows a lovely Byzantine *Madonna and Child*, while the *Last Judgment* scenes at the west end make a dramatic contrast. Leave time to climb the tower for fine views, and to see smaller and more intimate Santa Fosca; its arcaded porch is full of wheeling swifts.

If time permits, ask a boatman to row you across to San Francesco del Deserto from Burano. This Franciscan monastery, with its serene old church and gardens, is one of the lagoon's loveliest corners.

San Lazzaro degli Armeni and San Servolo

Since the 18th century, the island of San Lazzaro degli Armeni has been an Armenian monastery, a center of learning for this ancient branch of Christianity. Young Armenians come here to study. One of the monks will show you the church and museum. The monastery has run a polyglot printing press for more than 200 years; you can buy the items it produces.

San Servolo also was once a monastery island and Benedictine foundation that later became a hospital and asylum. Today it's a training center for a range of conservation techniques for architectural restoration.

San Michele 🚣 3, 41, 42

Murano 🚣 3, 4, 7, 13, 14, N

Museo Vetrario ✉ Fondamenta Giustinian 8 ☎ 041 739 586 🕑 Daily 10–6, Apr.–Oct.; 10–5, rest of year 🎟 $$

Basilica dei Santi Maria e Donato ✉ Campo San Donato ☎ 041 739 056 🕑 Mon.–Sat. 8–noon and 4–7, Sun. 3:30–7 🎟 Free

Museo del Merletto ✉ Piazza Baldassare Galuppi 187 ☎ 041 730 034; www.museomerletto. visitmuve.it 🕑 Daily 10–6, Apr.–Oct.; 10–5, rest of year 🎟 $$

Mazzorbo 🚣 12

Torcello 🚣 12 to Burano then shuttle boat 9

Basilica di Santa Maria della Assunta ☎ 041 296 0630 🕑 Daily 10:30–6, Mar.–Oct.; 10–5, rest of year 🎟 $; combined ticket $$$

Museo di Torcello ☎ 041 296 0630 🕑 Daily 10:30–5:30, Mar.–Oct.; 10–5, rest of year 🎟 $; combined ticket $$$

Santa Fosca ☎ 041 730 084 🕑 Daily 10–4:30 🎟 Free

San Francesco del Deserto 🚣 12 to Burano

Convento di San Francesco del Deserto ☎ 041 528 6863; www.sanfrancescodeldeserto.it 🕑 Guided tours only: Tue.–Sun. 9–11 and 3–5 🚣 12 to Burano, then with Lagunafla (www.lagunafla.it for details) or call Massimiliano (3479 922 959) 🎟 Free

San Lazzaro degli Armeni 🚣 20

Monastero Mekhitarista ☎ 041 526 0104 🕑 Daily 3 p.m. (guided tours only) 🚣 20 🎟 $$$

Above left to right: Looking across to the island of Burano, with its campanile; Burano's brightly painted houses are reflected in one of its canals

Regional Sights

> **Key to symbols**
> ➕ map coordinates refer to the region map on
> page 58 ⓦ admission charge: $$$ more than €7,
> $$ €4–€7, $ less than €4
> See page 5 for complete key to symbols

Roman remains at Aquileia

Aquileia

The flat plains south of Udine leave you unprepared for the treasure of Aquileia. The colony was established in 181 BC and by the fourth century had become a patriarchate, a region ruled by a prince-bishop or patriarch. The first patriarch was Theodore, who built a great basilica. Sacked by Attila and the Lombards, this early church was rebuilt several times and today is a superb blend of Romanesque and Gothic elements. Its chief glory is the jewel-like mosaic tiled floor whose Christian and pagan scenes are as fresh as when they were created in around AD 320. Look for the mosaic bestiary around the base of the 11th-century campanile and the 12th-century Byzantine frescoes in the shadowy crypt. Sleepy Aquileia also has two museums – the Archeological Museum displays everything from fine Roman sculpture to a reconstructed galley.

A stroll along the River Natissa will take you to the Museo Paleocristiano (Paleo-Christian Museum), a collection of more local Roman finds.

➕ C2

Tourist information ✉ Via Lulia Augusta ☎ 0431 919 491; www.turismofvg.it and www.aquileia.net ⓖ Daily 9–7, Jun.–Aug.; 9–1 and 2–6, Apr.–May and Sep.; Mon.–Sat. 9–3, rest of year

Basilica ✉ Piazza Capitolo ☎ 0431 919 719 ⓖ Basilica: daily 9–7, Mar.–Oct.; 9–1 and 2–5, rest of year. Bell Tower: daily 9:30–1:30 and 3:30–6:30, Mar.– Oct.; closed rest of year ⓦ Basilica free; Crypts $; Belltower $

Museo Archeologico ✉ Via Roma 1 ☎ 0431 91 016; www.museoarchaeo-aquileia.it ⓖ Tue.–Sun. 8:30–7:30 ⓦ $$

Museo Paleocristiano ✉ Piazza Pirano, Monastero delle Benedettine ☎ 0431 91 131 ⓖ Tue.–Sun. 8:30–1:45 ⓦ Free

Asolo

Asolo's charms gave the Italian language a new verb – *asolare*, meaning to pass the time in pleasant aimlessness. This medieval walled town, sprinkled with enchanting piazzas and pretty churches, is perhaps the loveliest in the Veneto. Famous figures have loved Asolo, among them 15th-century Caterina Cornaro, one of the few women to have played an important part in Venetian history. She became, through marriage, queen of Cyprus, but was duped out of the island by the Venetian state, which gave her Asolo as a consolation prize. The actress Eleanor Druse was born here in 1859. Famous as much for her love life as for her acting, she often came here to escape gossip and scandal, and although she died in far-off Pittsburgh, she is buried here. There's information on her life in the Museo Civico, which also devotes space to the English poet Robert Browning, who lived here for some time.

➕ B2

Tourist information ✉ Piazza Garibaldi 73 ☎ 0423 529 046; www.asolo.it ⓖ Mon.–Fri. 9–12:30, Tue., Thu. and Fri. also 3–6, Sat.–Sun. 9:30–12:30 and 3–6

Museo Civico ✉ Via Regina Cornaro 74 ☎ 0423 395 2313 ⓖ Sat.–Sun. 10–noon and 3–7 ⓦ $$

Opposite: The jagged peaks of the Dolomites contrast with fertile upland pastures

Drive
The Great Dolomites Road

Duration: 3 to 4 hours

This drive follows the route known as La Grande Strada delle Dolomiti (The Great Dolomites Road), built in 1909 to link Bolzano and Cortina d'Ampezzo. It runs 70 miles (110 kilometers) through Europe's most breathtaking mountain scenery and offers frequent opportunities to take a scenic side road or a cable car up a mountain slope. The road is well-maintained but inevitably twisting in places, so bear this in mind if you suffer from vertigo or travel sickness. The Dolomites were designated UNESCO World Heritage Site status in 2009.

From Bolzano (see page 76), take the SS241 along the Val d'Ega to the Lago di Carezza.
East of Bolzano, you leave the road over the Brenner Pass, one of the historic trans-Alpine routes, and head along the gorge of the Val d'Ega. This narrow corridor, edged with waterfalls, offers the first taste of the superb views along this route, with the Catinaccio and Latemar massifs rising on either side of the road. Make your first stop at the Lago di Carezza, a picture-postcard lake

whose deep blue waters reflect mountain ridges sprinkled with dark fir trees and punctuated with white gravel slides. The road climbs from the lake to the Passo di Costalunga (5,750 feet), the first of the high passes along this route, which marks the boundary between the Alto Adige and Trentino regions.

Continue on the SS241 through the Passo di Costalunga to Vigo di Fassa.
Once over the pass, the road descends through the Val di Fassa, running beside the River Avisio to Vigo di Fassa, a mountain resort town. Vigo makes a good starting point for hikers wanting to explore the Catinaccio range. There are trails catering to all levels of fitness and experience, and a cable car takes away the worst of the initial hike. You can hike south back to the Lago di Carezza.

About 1 mile (1.5 kilometers) outside Vigo, turn left onto the SS48 to Canazei.
The road becomes increasingly dramatic, with views of wild countryside, soaring mountains and constantly changing vistas as it hairpins its way to Canazei. This is another mountain resort town, catering to the winter skiers, summer climbers and walkers who make it their base. There's a choice of cable-car rides into the surrounding mountains.

Stay on the SS48, climbing steeply to the Passo Pordoi and on to Arabba.
Twenty-seven hairpin turns over 7 miles (12 kilometers) mark the next section of driving, leading to the Passo Pordoi (7,400 feet), one of the highest passes on the route. Enjoy the scenery

until you come to the village of Arabba, a cluster of hotels set in peaceful mountain pastureland. The huge massif to the south is the Marmolada; you can take a cable car up to the Porto Vescovo for a closer look at its icy slopes.

If you want to make this drive a round trip, turn left onto the SS243 for the Passo di Gardena. At Plan de Gralba, turn right onto the SS242. Stay on this road through Ortisei (where it becomes the SS242d) and after 2 miles (3.5 kilometers) branch left to Ponte Gardena, where you can join the SS12 south to return to Bolzano. To continue to Cortina, stay on the SS48 through Arabba and Pocol to Cortina d'Ampezzo.

You'll cross another pass on the way to Pocol. This is the Passo di Falzarego (8,200 feet). The descent to Cortina runs along the slopes of the Tofane massif to emerge into the stunning mountain bowl that encircles this chic resort.

Bolzano tourist information (see page 76)
Cortina d'Ampezzo tourist information ✉ Piazzetta San Francesco 8 ☎ 0436 3231; www.infodolomiti.it ⚅ Daily 9–12:30 and 3:30–6:30

The Dolomites have breathtaking vistas at every turn – this is Lago di Carezza

A statue of the 12th-century German bard Walther von der Vogelweide stands in Bolzano's Piazza Walther

Bolzano

Capital of the German-speaking Alto Adige region, mountain-hemmed Bolzano (Bozen) makes a good base for exploring the scenic splendors of the Dolomites (see page 74). This area ultimately became part of Italy at the end of World War I and retains a distinctly Teutonic flavor, which is manifested in its cuisine, language and efficiently run services. Head first for the café-fringed Piazza Walther, the central square, to visit the Gothic Duomo (Cathedral), with an eye-catching carved spire and yellow-and-green tiled roof. Its lovely Porta del Vino (Wine Door) is decorated with carvings of peasants working the vineyards, and was erected in 1387 when the church was granted a license to sell wine.

Nearby, the Chiesa dei Domenicani has Bolzano's best frescoes; you'll find a 14th-century cycle in Cappella di San Giovanni (St. John's Chapel) and 15th-century scenes of life in the cloisters. North from here lies the Piazza dell'Erbe, with its colorful daily market. Don't miss the Museo Archeologico, best known for Ötzi, the "ice man," a 5,000-year-old mummified body discovered in glacial ice in 1992. To experience the glorious mountains, you could take a cable car to Soprabolzano; from there a tiny tramway runs to the hamlet of Collalbo.

➕ A3

Tourist information ✉ Piazza Walther 8 ☎ 0471 307 000; www.bolzano-bozen.it ⏰ Mon.–Fri. 9–1 and 2–7, Sat. 9–2 ℹ For information on the Dolomites, visit the regional tourist office at Piazza Parrochia 11/12 ☎ 0471 000 000; www.suedtirol.info ⏰ Mon.–Fri. 8:30–6

Duomo ✉ Piazza Parrochia ⏰ Mon.–Fri. 10–noon and 2–5, Sat. 10–noon. Treasury: Tue.–Sat. 10–noon 🎟 Free

Chiesa dei Domenicani ✉ Piazza Domenicani ⏰ Mon.–Sat. 9:30–5, Sun. 12–6 🎟 Free

Museo Archeologico dell'Alto Adige ✉ Via del Museo 43 ☎ 0471 320 100; www.iceman.it ⏰ Daily 10–6, Jul.–Aug. and Dec.; Tue.–Sun. 10–6, Sep.–Nov. and Jan.–Jun. 🎟 $$$

Cividale del Friuli

Just a few miles from the border with Slovenia, the lovely town of Cividale del Friuli is a beguiling tangle of medieval streets and interesting buildings. It lies on the Natisone river and is one of the few places in Italy with tangible reminders of the Lombards. This Teutonic warrior race invaded Italy in the sixth century, establishing three dukedoms and leaving a sparse legacy of carvings and sculpture. The finest example is the Tempietto Longobardo (Lombard Temple); the eighth-century stucco arch features smiling saints, a peerless example of Lombard art.

There's more to be seen in the Museo Cristiano (Christian Museum), in the precincts of the 15th-century Duomo (Cathedral). Here you can admire the stunning Altar of Ratchis, an eighth-century masterpiece, and the octagonal Baptistery of Callisto, made from fifth-century stone and marble fragments. The cathedral's main draw is the silver pala (altarpiece).

🕂 C2

Tourist information ✉ Piazza Paolo Diacono 9–10 ☎ 0432 710 460; www.comune.cividale-del-friuli.ud.it or www.cividale.net ⏲ Daily 9:30–12:30 and 3:30–6 **Tempietto Longobardo** ✉ Via Monastero Maggiore 34 ☎ 0432 700 867 ⏲ Mon.–Sat. 9:30–12:30 and 3–6:30 (closes 5 p.m. Oct.–Mar.), Sun. 9:30–1 and 3–7:30 (2:30–6:30 p.m. Oct.–Mar.) 🖐 $ **Museo Cristiano** ✉ Via Candotti 1 ☎ 0432 773 0403 ⏲ Wed.–Sun. 10–1 and 3–6, Apr.–Sep.; Sat.–Sun. 10–1 and 3–6, rest of year. Open other days by appointment (☎ 0432 730 403) 🖐 $$

Merano

Staid and placid Merano (Meran), with its Mediterranean-type mild climate and thermal springs, provides a splendid contrast to the dramatic mountain scenery that surrounds it. The town attracted wealthy central Europeans at the beginning of the 20th century. They came here to "take the cure" and to walk in its parks and along its promenades. The most famous is the Passeggiata d'Inverno e d'Estate (Winter and Summer Path), which runs along the banks of the Passirio river. Higher up, you can enjoy the winding Passeggiata Tappeiner, which runs through vineyards above the town.

The Via dei Portici marks Meran's historic center. The streets are a mix of local rustic architecture, chic shops and fin-de-siècle elegance. The Gothic cathedral and ivy-clad castle are worth a visit. However, for the true Meran experience, take a dip in the thermal baths. The town makes an excellent base from which to explore the Texelgruppe mountains, about 6 miles away, or the far more dramatic Ortles range, an incredible area of rocks and glaciers.

🕂 A3

Tourist information ✉ Corso della Libertà 45 ☎ 0473 272 000; www.merano.eu ⏲ Mon.–Fri. 9–1 and 2–6, Sat. 9:30–12.30 and 2:30–5 🛈 Third week in Oct.: Grape Fest with processions, concerts, and wine and food tastings

Padova

The Veneto's most important economic center and a major university city, Padova (Padua) was heavily bombed during World War II. The subsequent rebuilding makes first impressions less than immediately alluring. But there are some real gems here, chief among them the frescoes by Giotto in the Scrovegni Chapel. Painted in the early 1300s, the scenes of the life of Christ and his Blessed Mother are one of the turning points of Western art development, with a wholly innovative naturalism. Also visit the Civic Museum next door before heading through the city to visit the Basilica di Sant'Antonio, a many-domed church dedicated to Padua's own St. Anthony. Outside stands the fine equestrian statue of the mercenary Gattamelata (Honey Cat), sculpted by Donatello in 1453. Down Via del Santo from the basilica, you'll find Padua's two main squares, the Piazza della Frutta and the Piazza delle Erbe. Morning is the best time here; the daily fruit and vegetable markets are in full swing. The extraordinary building between the two squares is the Palazzo della Ragione, which contains a huge wooden model of a horse, made for a joust in 1466.

🕂 B1

Tourist information ✉ Stazione Ferroviaria ☎ 049 875 2077; www.turismopadova.it Also offices at ✉ Galleria Pedrocchi ☎ 049 876 7927 and ✉ Piazza del Santo ☎ 049 875 3087 ⏲ Pedrocchi Office: Mon.–Sat. 9–1:30 and 3–7; Stazione Office: Mon.–Sat. 9–7, Sun. 9:15–12:30; Piazza del Santo office: Mon.–Sat. 9–1:30 and 3–6, Sun. 10–1 and 3–6, Mar.–Oct.; closed rest of year 🛈 You can take a cruise along the Brenta river from Padua to Venice from March through early November, visiting some of the villas en route. Details from Padova Navigazione ☎ 041 241 3296; www.ilburchiello.it

Cappella degli Scrovegni and Musei Civici
✉ Piazza Eremitani 8 ☎ Call center: 049 201 0020;
www.cappelladegliscrovegni.it ⊕ Museum: Tue.–Sun.
9–7; Chapel: daily 9–7, Jan. and Feb.; also open some
evenings, rest of year. Hours may vary (entry included
with Padova Card, valid for other city attractions. Chapel
visits, lasting 20 minutes, must be pre-booked online or
by phone Mon.–Fri. 9–7, Sat. 9–6) 🎫 $$$
Basilica di Sant'Antonio ✉ Piazza del Santo ☎ 049
822 5652; www.basilicadelsanto.it ⊕ Daily 6:20 a.m.–
7 p.m. (7:45 p.m., Apr.–Oct.) 🎫 Free
Palazzo della Ragione ✉ Piazza delle Erbe ☎ 049 820
5006 ⊕ Tue.–Sun. 9–7, Feb.–Oct.; 9–6, rest of year
🎫 $$

Treviso

Home to the Benetton company, Treviso
is an alluring provincial town enclosed
by 16th-century walls, with canals, long
porticoes and frescoed facades. The main
street is the Calmaggiore. This leads
right through the center, beautifully
rebuilt and restored after heavy bombing
in both world wars. Treviso's cathedral
is the Duomo San Pietro, where you'll
find an impressive crypt with a thicket
of 12th-century columns. Treviso is
noted for the production of radicchio,
the red-leaf salad vegetable. Wine lovers
can use Treviso as the gateway to some
of the Veneto's best wine areas; two wine
trails head out from the town of
Conegliano to the north.

✚ B2
Tourist information ✉ Palazzo Scotti, Via S. Andrea 3
☎ 0422 547 632; www.turismo.provincia.treviso.it
⊕ Mon. 9–1, Tue.–Fri. 9–1 and 2–6, Sat. 9–1 and 3–6,
Sun. 9:30–1
Duomo San Pietro ✉ Piazza del Duomo ⊕ Mon.–Fri.
7:30–noon and 3:30–7, Sat.–Sun. 7:30–1 and 3:30–8
(hours may vary) 🎫 Free

Trieste

With its superb Piazza dell'Unità d'Italia
opening to embrace the sea, Trieste rates
as one of Italy's finest port cities.
Founded in Roman times, Trieste's
ownership over the centuries has swung
back and forth between the different
powers whose interests lay in this corner
of the Adriatic. Thus Italian, Austro-
Hungarian and Slavic influences have
all shaped today's city, which finally
became part of Italy in 1954.

 Trieste is set on the slopes of a
limestone plateau overlooking the sea
and owes much of its appearance to the
Austrian Empress Maria Teresa, who
constructed the 18th-century city center
as a fitting background for its role as the
main Habsburg southern port. This
central area has good shops and wide
streets, well worth a visit before you
climb through the remnants of Roman
and medieval Trieste to the hilltop
Castello (Castle) and Cattedrale di San

The town of Verona, immortalized by William Shakespeare in *Romeo and Juliet*, lies on the Adige river

Giusto (St. Just's Cathedral). The main museums in town are the Museo Revoltella, the Museo di Storia e dell'Arte (History and Art Museum) and the Museo Morpurgo. Or you could follow the footsteps of James Joyce, the Irish author of *Ulysses*, who lived here for many years.

By far the nicest attraction is the idiosyncratic Castello di Miramare, a wonderfully situated castle overlooking the sea and standing in delightful gardens. It was built for the Archduke Ferdinand Maximilian (later Emperor of Mexico) in the 1860s.

➕ C2

Tourist information ✉ Via dell'Orologio 1 (corner of Piazza Unità d'Italia) ☎ 040 347 8312; www.turismofvg.it ⏰ Mon.–Sat. 9–6, Sun. 9–1

Cattedrale di San Giusto ✉ Piazza della Cattedrale ☎ 040 309 666 ⏰ Daily 8–noon and 3.30–7:30 (longer in summer) 🎟 Free

Museo Revoltella ✉ Via Armando Diaz 27 ☎ 040 675 4350; www.museorevoltella.it ⏰ Wed.–Mon. 10–7; some later opening in Jul. and Aug. 🍴 Terrace bar open Jul.–Sep. 🎟 $$

Museo di Storia e dell'Arte ✉ Piazza Cattedrale 1 ☎ 040 308 686; www.triestecultura.it ⏰ Tue.–Sun. 9–1 🎟 $

Museo Morpurgo ✉ Via Imbriani 5 ☎ 040 636 969; www.triestecultura.it ⏰ Tue. and Thu.–Sun. 9–1, Wed. 9–7 🎟 $

Castello di Miramare ✉ Viale Miramare ☎ 040 224 143; www.castello-miramare.it ⏰ Castle: daily 9–7; Gardens: daily 8–7, Apr.–Sep.; 8–6, Mar. and Oct.; 8–5, rest of year 🎟 $$; Gardens free

Verona

One of northern Italy's most captivating cities, Verona lies on the banks of the Adige river. Start your tour in the sweeping Piazza Brà, the largest square. It's dominated by the first-century Arena, one of the world's largest surviving Roman amphitheaters and scene of Verona's famous summer opera festival.

The pedestrian Via Mazzini, with its swanky shops and cafés, leads to the heart of Verona, around the intimate Piazza dell'Erbe. Lined with loggias, town houses and Renaissance palaces, the piazza also has been the site of the market since medieval times. From here, head down Via Cappello for a glimpse of the Casa di Giulietta (Juliet's House), complete with balcony. Shakespeare based his tragedy on true families, the Cappelli and Montecchi, although Romeo and Juliet are fictional. This hasn't deterred thousands of modern lovers from leaving their initials on every available surface of the house's walls.

Behind the Piazza dell'Erbe lies the stunning ensemble of the Piazza dei Signori; there are wide views from the top of the Torre dei Lamberti (Lamberti Tower). Don't miss the Arche Scaligeri (Scaligeri Monuments), the superb Gothic funerary monuments to Verona's medieval ruling family. The main figure is Cangrande (Big Dog), protector of Dante and a great artistic patron.

North from here lies the Duomo (Cathedral) and Sant' Anastasia, Verona's largest church, built from 1290 to 1481. Nearby, you can see a careful reconstruction of the first-century Ponte Pietra (Stone Bridge); the original was bombed in World War II.

Across the river stands the remains of the Roman theater. Head parallel with the river to the Castelvecchio, the medieval fortress seat of the Scaligeri. It houses the city's Museo Civico d'Arte (Civic Art Museum). Another short walk will bring you to the church of San Zeno, a superb Romanesque basilica built atop an earlier church in 1117. Its lovely bronze doors are enclosed by marble bas-reliefs and topped by a "Wheel of Fortune" rose window. Inside, don't miss Mantegna's lovely Madonna and Saints over the high altar.

➕ A2

Tourist information ✉ Via degli Alpini 9 ☎ 045 806 8680; www.tourism.verona.it ⏰ Mon.–Sat. 9–7, Sun. 10–4, Feb.–Nov.; Mon.–Sat. 1–6, Sun. 10–4, rest of year 🏳 The VeronaCard ($$$) is valid for two or five days and covers admission to museums, churches and monuments

Arena ✉ Piazza Brà ☎ 045 800 3204; box office 045 800 5151; www.arena.it ⊙ Mon. 1:30–7:30, also Tue.–Sun. 8:30–7:30; hours vary during opera season (Jul.–Sep.) 📱 $$ ❶ Reserve well in advance for opera

Casa di Giulietta ✉ Via Cappello 23 ☎ 045 803 4303 ⊙ Mon. 1:30–7:30, Tue.–Sun. 8:30–7:30 📱 $$

Torre dei Lamberti ✉ Piazza dei Signori, Cortile Mercato Vecchio ☎ 045 927 3027 ⊙ Daily 8:30–7:30 📱 $$

Duomo ✉ Piazza del Duomo ☎ 045 592 813; www.chieseverona.it ⊙ Mon.–Sat. 10–5:30, Sun. 12:30–6, Mar.–Oct.; Tue.–Sat. 10–1 and 1:30–5, Sun. 1:30–5, rest of year 📱 $

Sant' Anastasia ✉ Corso Sant' Anastasia ☎ 045 592 813 ⊙ Mon.–Sat. 9–6, Sun. 1–6, Mar.–Oct.; Tue.–Sat. 10–1 and 1:30–5, Sun. 1–5, rest of year 📱 $

Castelvecchio and Museo Civico d'Arte ✉ Corso Castelvecchio 2 ☎ 045 592 985 ⊙ Mon. 1:30–7:30, Tue.–Sun. 8:30–7:30 📱 $$

San Zeno ✉ Piazza San Zeno ☎ 045 592 813 ⊙ Mon.–Sat. 8:30–6, Sun. 12:30–6, Mar.–Oct.; Tue.–Sat. 10–1 and 1:30–5, Sun. 12:30–5, rest of year 📱 $

Vicenza

Vicenza grew rich in the second half of the 20th century on textiles, electronics and printing. Prosperity has given the city polish without detracting from its charm. The center is an amalgam of Gothic architecture, as well as the classical buildings of the great 16th-century architect Andrea Palladio. Vicenza's main street, Corso Andrea Palladio, commemorates him and is lined with examples of his work. One of his palaces houses the Museo Civico, with masterpieces by Tiepolo and Tintoretto.

The mid-13th-century church of Santa Corona houses two superb paintings, Giovanni Bellini's *Baptism of Christ* and the *Adoration of the Magi* by Paolo Veronese. Nearby is the Gallerie di Palazzo Montanari, where a splendid baroque palace houses two collections, a range of intimate domestic paintings by Longhi, Guardi and other Venetian artists, and a huge collection of richly colored Russian icons. Across Piazza

Matteotti is Palladio's Teatro Olimpico (Olympic Theater), Europe's oldest indoor theater, which opened in 1585. Palladio died before it was completed; the astonishing backdrop of a classical city behind the stage was added by Vincenzo Scamozzi.

Head south from here to the Piazza dei Signori, the heart of the centro storico (historic center), to visit the basilica, Palladio's first major project and the one that made his reputation. The building facing the basilica is the Loggia del Capitaniato, a late and unfinished Palladian structure built for the Venetian military commander. Behind here, vendors in the Piazza dell'Erbe sell fruits and vegetables as they have since medieval times – a good place to shop or enjoy a drink at one of the cafés.

Leave time to take in one of Palladio's famous villas. The Villa Capra (La Rotonda) was built as a pleasure pavilion, its balanced classical lines providing the inspiration for many public buildings in the United States.

➕ A2

Tourist information ✉ Piazza Matteotti 11–12 ☎ 0444 320 854; www.vitourism.it ⊙ Daily 9–1 and 2–6 ❶ There are various cards offering free access or reduced ticket prices to a range of Vicenza attractions including Palladio Card ($$$)

Museo Civico ✉ Palazzo Chiericati 39 ☎ 0444 222 811 ⊙ Tue.–Sun. 9–5 📱 $$$ (combined ticket with Teatro Olimpico)

Santa Corona ✉ Contrà Santa Corona ☎ 0444 321 924 ⊙ Tue.–Sun. 9–5, Sep.–Jun.; Tue.–Sun. 9–7, Jul.–Aug. 📱 Free

Gallerie di Palazzo Leoni Montanari ✉ Contrà Santa Corona 25 ☎ 800 578 875; www.palazzomontanari. com ⊙ Tue.–Sun. 10–6 📱 $

Teatro Olimpico ✉ Piazza Matteotti 11 ☎ 0444 222 800; www.olimpico.vicenza.it ⊙ Tue.–Sun. 9–6, Jun.–Aug.; 9–5, rest of year 📱 $$$ (combined ticket with Museo Civico)

Basilica ✉ Corso San Felice Fortunato 219 ☎ 0444 323 681 ⊙ Tue.–Sun. 9–5 📱 Free

La Rotonda, Villa Capra ✉ Via Rotonda 45 ☎ 0444 321 793 ⊙ Villa: Wed. and Sat. 10–noon and 3–6, mid-Mar. to Nov.; Gardens: Tue.–Sun. 10–noon and 3–6, mid-Mar. to early Nov. 📱 Villa $$$; Gardens $$

Winter Sports

Italy's mountains offer a vast range of skiing, with good facilities and a relaxed atmosphere. With the Alps right on their doorstep, many northern Italians are avid skiers and head for the slopes most weekends during the season. The Valle d'Aosta area in the northwest gives access to Mont Blanc and the splendid Gran Paradiso, but Italy's favorite winter play area is the Dolomites in the northeast. The Via Lattea (Milky Way) resorts, including Sestriere, Sansicario, Sauze d'Oulx, Cesana, Claviere and Bardonechhia, an hour's drive from Turin, are also popular.

Where To Go

From Christmas through March, the Dolomites offer some of Europe's best skiing in fantastically beautiful mountain scenery. Although Italians are generally much more relaxed about skiing than the Swiss or French, their resorts are excellently run, with well-tended pistes (slopes) and plenty of access via cable cars, chairlifts and drags. The main resorts are Cortina d'Ampezzo, east of Bolzano (see page 76), and Madonna di Campiglio, on the fringe of the Dolomiti di Brenta. Both towns are among Europe's most stylish international winter sports centers, offering superb facilities and steep prices to match. If you're looking for good value for your money, head for the Val Gardena or the Val Badia; both are noted for good snow and good value. Wherever you go, you'll find the full range of ski runs, schools, classes and personal guides, plus snowboarding, which is very popular in Italy.

Cross-country skiers can use the miles of well-groomed tracks; two of the best centers are Ortisei and Dobbiaco in the Val Gardena. Non-skiers will find lovely Alpine walks through silent woods, sleigh rides, bars and restaurants where you can enjoy lunch or a drink, and resort activities such as swimming, ice-skating and some of the most tempting window-shopping in Europe. Après ski offerings range from a quiet dinner in a wood-paneled restaurant to throbbing discos and smoky piano bars.

Accommodations

The best way to experience Italian winter sports is to book a package during the *settimane bianche* (white weeks). These generally fall during the quiet weeks of January and February and are a superb value. Contact the regional tourist boards for details.

Valle d'Aosta tourist information ✉ Piazza Emilio Chanoux 2 ☎ 0165 236 627; www.regione.vda.it
Trentino-Alto Adige tourist information ✉ Via Manci 2 ☎ 0461 216 000; www.visittrentino.it

Skiers enjoy great views, snow and brilliant sunshine in the Dolomites

Tuscany, Umbria and the Marche

Opposite: The view around San Gimignano from the top of the Torre Grossa, one of 15 remaining towers

Tuscany, Umbria and the Marche

The political regions of Tuscany (Toscana), Umbria and the Marche cut right across north-central Italy. This is the country's Renaissance heartland, where the great 14th-century upsurge of culture and the arts truly began. Its timeless landscapes epitomize the visitor's dream of Italy. Prosperous cities, a sound infrastructure, an abundance of history, art and culture, and good food and wine make this area one of Italy's most-visited. Bear this in mind when planning your trip; art-lovers will do best out of season when museums and galleries are less crowded, while the countryside looks its dazzling best during May and June.

Tuscan Towns and Villages

Florence is Tuscany's major city and the capital of this thriving region, with

high-technology industry, a university and a rich agricultural community. It's also among Italy's most popular tourist spots. Visitors seem to outnumber locals in many parts of the city, but Florence has a life of its own that few visitors experience. Local life is more accessible in the region's lesser cities, many of which deserve a day's visit.

Medieval Siena is the perfect contrast to Florence, while Pisa contains one of Europe's most perfect architectural ensembles. Lucca, Cortona and Volterra have much to offer, and are all set in contrasting and beautiful landscapes. You also may appreciate San Gimignano,

San Gimignano is surrounded by vineyards

the best-known hill town, and Montalcino, Montepulciano and the city of Pienza in the south.

Traveling in Tuscany

To enjoy the beauty of Tuscany at its best, rent a car for the freedom it allows to explore off-the-beaten-track roads and villages. Tourists are important to the Tuscan economy, and facilities are excellent, with a wide range of accommodations and restaurants throughout the region. English is widely spoken, particularly in the main tourist centers, and levels of courtesy and service are generally high. You'll find that many Tuscans are reserved and rational people, not given to the dramatic outbursts found in other parts of Italy. Accustomed to an annual influx of international visitors, they are professional and reliable. In Tuscany, as everywhere in Italy, a few words of Italian will work wonders.

Rural Tuscany

For many people, Tuscany encapsulates Italian countryside. Rolling hills, vineyards, olive groves and glowing wheatfields punctuated by pencil-thin cypress trees are quintessentially Italian, and all can be found in Tuscany. There's

more: Head north to explore the Alpi Apuane, where you'll find dramatic mountains, their flanks glistening white with marble quarries. Or discover the scenic splendors of the Garfagnana, Tuscany's "Little Switzerland." South of Siena lie the rolling wheatlands and bare clay slopes of the *crete*, a strange, almost lunar landscape, while along the coast stretch the melancholy plains and low hills of the Maremma. Eastern Tuscany, an area still largely unexplored by visitors, has more wooded hills, punctuated by deep river valleys planted with corn and tobacco.

The Green Heart of Italy

Recent years have seen Umbria emerge from Tuscany's shadow as a fascinating and beautiful area well worth visiting in its own right. Many visitors prefer its less crowded cities. This is a varied, tranquil and lovely region and is well-deserving of its title, *il cuore verde d'Italia* (the green heart of Italy). Historically poor and undeveloped, the region's infrastructure and economy have taken huge strides during the last 30 years. Growing prosperity blends with the traditional to attract growing numbers of visitors.

Part of Umbria's charm is its largely untouched countryside, scattered with historic hill towns, each increasingly able to cater to visitors' needs. The landscape includes gentle hills, vineyards, woodland and the dramatic peaks of the Monti Sibillini to the east.

A traditional Tuscan farmhouse in the lovely area that lies between Volterra and San Gimignano

The whole region is permeated by a hazy blue light distinctively Umbrian. The light is quite appropriate to mystical Umbria, the birthplace of St. Francis and St. Benedict.

Umbrian People and Places

Courteous and friendly, the Umbrians are welcoming and kind. Outside the main towns, few people speak more than a few words of English, but they do have time for, and patience with, visitors. Many of the remote areas are inhabited by people whose way of life has seen little change for decades. But accommodations are very easy to find, restaurants are excellent and roads, towns and villages are still relatively quiet. The main attractions are Perugia, Umbria's capital; Assisi, with its Franciscan associations; and Orvieto, for its superb Duomo (Cathedral). Make sure to leave time for historic Spoleto and Gubbio, and don't neglect the smaller towns of Spello, Todi and hilltop Trevi. Lovers of unspoiled scenery will find some of the best in the wild uplands above Norcia.

A Place Apart – the Marche

Daunted by the barrier of the Apennines, relatively few visitors penetrate the Marche, a wonderfully varied region with mountains, jumbled hills and valleys, fertile plains and a long coastline. The northern part of this area has the most to offer. Incomparable Urbino is one of Italy's most perfect Renaissance towns. San Leo is dramatically situated, San Marino is popular and Pesaro, with two miles of beach, draws sun-seekers from all over Europe.

To the south lies picturesque Ascoli Piceno in the Tronto valley, possibly the most logical route to the Marche from Umbria. Hotels and restaurants, particularly on the coast, are more than adequate, but the road system away from the coast still lags behind those of many other Italian regions.

A quiet street in hilltop Montalcino

Florence

Florence (Firenze) is the capital of Tuscany and one of the world's great artistic shrines. In no other city can the development of Renaissance art be traced so comprehensively in such a relatively small space. Florence can be overwhelming for the wrong reasons: the heat, crowds and traffic mar many people's enjoyment. At first sight, the city can seem somewhat architecturally dour, with narrow streets and overpowering buildings, but it's the contents of the buildings that people come to see, so be prepared to spend much of your time inside.

Background

The Roman city of Florentia re-emerged as an independent city-state, in the 12th century, its prosperity based on wool, banking and commerce. Between the early 14th and late 15th centuries, the Medici were the pre-eminent family; they ruled Florence and later Tuscany until the 18th century. During World War II, Florence was occupied by the Germans; because of its artistic importance, they declared it an open city. Huge damage was caused to the city and its treasures when the Arno river burst its banks in 1966 (see page 96).

The graceful curve of the dome of Florence's cathedral, with the city beyond

The Medici Balls

On buildings and statues all over Florence you'll notice the Medici emblem, a cluster of red balls *(palle)* set on a gold background. This is the coat-of-arms of the city's ruling family, with which they adorned every building owned by or connected to them. The number of balls varied throughout the centuries, so you'll notice any number between five and 12. Their original meaning is obscure, but most historians agree they derive from either medicinal pills (family members were once apothecaries) or coins, a reference to the Medici interests in banking and money-lending.

Plan Ahead

Choose the time of your visit carefully; although the city is less crowded in the winter, there is no time of year when Florence is empty. Winter temperatures are better for sightseeing, as few public buildings and museums in Florence are air-conditioned. Above all, don't do too much. See what you want to see, not what you feel you should see. Be prepared to walk a fair amount; many major attractions, however, are in the city center. Reserve tickets online and in advance to avoid the worst crowds at museums. Otherwise arrive sharp at opening time or go late in the day.

Venture off the tourist circuit and explore the quieter back streets and hidden piazzas, where you'll find neighborhood stores, artisans' workshops and atmospheric corners.

The City

Florence's highlights lie close together on the north bank of the Arno river. You should see the Piazza della Signoria, which contains the Palazzo Vecchio, the Piazza del Duomo with the cathedral and baptistery, and the Uffizi and Bargello galleries. Many superb works of art are in the city's churches; Santa Maria della Carmine for Masaccio, Santa Croce for Giotto, San Marco for Fra Angelico and San Lorenzo for Michelangelo top the list. Be sure to take in the Ponte Vecchio bridge, the elegant stores on and around the Via de' Tornabuoni and the markets.

Friendly Eating

Florence is packed with restaurants of every type, and a meal here can be memorable. Many restaurants are specifically aimed at tourists, with prominently displayed fixed-price menus; eateries patronized by locals are usually a good bet. As a general rule, you'll find the cheaper restaurants near the railroad station, chic places in the city center, and small and friendly eating houses on the south side of the Arno river.

Lunch is served any time after 12:30 p.m. and dinner begins around 7:30 p.m. For a simple lunch, try a slice of freshly baked pizza-to-go or a quick snack in a bar or traditional wine shop, a *fiaschetteria*. The food markets are tempting. Tuscan food is simple and excellent, with plenty of soups, pork products, broiled meats and vegetables. Bean dishes are especially popular – other Italians nickname Tuscans *mangiafagioli*, bean-eaters. The most famous wine is Chianti, but also look for Brunello di Montalcino. Vino Nobile is a superb wine from Montepulciano.

Shopping

Florence is home to some of Italy's finest shops and most intriguing boutiques. Leather goods such as shoes, bags and accessories are famous, as are fine china, bed and table linen, and gold jewelry. Designer-label fans can visit Pucci and Gucci on their home ground, and

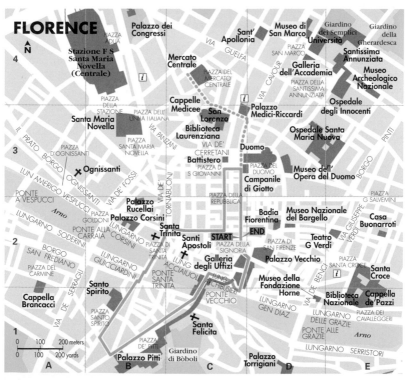

The Firenze Card

The Firenze Card, valid for 72 hours, entitles you to travel on public transportation free of charge, as well as allowing admission to more than 30 museums in Florence (€50; www.firenzecard.it). Check the website for participating museums. The pass must be activated at the first museum visited or the first bus/tram boarded.

brilliantly glazed majolica pottery, marbled paper, prints and antiques make tempting souvenirs.

Via de' Tornabuoni and the cluster of surrounding streets house the most elegant stores; less expensive fashion can be found around Piazza della Repubblica and Via dei Calzaiuoli, while jewelers line the Ponte Vecchio, their home since the 16th century. There are many factory leather outlets near Santa Croce.

The main street market is the huge Mercato San Lorenzo, which has the added bonus of its proximity to the Mercato Centrale, Florence's central food market. Most stores will ship goods direct to the United States.

Entertainment

Many tourists are content to round off the day with a leisurely dinner and evening stroll, but Florence also offers a good range of theaters, concerts, opera, ballet, movie theaters, clubs and discos. Summer visitors can catch one of the two big cultural festivals, the Estate Fiesolana or the Maggio Musicale Fiorentino. Concerts, opera and ballet are often performed outdoors in a historic setting. Look for the free monthly tourist magazine *Florence Concierge* (Concierge Tourist Information); it has full listings and lots of other helpful information.

Essential Information

Tourist Information
Via Cavour 1r ☎ 055 290 832/3
Piazza della Stazione 4 ☎ 055 212 245;
www.firenzeturismo.it and www.comune.fi.it
Piazza di San Giovanni 1 ☎ 055 288 496

Urban Transportation
Buses run from Santa Maria Novella station all over town. Tickets must be purchased from machines or tobacco shops before boarding. They are valid for unlimited journeys over a period of 90 minutes; 24-hour, 3-day and weekly passes are also available. Pick up a schedule from the ATAF office (✉ Piazza Stazione ☎ 800 424 500; www.ataf.net). Stamp the tickets as you get on; look for the

orange box on the bus. Taxis can be hailed at various locations or ordered from Taxi Firenze (☎ 055 4390) or Radio Taxi (☎ 055 4242 or 055 4798).

Airport Information
Most visitors arrive and leave from Pisa's Aeroporto Galileo Galilei (☎ 050 849 300 for flight information or ☎ 050 849 111; www.pisa-airport.com), connected to Florence's Santa Maria Novella railroad station by regular trains (journey time about 75 minutes). Florence's own airport, Amerigo Vespucci International Airport, is at Perètola (☎ 055 306 1300; www.aeroporto.firenze.it), 4 miles from the city and easily reached by bus or taxi.

Climate – average highs and lows for the month

Jan.	Feb.	Mar.	Apr.	May	Jun.	Jul.	Aug.	Sep.	Oct.	Nov.	Dec.
10°C	12°C	15°C	18°C	23°C	27°C	31°C	30°C	26°C	21°C	14°C	10°C
50°F	54°F	59°F	64°F	73°F	81°F	88°F	86°F	79°F	70°F	57°F	50°F
1°C	2°C	5°C	7°C	11°C	14°C	17°C	17°C	14°C	10°C	5°C	2°C
34°F	36°F	41°F	45°F	52°F	57°F	63°F	63°F	57°F	50°F	41°F	36°F

Florence Sights

Cappella Brancacci

Comprehensively and sensitively restored in the 1980s, the 13th-century Cappella Brancacci frescoes represent a pivotal point in art development. Commissioned in 1424 by Felice Brancacci, a wealthy merchant, the cycle illustrates the life of St. Peter. It was painted by Masolino, his dazzling pupil Masaccio, and Filippino Lippi, who completed the work 60 years later. Masaccio's radiant work, with its superb handling of light and space, drama and realism, was an inspiration for many other Renaissance artists. Highlights are the *Tribute Money*, with its weighty figures, the heart-rending *Expulsion from Paradise and St. Peter Healing the Sick*.

✚ A1 ⊠ Santa Maria del Carmine, Piazza del Carmine ☎ 055 238 2195; www.museicivicifiorentini.it/brancacci 🕔 Mon. and Wed.–Sat. 10–5, Sun. 1–5 🚇 D 🅥 $$ (combined ticket with Palazzo Vecchio. Reservations required)

Cappelle Medicee

Set behind San Lorenzo is Florentine architect Filippo Brunelleschi's serene 1419 structure that served as the Medici parish church. The Cappelle Medicee (Medici Chapels) were built as the mausoleum for Florence's most powerful family. Family members were interred in the crypt, the Sagrestia Nuova (New Sacristy) and Buontalenti's grandiose domed *Chapel of the Princes*. The Sagrestia Nuova was built by Michelangelo between 1520 and 1534 and contains some of his most powerful sculpture. Reclining figures representing *Night, Day, Dawn and Dusk* decorate the tombs of Lorenzo, Duke of Urbino, and Giuliano, Duke of Nemours. The chapel

also contains the artist's lovely *Madonna and Child*, as well as charcoal drawings thought to be by the master.

✚ C3 ⊠ Piazza Madonna degli Aldobrandini 6 ☎ 055 238 8602; www.uffizi.com 🕔 Daily 8:15–5; closed second and fourth Sun. and first, third and fifth Mon. of the month 🚇 C1 🅥 $$

Duomo, Battistero and Campanile di Giotto

The richly marbled Gothic Duomo (Cathedral) of Santa Maria del Fiore was built between 1296 and 1436 on the site of a seventh-century church. Pass through the cathedral's austere interior, with its fine Uccello fresco, to climb the 463 steps (no elevator) to the top of Brunelleschi's dome, its herringbone brickwork copied from the Pantheon in Rome. The chief draw of the marble Battistero (Baptistery), probably built between the fifth and seventh centuries and marble-covered in the 11th and 13th centuries, is the three sets of bronze doors with their Old Testament scenes. Pisano cast the south pair in 1326, and they inspired Ghiberti to design the north and east doors in the 1400s; the originals are in the Museo dell'Opera del Duomo. The graceful campanile was designed by Giotto and built by Pisano and Talenti between

Inside Santa Maria del Fiore (the Duomo)

1334 and 1359. Its pink, green and white marble walls are decorated with copies of the original relief sculptures, also displayed in the Museo dell'Opera.

✚ C3–D3 ✉ Piazza del Duomo ☎ 055 230 2885; www.operaduomo.firenze.it ◉ Cathedral: Mon.–Wed. and Fri. 10–5, Thu. 10–3:30 (Thu. times vary during the year), Sat. 10–4:45 (10–3:30 on last Sat. of month), Sun. 1:30–4:45 (call for more hours). Dome: Mon.–Fri. 8:30–7, Sat. 8:30–5:40. Baptistery: Mon.–Sat. 12:15–7, Sun. plus first Sat. of month 8:30–2. Museo dell'Opera: Mon.–Sat. 9–7:30, Sun. 9–1:45, closed public holidays. Campanile: daily 8:30–7:30 (last admission 6:40 p.m.) 🚌 23, 71; electric bus C1, C2 🚇 Cathedral free; Baptistery $$; Museo dell'Opera $$; Campanile $$

Galleria degli Uffizi

Arguably the world's greatest collection of Renaissance paintings, the Galleria degli Uffizi (Office Gallery) is an elegant arcaded building designed by Giorgio Vasari. Here, in chronological order, are paintings representative of the greatest names in art from the 13th through 18th centuries. You can trace the technical development of painting through masterpieces of perspective such as Uccello's *Battle of San Romano* (*c*1456), while Renaissance neo-Platonic philosophy is expressed in the iconography underlying Botticelli's beautiful *Birth of Venus* and *Primavera*.

Don't miss Piero della Francesca's austere double portrait of Federico da Montefeltro and his wife, Battista Sforza, Leonardo da Vinci's sublime *Adoration of the Magi* and Titian's *Venus of Urbino*. Come early or late to avoid the lines; it is also possible to reserve your visit in advance.

✚ C2 ✉ Piazzale degli Uffizi 6 ☎ 055 238 8651; www.polomuseale.firenze.it/musei/uffizi ◉ Tue.–Sun. 8:15–6:50 (occasional late opening in summer) 🚌 In pedestrian zone, but 23 and 71 run on eastern flank of museum; electric bus C1 🚇 $$ ($$$ mid-Jun. to early Nov.) ℹ Book in advance (☎ 055 294 883) or online

Galleria dell'Accademia

Founded as an art school in 1784, the Academy Gallery today houses the world's most important collection of Michelangelo sculptures. The main attraction is his *David*, possibly the most famous in the history of sculpture. Other sculptures by the artist include the four *Prisoners*, the figures struggling to escape the stone. The gallery also has work by other Renaissance artists.

✚ D4 ✉ Via Ricasoli 58–60 ☎ 055 238 8612; www.polomuseale.firenze.it/musei/accademia ◉ Tue.–Sun. 8:15–6:50 🚌 1, 7, 10, 20; electric bus C1 🚇 $$ ($$$ mid-Jul. to Aug.)

Giardino di Boboli

Florence's green lung is a revelation of geometric garden design. Laid out for the Medici in 1550 and open to the public since 1766, the Giardino di Boboli (Boboli Gardens) are truly Renaissance in spirit, an amalgam of nature and artifice. Fountains, crumbling statues, aromatic shrubs, trees and pools combine to create a garden very different from the Anglo-Saxon ideal. Highlights include the offbeat statue of Bacchus astride a tortoise and the 1785 Limonaia, where citrus trees were once stored to protect them from winter frosts.

✚ C1 ✉ Piazza dei Pitti 1 ☎ 055 238 8786; www.polomuseale.firenze.it ◉ Daily 8:15–7:30, Jun.–Aug.; 8:15–6:30, Apr., May, Sep. and Oct.; 8:15–5:30, Mar.; 8:15–4:30, Nov.–Feb. Closed first and last Mon. of month 🚌 11, 36; electric bus B 🚇 $$

Museo di San Marco

Rebuilt in 1437 and decorated by Fra Angelico, the convent attached to the church of San Marco is one of Florence's treasures. It's a peaceful religious house where each of the 44 cells is adorned with a tiny fresco to aid prayer. Designed by Michelozzo in 1437, it was funded by Cosimo il Vecchio, the first truly prominent Medici. The pilgrims' hall contains many paintings by Angelico and his school, and more are found in the cloisters and on the stairs, notably the *Annunciation*. The great Dominican reformer Savanarola was prior here at the end of the 15th century.

✚ D4 ✉ Piazza San Marco 3 ☎ 055 238 8608;

Walk
The Heart of Florence

Refer to route marked on city
map on page 89

This walk (about 2 hours long) takes
you through the heart of historic
Florence and is useful for getting
your bearings.

Start in the Piazza della Signoria.
This square is the historic center of
Florentine power, as is evident from the
looming Palazzo Vecchio, the elegant
Loggia dei Lanzi and the numerous
sculptures.
**Head toward the Arno river through the
Piazzale degli Uffizi, with the Galleria degli
Uffizi on your left. Turn right onto the
Lungarno Archibusieri to the Ponte Vecchio,
Florence's oldest bridge.**
Cross the bridge and walk along the Via
de' Guicciardini to the monumental
Palazzo Pitti, which houses another of
Florence's major art collections. Cross
the Piazza dei Pitti to the Piazza San
Felice, then cut right down the Via
Mazzetta to Piazza Santo Spirito, with its
lively atmosphere and great Brunelleschi
church. Walk down Via del Presto di

San Martino to the church's right, and
across Piazza Frescobaldi to re-cross the
river on the beautiful Ponte Santa
Trinita. Continue along Via de'
Tornabuoni, where you'll find stores
such as Versace and Gucci. Then take
a right along Via Porta Rossa to the
Mercato Nuovo, with its famous brass
boar, the Porcellino. This is a great, but
touristy, place for souvenir shopping.
 A left turn here onto Via Calimala
leads through the grandiose 19th-
century Piazza della Repubblica,
scattered with tempting sidewalk cafés,
to Via Roma. This street opens up onto
the Piazza San Giovanni, where you turn
right to visit the religious heart of the
city, the Piazza del Duomo, with the
city's cathedral, baptistery and
campanile.
**An option for hearty walkers is a detour
north from the cathedral to San Lorenzo,
the great Medici church, and up Via dell'
Ariento to Florence's Mercato Centrale, the
city's major produce market, housed in a
superb 19th-century cast-iron structure.
Return to the cathedral.**
For a shorter route from the cathedral,
turn left onto the Via dei Calzaiuoli.
A few blocks down on the right is the
church of Orsanmichele, Florence's
medieval guild church, with its
Renaissance sculptures and Bernardo
Daddi fresco. Via dei Calzaiuoli leads
back to the Piazza della Signoria.

The 14th-century Campanile, designed by Giotto, stands alongside the Duomo

Jewelers' shops and houses line the Ponte Vecchio, one of the world's most famous bridges

www.polomuseale.firenze.it ⊙ Mon.–Fri. 8:15–1:50, Sat.–Sun. 8:15–4:50; closed second and fourth Mon. of the month 🚌 7, 10, 25; electric bus C1 ✋ $$

Museo Nazionale del Bargello

The Bargello was built in 1255 as the first seat of Florence's government, and went on to house the law courts. In 1574 it passed to the police department and served as a prison until 1859. It opened as a museum in 1865. Today it houses Italy's finest collection of Renaissance sculpture. Airy rooms surround a spacious courtyard and you'll find works by Michelangelo, Cellini and Giambologna. The vaulted first-floor hall has the museum's masterpieces: Donatello's jaunty bronze *David*, the first free-standing nude to be modeled since Roman times, his fine *St. George*, and the baptistery door reliefs by Brunelleschi and Ghiberti.

✚ D2 ✉ Via del Proconsolo 4 ☎ 055 238 8606; www.polomuseale.firenze.it ⊙ Daily 8:15–1:50. Closed first, third and fifth Sun. and fourth Mon. of month. Ticket offices close at 1:20 p.m. 🚌 23, 71; electric bus C2, C3 ✋ $$

Palazzo Medici–Riccardi

Designed by Michelangelo in 1444, the the Palazzo Medici-Riccardi's solid exterior of heavy rusticated stonework is lifted by the beautiful courtyard, with its sgrafitto decoration. The interior contains the Cappella dei Magi, a tiny chapel totally covered with charming frescoes. Executed by Benozzo Gozzoli from 1459 to 1463, they show the Magi, gorgeously dressed in contemporary high fashion, walking through an idealized Tuscan landscape rich with flowers and birds.

✚ C3 ✉ Via Cavour 3 ☎ 055 276 0340; www.palazzo-medici.it ⊙ Thu.–Tue. 9–7; reserve tickets in advance for Cappella dei Magi 🚌 1, 11, 14, 17, 23; electric bus C1 ✋ $$

Palazzo Pitti

This palace was the Medici residence from 1550 until 1743, when they bequeathed their collections to the city. It now houses six museums, including the Galleria Palatina and the Museo degli Argenti. The former is primarily a painting gallery, where you'll find

which overlooks the square where executions took place, riotous crowds assembled and religious fanatics preached. The square itself and the graceful Loggia dei Lanzi display an impressive range of sculptures. The horseman, a statue by Giambologna dated 1595, is Duke Cosimo I, the Medici who brought all of Tuscany under military rule. Don't miss Benvenuto Cellini's *Perseus*, who holds aloft Medusa's head.

➕ C2 ✉ Piazza della Signoria 🍽 Bars and restaurants nearby 🚌 In pedestrian zone

Ponte Vecchio

Not the most beautiful Florentine bridge, but certainly the most photographed, the Ponte Vecchio (Old Bridge) was built in 1345 to replace an earlier one. It is lined with shops, exclusively goldsmiths and jewelers since 1593. Above them runs a corridor used by the Medici to travel from the Pitti to the Uffizi. It was the only bridge not destroyed by the Germans during World War II, and it also survived the floods in 1966.

➕ C2 ✉ Ponte Vecchio 🚌 In pedestrian zone

Santa Croce

This huge Franciscan preaching church, damaged by the 1966 floods, was built in 1294 – although the marble facade dates from 1863, funded by Englishman Sir Francis Sloane. The interior of the basilica contains superb early Gaddi frescoes that tell the story of the Santa Croce (Holy Cross). The Bardi and Peruzzi chapels feature frescoes by Giotto. Michelangelo is buried here, as are Galileo Galilei, Machiavelli and Antonio Rossini. In the cloisters stand a small museum and the beautiful Cappella dei Pazzi (Pazzi Chapel), designed by Brunelleschi in the 1430s.

➕ E2 ✉ Piazza Santa Croce ☎ 055 246 6105 (museum); www.santacroceopera.it 🕐 Mon.–Sat. 9:30–5:30; Sun. 1–5:30 (last entry 5 p.m.) 🚌 14, 23; electric bus B, C 🍽 Enoteca Pinchiorri, see page 205 🎟 $$ (combined ticket includes museum)

Raphael's *Madonna of the Chair, Mary Magdalene* by Titian and some fine portraits. The art objects in the Museo degli Argenti mostly represent a triumph of expensive bad taste, although the Roman glass and cameo collection is good. The Pitti also houses the Appartamenti Monumentali (State Rooms), the Galleria del Costume (Costume Museum), the Galleria d'Arte Moderna (Modern Art Gallery) and the Museo delle Porcellane (Porcelain Museum).

➕ B1 ✉ Piazza dei Pitti 📷 Galleria Palatina, Museo degli Argenti 055 294 883 (tickets); www.polomuseale. firenze.it (information) 🕐 Galleria Palatina: Tue.–Sun. 8:15–6:50, Feb.–Dec. Museo degli Argenti: daily 8:15–6:50, Jun.–Aug.; 8:15–6.30, Apr.–May and Sep.–Oct.; 8:15–5:30, Mar.; 8:15–4:30, Nov.–Feb. (closed first and last Mon. of month) 🚌 11, 36, 37; electric bus B 🎟 Palatina $$$; Argenti $$; combined ticket includes Boboli and Bardini gardens, and Costume and Porcelain museums

Piazza della Signoria

Piazza della Signoria was the center of Medici and Florentine power. The council met in the Palazzo Vecchio,

The Flood of 1966

As you walk the streets of Florence, keep an eye open above your head for the small stone plaques on many buildings; they mark the height to which the floodwaters of the Arno river rose on the night of November 4, 1966. It was an event that proved a catastrophe for the city and its art.

October 1966 was a very wet month throughout Italy, while the first two days of November saw 18 inches of rain fall in the Florence area. Water pressure rose dangerously in an upstream reservoir, and the authorities, fearing its dam might break, opened the sluices. They failed to warn anyone in the city of Florence; only the jewelers whose shops lined the Ponte Vecchio were alerted by their own night watchman who noticed that the bridge was shaking as the waters rose. As the traders cleared their stock, they asked watching police if the alarm had been officially raised, only to be told that no orders had been received.

Shortly after, the banks of the Arno could no longer contain the unprecedented tons of water. They broke, releasing a flash flood of more than 500,000 tons of water and mud that poured with startling speed through the city. Thirty-five Florentine citizens were drowned in the first onrush, many trapped in the underpass of Santa Maria Novella railroad station. The muddy floodwaters mixed with heating oil stored in basements and cellars, and it was this ghastly cocktail that did the harm. Damage to homes, shops and businesses was huge, with many families losing all their possessions.

Above: Cars re-emerging as the waters subside and the scale of the damage becomes apparent

The world's attention, though, was focused on the damage to works of art, particularly in the Santa Croce area, one of the lowest parts of Florence. More than 3,000 paintings were damaged, some irretrievably. Antiquities were destroyed, and thousands of priceless books and manuscripts were lost.

Within days, voluntary workers, many of them art students, were arriving to begin the rescue operation. They worked nonstop in appalling conditions heaving artworks to safety and starting the drying-out process on books and manuscripts.

Money poured in from all over the world, and by the following summer Florence was itself again – at least superficially. Behind the scenes, however, the task of art restoration was immense and, almost 50 years later, work still continues on paintings, sculpture, books and manuscripts.

One beneficial result of the disaster was the tremendous strides made in the development of restoration techniques to cope with the flood's effects. Frescoes had to be stabilized, oil paintings painstakingly reassembled from fragments, and priceless books dried and cleaned.

Later projects throughout Italy, such as the restoration of such major works as Michelangelo's frescoes in the Sistine Chapel in Rome and Piero della Francesca's frescoes in Arezzo, owe much to the efforts in Florence. International co-operation among restorers all over the world forged ahead, and galleries and museums worldwide have profited from the city's restoration challenges.

Regional Sights

Key to symbols

➕ map coordinates refer to the region map on pages 84–85 🅱 admission charge: $$$ more than €7, $$ €4–€7, $ less than €4

See page 5 for complete key to symbols

Arezzo

Well-heeled Arezzo, its modern wealth based on the fact that it is the world's largest manufacturing center of gold, spreads down a hill above the Arno valley in eastern Tuscany.

A major Etruscan city, it thrived under the Romans and was a prosperous medieval republic until 1384, when it was annexed by Florence. Today, Arezzo's chief glory is the superb fresco cycle, *The Legend of the True Cross*, by the enigmatic Renaissance artist Piero della Francesca, in the church of San Francesco. Lengthily and superbly restored in the 1990s, these luminous paintings, executed between 1452 and 1466, tell the story of the cross used to crucify Christ.

Near San Francesco is the Pieve di Santa Maria, an earlier Romanesque church with an exuberant facade and Pietro Lorenzetti's glowing high altar polyptych showing the *Madonna and Child with Saints*. The church is backed by the Piazza Grande, a sloping medieval square with a loggia on its north side. The piazza is the scene of Arezzo's major festival, the *Giostra del Saraceno*, a jousting display preceded by costumed processions.

The Duomo (Cathedral) stands at Arezzo's highest point; constructed over more than four centuries, its facade was finally finished in the 20th century. Inside there are glowing stained-glass windows; Guido Tarlati's tomb, said to have been designed by Giotto; and the tiny fresco *Magdalene*, another work by Piero della Francesca. Elsewhere,

Arezzo's shops offer temptations; the town is a noted antiques center, with a monthly antiques fair, *Fiera Antiquaria*, on the first Sunday of each month.

➕ C2

Tourist information (APT) ✉ Palazzo Comunale, Piazza della Libertà 1 ☎ 0575 401 945; www.apt. arezzo.it 🕔 Mon.–Fri. 11–1 and 2–4, Sat.–Sun. 11–4, also 24/7 touch-screen information at Piazza della Repubblica 28

San Francesco ✉ Piazza San Francesco 1 ☎ 0575 20 630; www.pierodellafrancesca.it 🕔 Church: Mon.–Fri. 9–6:30, Sat. 9–5:30, Sun. 1–5:30 🅱 Free 🅸 Guided visits to the frescoes every 30 mins during opening hours, must be booked in advance on 0575 352 727 ($$)

Pieve di Santa Maria ✉ Corso Italia 7 ☎ 0575 22 629 🕔 Daily 8–1 and 3–7, May–Sep.; 8–noon, 3–6, rest of year 🅱 Free

Duomo ✉ Piazza del Duomo ☎ 0575 23 991 🕔 Daily 7/8:30–12:30 and 3–6:30/7 🅱 Free 🅸 Giostra del Saraceno is held on first Sun. in Sep. and third Sun. (or second last Sun.) of Jun.

Ascoli Piceno

Ascoli Piceno stands in a steep hollow 15 miles from the Adriatic coast. The streets still follow those of the Roman colony established after the defeat of the Picini, an early tribe. The heart of the town is the Piazza del Popolo, an ensemble of medieval and Renaissance buildings, all made of the travertine stone of which Ascoli is constructed.

On the piazza's north side stands the lovely Gothic San Francesco church, with its graceful five-arched loggia and slender bell towers. Other delights include the Duomo (Cathedral), which contains an art gallery and an archeological museum; and the tangle of beguiling streets at the top of the Via del Trivio above the Tronto river.

➕ E1

Tourist information ✉ Piazza del Popolo ☎ 0736 253 045; www.rinascita.it 🕔 Mon.–Fri. 9–12:30 and 3–6:30, Sat.–Sun. 9–1 (hours can vary and may be longer in summer)

San Francesco ✉ Piazza del Popolo ☎ 0736 259 496 🕔 Daily 8–12:30 and 3:30–7 🅱 Free

---

Opposite: San Gimignano, known as the City of Towers or Medieval Manhattan

Duomo ✉ Piazza Arringo ⏱ Daily 8–12:30 and 4–8 💺 Free

Pinacoteca Civica ✉ Palazzo Arringo, Piazza Arringo 7 ☎ 0736 298 213; www.ascolimusei.it ⏱ Tue.–Sun. 10–7, mid-Mar. to Sep.; Tue.–Fri. 10–5, Sat.–Sun. 10–7, rest of year. Guided visits daily at 10:30, noon, 3, 4:15 and 6 💺 $$$

Museo Archeologico ✉ Piazza Arringo 28 ☎ 0736 253 562; www.archeomarche.it ⏱ Tue.–Sun. 8:30–7:30 💺 $ ℹ Quintana is held on the first Sun. in Aug.

Assisi

The town of Assisi is inextricably linked with St. Francis (1182–1226), the founder of the Franciscan order, and is visited by pilgrims from all over the world. In late 1997, Assisi was damaged by a series of earthquakes, and the Basilica di San Francesco lost some of its lesser treasures forever. The lower church, built around 1228, and the upper church have reopened, and the 28 panels of Giotto's *Life of St. Francis* have been restored. The most powerful of the lower church frescoes are Simone Martini's *Life of St. Martin* and Lorenzetti's *Deposition and Crucifixion.*

At the opposite end of town is Santa Chiara, the burial place of St. Clare, the companion of St. Francis and founder of the Poor Clares, the Franciscan nuns. The square outside this pink-and-white striped Gothic building offers lovely

Vineyard near Castellina in Chianti

views. Above the square stands the Duomo (Cathedral); built from 1140 to 1253, it has a beautiful Romanesque facade. Back toward the basilica is the Piazza del Comune, a lovely medieval square on the probable site of the Roman forum. The focal point is the superb first-century Tempio di Minerva. The Pinacoteca Comunale (Art Gallery) occupies an old town house. The San Damiano is a country church and convent where St. Francis composed the *Canticle to the Sun.* Equally lovely is the Eremo delle Carceri, a monastery and retreat for St. Francis.

➕ D2

Tourist information ✉ Piazza del Comune 9 ☎ 075 813 8680 or 075 813 8681; www.conoscerelumbria. regioneumbria.eu or www.lamiaumbria.it ⏱ Mon.–Sat. 8–2 and 3–6, Sun. 10–1 and 2–5, Apr.–Sep.; Mon.–Sat. 8–2 and 3–6, Sun. 9–1, rest of year

Basilica di San Francesco ✉ Piazza San Francesco 2 ☎ 075 819 001, 075 819 0084 (information office); www.sanfrancescoassisi.org ⏱ Lower Church: Mon.–Sat. 6–5:45, Sun. 6–7:15; Upper Church: Mon.–Sat. 8:30–5:45, Sun. 8:30–6:45. Hours may vary 💺 Free

Basilica di Santa Chiara ✉ Piazza Santa Chiara ☎ 075 812 282 ⏱ Daily 6:30–noon and 2–7, Apr.–Sep.; 6:30–noon and 2–6, rest of year 💺 Free

Duomo ✉ Piazza San Rufino ☎ 075 816 016 ⏱ Daily 8–1 and 3–7, Apr.–Sep.; 8–noon and 2–6, rest of year 💺 Free

Pinacoteca Comunale ✉ Via San Francesco 10 ☎ 075 812 033; information line (in Italy) 199 194 114 ⏱ Daily 10–1 and 2–6, mid-Mar. to mid-Oct.; 10–1 and 2–5, rest of year 💺 $

San Damiano ✉ Via San Damiano ☎ 075 812 273 ⏱ Daily 10–12:30 and 2–6 💺 Free

Eremo delle Carceri ☎ 075 812 301; www.eremocarceri.it ⏱ Daily 8:30–6:30, May–Sep.; 8:30–5:30, rest of year 💺 Free

Chianti

Between Florence and Siena lies Chianti, an area of wooded hills and vineyards dotted with intriguing villages and threaded by winding back roads. The most famous product is wine; trademark Gallo Nero (Black Cockerel) is known all over the world.

Chianti's good climate and fascinating surroundings have been attracting northern Europeans since the 1960s, and international visitors have bought and converted many of the lovely old houses, while once-unspoiled hill towns such as Radda in Chianti and Gaiole are now packed with visitors. The best way to enjoy this region is to leave the main roads. Explore the woods and smaller villages and sample the wines at any of several hundred vineyards as you go.

Wine lovers will enjoy Greve in Chianti; in September it's the scene of the area's biggest wine fair. Greve has a lively Saturday market in its main piazza, where you'll also find a statue of Giovanni da Verrazzano, the discoverer of New York Harbor in 1524.

Greve in Chianti ✚ B3

Tourist information ✉ Piazza Matteoti 11, Greve in Chianti ☎ 055 854 6299; www.firenzeturismo.it ◉ Daily 10–1 and 3–7, Apr.–Oct. 🚩 Greve Wine Fair is held in Sep.; further details from the tourist office

Gubbio

Few tourists venture as far as Gubbio, tucked beneath rolling mountains near Umbria's eastern border. But this charming town, once the most important *comune* between Rome and Ravenna, is rich in quaint streets, superb old palaces, churches and paintings. Start a tour at the bottom of the Old Town, where you'll find the church of San Francesco, with an engaging fresco (1410) by Ottaviano Nelli, and the 14th-century Loggia dei Tiratori, Italy's best-preserved example of a weaver's shed, where wool was spread to dry away from direct sunlight.

Up the hill stands the solid bulk of the 14th-century battlemented Palazzo dei Consoli, Gubbio's civic masterpiece, fronted by the sweeping Piazza Grande. It now houses the town's museum and art gallery. Nearby stand the cathedral and the Palazzo Ducale, built by Federico da Montefeltro, the Duke of neighboring Urbino (see page 113), in 1470. From here, you can climb Monte Ingino, which rises above the town, to visit the Basilica di Sant' Ubaldo, Gubbio's patron saint. The gigantic wooden *ceri* (candles), each weighing up to 400kg (880 pounds), carried in the *Corsa dei Ceri*, a famous race and festival held May 15, are stored here.

✚ D2

Tourist information ✉ Via della Repubblica 15 ☎ 075 922 0693; www.comune.gubbio.pg.it ◉ Mon.–Fri. 8:30–1:45 and 3–6, Sat. 9–1 and 3–6, Sun. 9:30–12:30

Museo Civico ✉ Piazza Grande ☎ 075 927 4298 ◉ Daily 10–1 and 3–6, Apr.–Sep.; 10–1 and 2:30–5:30, rest of year 🤚 $$

Lago Trasimeno

Italy's fourth largest lake is a shallow expanse of warm water fringed with beaches and laid-back little towns. Lago Trasimeno (Lake Trasimeno) makes an excellent stopping point for a couple of days of relaxation. Castiglione del Lago, on the western shore, has a fine fortified 16th-century castle jutting into the lake and some pleasant swimming beaches.

Passignano, on the opposite shore, is a friendly town with a lakeside promenade and good bars and restaurants. In the hills behind Passignano you'll find Castel Rigone, a pretty village with fantastic views. Tuoro is another hill village above the lake; between here and Passignano is the site of Hannibal's great defeat of the Romans in 217 BC. Village names such as Sanguineto (Place of Blood) and Ossaia (Place of Bones) are permanent reminders of the great Carthaginian general.

✚ C2

Castiglione del Lago tourist information ✉ Piazza Mazzini 10 ☎ 075 965 2484 ◉ Mon.–Sat. 9–1 and 3:30–7, Sun. 9–1 and 4–7, Apr.–Oct.; Mon.–Fri. 9–1 and 3:30–7, Sat. 9–1, rest of year

Passignano tourist information ✉ Piazza Trento e Trieste 6 ☎ 075 827 635 ◉ Mon.–Sat. 10:30–12:30 and 4–7, Sun. 10:30–12:30, Jun.–Sep.; Fri.–Sat. 3–6:30, Sun. 10–12:30, rest of year 🚢 Boats run daily to Isola Maggiore, Trasimeno's largest inhabited island, from Passignano. Contact APM (☎ 075 506 781; www.trasimeno.ws) for further information

Drive
Eastern Umbria to the Vale of Spoleto

Duration: 3.5 to 4 hours

This drive starts in remote Gubbio (see page 101), a stone-built, fortress-like town in the hills of northeast Umbria.

From Gubbio, take the SS298 heading southwest through the hills toward Perugia.
This scenic road takes you past villages and farms to join the *superstrada* (highway) SS3bis in the upper valley of the Tiber river. The highway proceeds to Rome and Ostia.
Turn left onto the SS3bis and continue for 6 miles (10 kilometers) before joining the

SS147 south (marked Assisi, Foligno and Spoleto). At the Assisi exit, follow the signs up the hill toward the town.
The huge domed church in the lower modern part of Assisi is Santa Maria degli Angeli. It was begun in 1569, although the present building dates from 1832. The basilica is constructed around the Porzuincola, the tiny chapel where St. Francis lived in the earliest days of the Franciscan movement. In the garden you can see thornless rose bushes; according to legend they are the descendants of those into which the saint threw himself while grappling with temptation. As he fell they lost their spines, while their leaves became stained with drops of blood.
Do not drive into Assisi unless you have hotel reservations; the streets are narrow and steep, and there is no municipal parking. Leave your car in one of the pay parking lots outside town and walk (see page 100). From Assisi you can take the unclassified, part-dirt road over Monte Subasio to Spello (see page 112), and then join the SS75 to Foligno.
This beautiful route leads through upland meadows, carpeted in spring and

Looking out across a fertile vineyard and toward the medieval town of Montefalco

early summer with spreads of wildflowers. From the road there are wide views over the plain. It's the perfect spot for a picnic. You wander on the grassy slopes and along the little trails on the mountain's heights.

Alternatively, head straight for Foligno on the SS75. Turn right at Foligno across the plain and continue for about 4.5 miles (7.5 kilometers) to Bevagna.

The main square of this sleepy and undiscovered town contains two of Umbria's finest Romanesque churches, San Silvestro and San Michele. They were both built at the end of the 12th century. The facade of San Silvestro, now deconsecrated, was constructed using old fragments of Roman buildings; its shadowy interior has a marvelous sunken crypt. San Michele's facade was embellished with a rose window in the 18th century; look for the quirky gargoyles over the doorway.

From Bevagna, continue about 4 miles (6.5 kilometers) southeast to Montefalco.

Montefalco is a superbly located town packed with artistic delights and noted for its fine wines. Made with the

Sagrantino grape, found nowhere else in Europe, the pick of these full-flavored reds is perhaps Sagrantino Passito, a stunning sweet red dessert wine. Montefalco's chief attraction is the fresco cycle by Benozzo Gozzoli in the church of San Francesco, now a museum. Painted in 1452, the cycle depicts scenes from the life of St. Francis with charming detail. Other treasures include Perugino's 1503 Nativity, complete with a fine view of Lake Trasimeno (see page 101) in the background. The nearby church of Sant'Agostino contains mummies of local holy people, while the church of Santa Chiara contains the preserved body of St. Chiara of Montefalco.

From Montefalco, head east across the plain through San Luca to Fabbri). Pick up the SS3, which will take you south to Spoleto (see page 112).

Montefalco www.montefalco.it

Museo Civico di San Francesco ✉ Via Ringhiere Umbra 6 ☎ 0742 379598 🕐 Daily 10:30–1 and 3–7, Jun.–Jul.; 10:30–1 and 3–7:30, Aug.; 10:30–1 and 2–6, Mar.–May and Sep.–Oct.; Tue.–Sun. 10:30–1 and 2:30–5, rest of year 💺 $$

The Church of San Michele in Foro, Lucca

Lucca

Set in northern Tuscany at the foot of the Alpi Apuane, Lucca, with its tree-lined encircling walls, magnificent churches and solid provincial prosperity, is instantly appealing. There are three outstanding churches here, all built and decorated in the ornate 13th-century style known as Pisan Romanesque.

San Michele in Foro dominates the main piazza. Its exuberant facade is a riot of columns, grotesques and carvings. Nearby, the Duomo (Cathedral) is fronted by a superb portal carved by Nicola Pisano. The interior houses the Tempietto, a shrine containing the venerated icon known as the *Volto Santo* (Holy Face). To the north is San Frediano; its facade glitters with 13th-century mosaics and its interior boasts a 12th-century font. Near here, just off Lucca's main shopping street, you'll find the Piazza Anfiteatro, a glorious oval built around the Roman amphitheater. Lucca's best museum is the Museo Nazionale Guinigi with its collection of art, sculpture and furniture. Be sure to leave time to walk the 16th-century walls and look for the Torre Guinigi, a 15th-century tower.

Near Lucca is a group of elegant country villas, the summer homes of wealthy citizens of the 15th through 18th centuries. Many have superb gardens that are open to the public.

Details about the gardens can be obtained from the tourist information office. The birthplace of Giacomo Puccini is at Corte San Lorenzo.

⊞ B3

Tourist information ⊠ Piazza Santa Maria 35 ☎ 0583 919 931; www.luccatourist.it, www.luccaturismo.it or www.accademiadelturismo.com ◷ Daily 9–7:30, Apr.–Oct.; Mon.–Sat. 9–noon and 3–6, rest of year ⓘ An English-language audio guide to Lucca is available from the tourist office

San Michele in Foro ⊠ Piazza San Michele ☎ 0583 48 459 ◷ Daily 9–noon and 3–6, mid-Mar. to Oct.; 9–noon and 3–5, rest of year ⓦ Free

Duomo di San Martino ⊠ Piazza San Martino ☎ 0583 490 530; www.museocattedralelucca.it ◷ Daily 7–5:45. Sacristy: daily 10–6, Apr.–Oct.; Mon.–Fri. 10–2, Sat.–Sun. 10–5, rest of year ⓦ Cathedral free; Tomb of Ilaria Carretto $

San Frediano ⊠ Piazza San Frediano ☎ 0583 493 627 ◷ Daily 9–noon and 3–6, mid-Mar. to Oct.; 9–noon and 3–5, rest of year ⓦ Free

Museo Nazionale Guinigi ⊠ Via della Quarquonia ☎ 0583 496 033 ◷ Tue.–Sat. 8:30–7:30, Sun. 8:30–1:30 ⓦ $$ (combined ticket with Palazzo Mausi)

Casa Natale di Puccini ⊠ Corte San Lorenzo 9 ☎ 0583 584 028; www.fondazionegiacomopuccini.it ◷ Daily 10–6, Apr.–Oct.; 11–5, rest of year ⓦ $$$

Montalcino

Hilltop Montalcino, encircled by walls and dominated by its Rocca (fortress), was independent until 1260, when it became part of Siena. Montalcino heroically held out until 1555 as the last bastion of Sienese independence against the Florentines. This role is still commemorated during Siena's Palio (see page 115). Centuries of stagnation followed, until the 1960s saw the revival of its famous wine, Brunello di Montalcino, and the growth of tourism.

First explore the striking 14th-century fortress, and climb the walls for superb views over the idyllic southern Tuscan landscape. The fortress also contains a busy a wine cellar where you can buy or sample superlative red wines. The Museo Civico e Diocesano d'Arte Sacra houses high-quality Sienese paintings and sculpture; among the finest is Sano di Pietro's *Madonna dell'Umiltà*, a rare portrayal of a kneeling Mary.

Take the road south to the Abbazia di Sant'Antimo, a 12th-century Benedictine abbey that stands alone amid olive trees and cypresses on the Francigena, one of Europe's ancient pilgrim routes. This glorious Romanesque building is noted for the carving on its pillars and its luminous interior.

☩ B2

Tourist information ✉ Costa del Municipio 1 ☎ 0577 849 331; www.terresiena.it ⊕ Daily 10–1 and 2–7, Apr.–Oct.; Tue.–Sun. 10–1 and 2–5:45, rest of year ⓘ Torneo della Apertura della Caccia (second Sun. in Aug.) and Sagra del Tordo (last Sun. in Oct.) feature costumed processions, archery tournaments and street banquets **Rocca** ✉ Piazzale Fortezza ☎ 0577 849 211 ⊕ Daily 9–8, Apr.–Oct.; 10–6, rest of year ⓦ Free; Tower $$ **Museo Civico e Diocesano d'Arte Sacra** ✉ Via Ricasoli 31 ☎ 0577 846 014 ⊕ Tue.–Sun. 10–1, 2–5:50, Apr.–Oct.; 10–1 and 2–5:40, rest of year ⓦ $$ (combined ticket with Rocca) **Abbazia di Sant'Antimo** ☎ 0577 835 659; www.antimo.it ✉ Castelnuovo dell'Abate ⊕ Mon.–Sat. 10:15–12:30 and 3–6:30, Sun. 9:15–10:45 and 3–6. Hours may vary ⓦ Free

Montepulciano

The highest of southern Tuscany's hilltop towns, Montepulciano sprawls down a narrow ridge, its picturesque side streets opening to gracious squares where you'll find a fascinating mixture of medieval, Renaissance and baroque architecture in churches and palaces. Following an alliance with Florence in 1511, money poured into the town, resulting in superb civic and private buildings designed by the architects Sangallo and Vignola. The focus is the Piazza Grande, where there are wonderful views from the Palazzo Comunale. The brick-faced cathedral has a serene Renaissance interior containing some great works of art, notably the glowing *Assumption* painted by Taddeo di Bartolo in 1401.

You can see more art in the Museo Civico before heading beyond the walls to San Biagio (St. Blaise), a glowing, honey-colored pilgrimage church designed by Antonio da Sangallo in 1518. Leave time to taste the town's red wine, the Vino Nobile, which you'll find in wine shops all over Montepulciano.

☩ C2

Tourist information ✉ Piazza Don Minzoni 1 ☎ 0578 757 341; www.terresiena.it or www.montepulciano.com ⊕ Mon.–Sat. 9:30–12:30 and 3–6, Sun. 9:30–12:30 ⓘ Cantiere Internazionale d'Arte (www.fondazionecantiere.it), a contemporary music festival, is held Jul.–Aug.; Bravio delle Botti, with costumed processions, a barrel race and street banquets, is on the last Sun. in Aug. **Palazzo Comunale** ✉ Piazza Grande ☎ 0578 712 243 ⊕ Mon.–Sat. 10–6 but call for latest times ⓦ $ **Museo Civico** ✉ Palazzo Neri-Orselli, Via Ricci 10 ☎ 0578 717 300 ⊕ Tue.–Sat. 10–1 and 3–6, Sun. 10–7, Apr.–Sep.; Tue.–Sun. 10–1 and 3–5, rest of year ⓦ $$ **San Biagio** ✉ Via di San Biagio ⊕ Daily 8:30–6:30 ⓦ Free

Norcia

Norcia is a low-key, friendly town. Tucked away in eastern Umbria at the foot of some of the region's most dramatic mountains, this solid little walled town is famed as the birthplace of St. Benedict, founder of the Benedictine order and patron saint of Europe.

The church of San Benedetto lies on the main piazza; its Gothic facade dates from 1389. Within the interior are the remains of a Roman building, reputedly the birthplace of the saint and his sister, St. Scholastica. Across the square is the Castellina, a massive fortress designed by Giacomo da Vignola in 1563, which houses an interesting museum. Norcia is famous for food – prosciutto, salami, sausages and above all truffles, the black gold of Umbrian cuisine. You could fuel your appetite by hiking on the Piano Grande to the east; this unique upland plain, surrounded by grassy flower-covered mountains, is one of Umbria's least-known and most beautiful areas.

✚ D1

✉ Via Solferino 22 ☎ 0743 817 090;
www.orvietoturismo.it 🄒 Mon.–Sat. 10–noon and
3:30–5, May–Sep. ℹ Last two weekends of Feb. (or
last weekend of Feb. and first of Mar.) the Mostra
Mercato del Tartufo takes place with tastings of food
from the region, including the local prized black truffles
(www.neronorcia.it/mostramercato)

Orvieto

A crag formed by an ancient volcano
first attracted the Etruscans to the site of
modern Orvieto, where they built a
settlement, Volsinii. You can still view
Etruscan tombs here, but most visitors
are lured to Orvieto by what is arguably
Italy's finest Gothic Duomo (Cathedral).

Construction started in the 13th
century to celebrate the Miracle of
Bolsena. During Mass, the communion
host dripped blood on the altar cloth;
this was the origin of the feast of the
Body of Christ, which has continued for
centuries. The facade alone, glittering
with mosaics and liberally endowed with
sculpture, took more than 300 years to
complete. The best-known interior work
is Luca Signorelli's fresco *Last Judgment*
(1504), a taut and technically stunning
masterpiece that has been superbly
restored.

Other highlights include the Etruscan
collection in the Museo Claudio Faina
and the Pozzo di San Patrizio (St.
Patrick's Well), an engineering tour de
force with an impressive double ramp
leading 62 feet into living rock. Orvieto
is noted for its colorful *maiolica*
(majolica) pottery and other ceramics;
look for examples in stores in the streets
around the Piazza del Duomo.

✚ C1

Tourist information ✉ Piazza del Duomo 24
☎ 0763 341 772; www.orvietoturismo.it 🄒 Mon.–
Thu. 8–2 and 4–7, Sat.–Sun. 10–1 and 3–6
Duomo ✉ Piazza del Duomo ☎ 0763 343 592;
www.opsm.it 🄒 Mon.–Sat. 9:30–7, Sun. 1–5:30,
Apr.–Sep.; Mon.–Sat. 9:30–6, Sun. 1–5:30, Mar. and
Oct.; Mon.–Sat. 9:30–1 and 2:30–5, Sun. 2:30–5, rest of
year 🎟 Cathedral $; Cappella Nuova (Signorelli's *Last
Judgment*) $

Cappella Nuova ✉ Piazza del Duomo 🄒 Mon.–Sat.
9:30–7, Sun. 1–5:30, Apr–Sep.; Mon.–Sat. 9:30–6, Sun.
1–5:30, Mar. and Oct.; Mon.–Sat. 9:30–1 and 3:30–5,
Sun. 2:30–5, rest of year 🎟 $
Museo Claudio Faina ✉ Piazza del Duomo 29
☎ 0763 341 216; www.museofaina.it 🄒 Daily 9:30–6,
Apr.–Sep.; 9:30–6, Oct.; Tue.–Sun. 10–5, rest of year
🎟 $$
Pozzo di San Patrizio ✉ Viale Sangallo (near funicular
stop on Piazza Cahen) ☎ 0763 343 768 🄒 Daily
10–6:45, Apr.–Sep.; 10–5:45, rest of year 🎟 $$

Perugia

Umbria's capital, Perugia, is surrounded
by ugly modern suburbs, but it's worth
negotiating these to explore the
unspoiled, traffic-free, historic center.
Parking is difficult, so leave the car in
the lower town and use the escalators
(*scala mobile*) to rise painlessly up to the
hilltop core. Most of the main sights are
on or near Corso Vannucci, a wide and
gracious street running to Piazza IV
Novembre, where you'll find the Duomo
(Cathedral) and the exquisite 13th-
century Fontana Maggiore. This
two-basin fountain was sculpted by
Nicola and Giovanni Pisano and is
surrounded by statues and carvings;
those showing the months of the year
are particularly charming. The Palazzo
dei Priori, the town hall, also houses the
Galleria Nazionale dell'Umbria, one of
central Italy's most important art
collections, stunningly presented in light
and airy galleries. Here you can trace the
development of Umbrian painting, with
some superb Sienese and Florentine
works as an added bonus. Highlights
include Duccio's lovely *Madonna and
Child*, Fra' Angelico's heavenly blue
triptych *Madonna with Angels and Saints*,
and the radiant symmetry of Piero della
Francesca's great polyptych *Madonna
and Child with Saints* – note the use of
perspective in the *Annunciation* panel.

Umbria's great duo, Perugino and
Bernardino Pinturicchio, are represented
by numerous paintings, suffused with
light and color and perfectly
encapsulating the distinct Umbrian style.

Perugino also is the star of the Collegio del Cambio just down the street; he was commissioned in 1496 to decorate Perúgia's money changers' guild home, and he decorated the walls and ceiling with a fusion of classical and Christian themes. Close by, you can visit the Collegio della Mercanzia, the Merchants' Guild, to admire its 15th-century wood paneling. Perugia's other treasures include the graceful Renaissance Oratorio di San Bernardino, the grand and opulent church of San Pietro, and San Domenico, whose cloisters house the Museo Archeologico Nazionale dell'Umbria. Perugia's Corso Vannucci has a choice of shops where you can buy locally made chocolates.

➕ C2

Tourist information 🖂 Loggia dei Linari, Piazza Matteotti 18 ☎ 075 573 6458; www.umbria-turismo.it or www.conoscerelumbria.regioneumbria.eu 🕔 Daily 8:30–6:30 ℹ️ The Card Perúgia Città Pass ($$) is available in several versions and combines a variety of sights (tel: 075 572 3832; www.umbriaonline.com). Umbria Jazz Festival takes place mid-Jul. for 10 days (tel: 075 573 2432; www.umbriajazz.com). Eurochocolate, a huge festival devoted to chocolate, is held on the third week of Oct. tel: 075 502 5880; www.eurochocolate.com)

Duomo 🖂 Piazza IV Novembre 🕔 Daily 8–noon and 3:30–6 ✋ Free

Galleria Nazionale dell'Umbria 🖂 Palazzo dei Priori, Corso Vannucci 19 ☎ 075 5866 8410; www.gallerianazionaleumbria.it 🕔 Tue.–Sun. 8:30–7:30 ✋ $$

Collegio del Cambio 🖂 Corso Vannucci 25 ☎ 075 572 8599 🕔 Daily 9–12:30 and 2:30–5:30, Mar.–Oct.; Tue.–Sun. 9–noon and 2:30–5:30, rest of year ✋ $$ (combined ticket with Collegio della Mercanzia)

Collegio della Mercanzia 🖂 Corso Vannucci 15 ☎ 075 573 0366 🕔 Daily 9–12:30 and 2:30–5:30, Mar.–Oct.; Tue.–Sun. 9–noon and 2:30–5:30, rest of year ✋ $ ($$ with Collegio del Cambio)

Oratorio di San Bernardino 🖂 Piazza San Francesco ☎ 075 573 3957 🕔 Interior: daily 8–12:30 and 3:30–6 ✋ Free

San Pietro 🖂 Via Borgo XX Giugno ☎ 075 34 770 🕔 Daily 8–noon and 3–6, but often closed so check times ✋ Free

San Domenico and Museo Archeologico Nazionale dell'Umbria 🖂 Corso Cavour ☎ 075 572 7141 (museum) 🕔 Daily 8:30–7:30 ✋ Church free; Museum $$

Pienza

Pienza stands in the fertile landscape of southern Tuscany, with Monte Amiata to the south. Once known as

Pienza, with its fine cathedral and panoramic city walls, lies above the Val d'Orcia

Corsignano, it was the birthplace of Pope Pius II, Aeneas Sylvius Piccolomini, born in 1405. Elected to the papacy in 1458, Pius embarked on a plan to transform his native village into an "ideal city." He commissioned the architect Bernardo Rossellino to design a cathedral, papal palace and town hall. This core of the existing town is harmoniously grouped around a charming square and named after the Pope. You can walk through the town in about 10 minutes, but Pienza merits more time than this.

Start at the Duomo (Cathedral), with its lovely facade and interior inspired by the northern churches Pius had seen on his travels. The side chapels have some outstanding altarpieces by contemporary artists. Pius' residence, the Palazzo Piccolomini, stands next door; you can visit the papal apartments and admire the views from the triple-tiered loggia.

➕ C2

Tourist information ✉ Corso Il Rossellino 30 ☎ 0578 749 905; www.terresiena.it 🕐 Wed.–Mon. 10–1 and 3–6, mid-Mar. to Oct.; Sat.–Sun. 10–1 and 3–6, Nov. to mid-Mar.; Wed.–Mon. 10–1 and 2–5, Dec. 20–Jan. 6

Duomo ✉ Piazza Pio II 🕐 Daily 8–1 and 3–7 (closed during services) ✋ Free

Palazzo Piccolomini ✉ Piazza Pio II ☎ 0578 286 300; www.palazzopiccolominipienza.it 🕐 Tue.–Sun. 10–6:30, mid-Mar. to mid-Oct.; 10–4:30, mid-Oct. to mid-Mar. Closed mid- to end Nov. and early Jan. to mid-Feb. ✋ $$

Pisa

Pisa's famous structure, the Leaning Tower, is just one of a quartet of beautiful buildings that make up the Campo dei Miracoli (Field of Miracles). The Duomo (Cathedral), Battistero (Baptistery), Campo Santo and the tower itself date from Pisa's Golden Age. In the 11th through 13th centuries, the city was still a port and one of the leading Mediterranean maritime powers.

Today Pisa is a busy industrial and university city, surprisingly unspoiled in many areas. The earliest building of the cathedral complex is the black-and-white striped cathedral itself, begun in 1064 in the unmistakable Pisan-Romanesque style. The interior is mainly Renaissance, but the magnificent pulpit by Giovanni Pisano dates from 1302 and shows scenes from the life of Christ; look for the apse mosaic by Florentine Cimabue. Construction started on the Torre Pendente (Leaning Tower) in 1173; the spongy subsoil caused it to lean before it was half completed. By 1989 it was leaning more than 16 feet from upright and nearing its limits. The tower was stabilized in the 1990s and re-opened in December 2001.

The Baptistery, with its dome and Romanesque arcades, was built between the 12th and 13th centuries and is the largest in Italy. Along the north edge of Campo dei Miracoli runs the perimeter wall of the cemetery, or Campo Santo, once lavishly decorated with frescoes but destroyed during World War II.

It's worth going south toward the Arno river, where there are attractive streets and squares and a great daily food market. The riverbank is lined with fine palaces.

➕ A3

The unmistakable Leaning Tower of Pisa

The medieval town of San Gimignano rises on a hill overlooking the vast Elsa Plain

Tourist information ✉ Piazza Vittorio Emanuele 16 ☎ 050 42291, www.pisaunicaterra.it 🅒 Mon.–Sat. 9–7, Sun. 9–4 ✉ Airport ☎ 050 502 518 🅒 Daily 9:30 a.m.–11:30 p.m. ✉ Piazza Arcivescovado 8 ☎ 334 641 9408 🅒 Daily 9:30–7:30, Apr.–Sep.; 10–5, rest of year 🅸 A variety of combined tickets are available for Pisa's main sites
Duomo ✉ Piazza del Duomo 1 ☎ 050 835 011; www.opapisa.it 🅒 Daily 10–8, Apr.–Sep.; 10–7, Oct.; 10–12:45 and 2–5, Nov.–Feb.; 10–6, Mar. 🖐 $
Torre Pendente (Leaning Tower) ✉ Piazza del Duomo 17 ☎ 050 560 547. Tickets available at ticket office on Piazza del Duomo. No reservations by telephone, but book online at www.opapisa.it 🅒 Daily 8:30–10:30, Jun.–Aug.; 8:30–8, Apr.–Jun. and Sep.; 9–7, Oct.; 9:30–5:30, Nov. and Feb.; 10–5, Dec.–Jan.; 9–4:30, Mar. 🖐 $$$ 🅸 30-minute guided tours only
Battistero and Campo Santo ✉ Piazza del Duomo ☎ 050 835 011 🅒 Daily 8–8, Apr.–Sep.; 9–7, Oct.; 10–5, Nov.–Feb.; 9–6 Mar. 🖐 $$

Pistoia

Walls encircle Pistoia, one of Tuscany's least-visited cities. The town displays a 12th-century zebra-striped Duomo (Cathedral), a Gothic baptistery and some impressive palaces. Inside the Pisan-Romanesque cathedral you'll find sculpture by masters such as Verrocchio and Rossellino, although the most astounding artwork is the Dossale di San Jacopo (St. James' Altarpiece). This solid silver altar weighs almost a ton and is covered with 628 sculpted figures; started in 1287, it took almost 200 years to complete. The Piazza del Duomo also contains a Civic Museum, 14th-century baptistery and an older bell tower. Other churches include San Giovanni Fuoricivitas, a green-and-white, 12th- to 14th-century structure, and Sant'Andrea, which contains a 1297 pulpit by Giovanni Pisano.

July sees the town's famous Giostro dell'Orso, a medieval jousting tournament, preceded by a stream of spectacular processions.
➕ B3
Tourist information ✉ Piazza del Duomo 4 ☎ 0573 21 622; www.pistoia.turismo.toscana.it 🅒 Daily 8.30–12:30 and 3:30–7
Duomo (Cattedrale di San Zeno) ✉ Piazza del Duomo ☎ 0573 25 095 🅒 Daily 9–noon and 4–7. Cappella di San Jacopo: Mon.–Sat. 10–noon and 4–6, Sun. 11–noon and 4–6 🖐 Cappella di San Jacopo $

San Gimignano

Even without the famous towers, hilltop San Gimignano, known as "Medieval Manhattan," would be a town worth visiting. Crowded all year, your best option may be to stay a day or two. Once the day-trippers have gone, the town takes on a different atmosphere.

San Gimignano once boasted 72 towers, built by rival nobles in the 12th and 13th centuries. Fifteen of them have survived. You can climb one of the towers, the Torre Grossa, for astounding views. San Gimignano's picturesque streets are full of tempting shops, cafés and picturesque houses, and the town also is rich in art and history.

Sights cluster around the two main squares, the Piazza della Cisterna and the Piazza del Duomo. On the latter is the 13th-century Collegiata, one of the most frescoed churches in Tuscany, with scarcely an inch of wall left undecorated. Themes include the Creation and the Old and New Testaments, while the tiny Chapel of St. Fina depicts the life of San Gimignano's own saint. Other highlights include the Museo Civico, packed with lovely Gothic and Renaissance paintings, and the church of Sant'Agostino, on the northern end of town. It has luminous 15th-century Benozzo Gozzoli frescoes showing the life of St. Augustine, and the bonus of having few visitors.

✚ B3

Tourist information ✉ Piazza del Duomo 1 ☎ 0577 940 008; www.sangimignano.com or www.terresiena.it ◷ Daily 9–1 and 3–7, Mar.–Oct.; 9–1 and 2–6, rest of year

Torre Grossa and Museo Civico ✉ Piazza del Duomo ☎ 0577 990 348 ◷ Daily 9:30–7, Mar.–Oct.; 10–5:30, rest of year 🎟 $$

Collegiata ✉ Piazza del Duomo ☎ 0577 940 316 ◷ Mon.–Fri. 9:30–7:10, Sat. 9:30–5:10, Sun. 12:30–5:10, Apr.–Oct.; Mon.–Sat. 9:30–4:40, Sun. 12:30–4:40, Mar. and Nov.–Jan.; services only rest of year 🎟 Chapel $$

Sant'Agostino ✉ Piazza Sant'Agostino ◷ Daily 7:30–noon and 3–7, Apr.–Oct.; 7–noon and 3–6, rest of year 🎟 Free

Siena

The warm colors of Siena's stones and brickwork and the exuberant black-and-white stripes of its Duomo (Cathedral) make it instantly more appealing to many visitors than its larger neighbor, Florence. Large and prosperous in the 13th and 14th centuries, the city's population was devastated by the 1348 Black Death; Siena never recovered, thereby leaving a legacy of one of Europe's most perfectly preserved cities.

The sloping scallop-shaped square known as the Campo is the heart of Siena. Its south side is dominated by the magnificent 14th-century Palazzo Pubblico and the 320-foot belltower, the Torre del Mangia. Once the seat of civic government and still the city's town hall, the palace also is home to the Museo Civico, which contains many frescoed rooms. The chief draws are Simone Martini's 1315 Maestà, the charming equestrian portrait of *Guidoriccio da Fogliano* and Ambrogio Lorenzetti's

Siena's Campo is lined with medieval palaces and dominated by the Torre del Mangia

great 1338 frescoes *Allegories of Good and Bad Government.*

It's worth lingering in the Campo to enjoy an overpriced drink while you visualize Siena's ebullient medieval horse race, the Palio, which takes place in July and August. From here, head to the cathedral, a wonderful mix of Romanesque and Gothic, its splendid facade a riot of statuary. Inside you'll find masterpieces by Donatello, Pisano and the young Michelangelo.

The cathedral's floor is entirely covered with a sumptuous marble inlay showing biblical and allegorical scenes. These were completed from 1349 to 1547 by just about every leading artist of the time. Don't miss the Libreria Piccolomini, built to house the books of Pope Pius II (Enea Silvio Piccolomini). The walls were painted by Bernardino Pinturicchio in 1502 with scenes of the life of Pope Pius II. Near the cathedral you'll find the baptistery and the Museo dell'Opera, which contains works from the cathedral, including Duccio di Buoninsegna's supreme *Maestà.*

Opposite the cathedral stands Siena's medieval hospital, Santa Maria della Scala, which closed in the late 1990s. It's now an interesting museum where you can admire lively frescoes showing everyday medieval hospital life. Nearby there are more paintings in the Pinacoteca Nazionale, with a fine collection that traces the whole development of Sienese painting.

🚹 B2

Tourist information ✉ Piazza del Campo 56 ☎ 0577 280 551; www.terresiena.it 🕐 Daily 9–7

Duomo ✉ Piazza del Duomo ☎ 0577 286 300; www.operaduomo.siena.it 🕐 Mon.–Sat. 10:30–8, Sun. 1:30–6, Jun.–Aug.; Mon.–Sat. 10:30–7:30, Sun. 1:30–5:30, Mar.–May and Sep.–Oct.; Mon.–Sat. 10:30–6:30, Sun. 1:30–5:30, rest of year. 💷 $$$

Torre del Mangia ✉ Piazza del Campo ☎ 0577 226 230 🕐 Daily 10–7, mid-Mar. to Oct.; 10–4, rest of year 💷 $$ or $$$ with Museo Civico

Museo Civico ✉ Piazza del Campo ☎ 0577 226 230 🕐 Daily 10–7, mid-Mar. to Oct.; 10–6, rest of year 💷 $$$

Museo dell'Opera ✉ Piazza del Duomo 8 ☎ 0577 286 300; www.operaduomo.siena.it 🕐 Daily 10:30–7, Mar.–Oct.; 10:30–5:30, Nov.–Feb., except 26 Dec.–6 Jan. (10:30–7) 💷 $$

Santa Maria della Scala ✉ Piazza del Duomo 2 ☎ 0577 534 511/571; www.santamariadellascala.com 🕐 Daily 10:30–6:30, mid-Mar. to Oct.; 10:30–4:30, rest of year 💷 $$

Pinacoteca Nazionale ✉ Palazzo Buonsignori, Via San Pietro 29 ☎ 0577 286 143 🕐 Tue.–Sat. 8:15–7:15, Sun and Mon. 9–1 💷 $$

Sovana

Tiny Sovana rests in far southeast Tuscany, in the sparsely inhabited and undeveloped area called the Maremma. The area prospered in Etruscan, Roman and early medieval times, but its prosperity was later eroded by malaria. Don't miss Sovana, although neighboring Pitigliano, built on a spectacular rugged rock, also is worth a visit.

Fewer than 130 people live in Sovana; their houses line the broad brick expanse of the Via di Mezzo, which widens to form the tiny piazza. Here is Santa Maria, a tranquil 13th-century church that houses a unique ninth-century pre-Romanesque stone canopy over the altar. Opposite the church is a small museum. A flower-edged lane leads to the huge Duomo (Cathedral), which was built from the eighth to 12th centuries. From here you can explore the labyrinth of sunken Etruscan roads carved out of the tufa, which lead to Etruscan tombs. These date from about the seventh century BC and range from *colombari*, niches for funerary urns, to elaborately carved structures such as the Tomba Ildebranda.

🚹 C1

www.turismoinmaremma.it

Santa Maria ✉ Piazza del Pretorio ☎ 0564 614 074 🕐 Daily 9–1 and 3–7 💷 Free

Museo del Palazzo Pretorio ✉ Piazza del Pretorio 🕐 Tue.–Sat. 10–1 and 4–7 💷 $

Duomo 🕐 Daily 9–1 and 3–6 💷 Free

Tomba Ildebranda 🕐 Daily 9–7, Mar.–Nov.; Fri.–Sun. 10–5, rest of year 💷 $$

Spello

The enchanting medieval town of Spello rambles down the lower slopes of Monte Subasio in the Vale of Spoleto, the perfect place to catch a taste of unspoiled Umbria. Narrow streets lined with flower-hung houses, some classy food shops and good bars and restaurants all combine to make the town a tempting stopping point.

Five Roman gates give access; head through Porta Consolare to Via Cavour, the main street, where you'll find the church of Santa Maria Maggiore. Inside, three walls of the Cappella Baglioni are decorated with Pinturicchio's glowing frescoes (1501) showing scenes of the life of Mary, the mother of Jesus. Next door is the Pinacoteca Civica, with more works of art; farther uphill, the church of Sant'Andrea has another Pinturicchio (*Madonna with Child and Saints*)

➕ D2

Tourist information ✉ Piazza Matteotti 3
☎ 0742 301 009; www.comune.spello.pg.it ⏱ Daily 9:30–12:30 and 3:30–5:30

Santa Maria Maggiore ✉ Piazza Matteotti ⏱ Daily 8:30–12:30 and 3–7, Apr.–Oct.; 8:30–12:30 and 3–6, rest of year 🎫 Free

Pinacoteca Civica ✉ Piazza Matteotti 10
☎ 0742 301 497 ⏱ Tue.–Sun. 10:30–1 and 3–6:30, Apr.–Sep.; Tue.–Sun. 10:30–12:30 and 3:30–5:30, rest of year 🎫 $

Sant'Andrea ✉ Piazza Matteotti 30 ⏱ Daily 8–12:30 and 3–7 🎫 Free

Spoleto

Spoleto's fine old town spreads down the hill from the hilltop Rocca (Castle) to the Piazza del Mercato on the site of the Roman forum, with the still-intact Roman Arco di Druso nearby and the mostly intact first-century Teatro Romano (Roman Theater), which often stages open-air performances in summer. The 12th-century Duomo (Cathedral) is one of the loveliest in this region; the entire apse features the blues and golds of Filippo Lippi's frescoes; Sant'Eufemia is a superb Romanesque building that includes the interesting

Museo Diocesano, while Sant'Ansano has sixth-century frescoes. You can walk outside town to San Pietro, with its Lombard-Romanesque carvings on the facade; the route passes the Rocca and its excellent museum and crosses a gorge spanned by the magnificent 250-foot arches of the Ponte delle Torri, a monumental bridge and aqueduct rebuilt in the 14th century. June and July see the Spoleto Festival, Italy's most prestigious international arts festival.

➕ D1

Tourist information ✉ Piazza della Libertà 7
☎ 0743 220 773; www.visitspoleto.it ⏱ Mon.–Fri. 8:30–1:30 and 4–7, Sat. 9:30–12:30 and 4–7, Sun. 9:30–12:30

Rocca Albornoziana ✉ Piazza Campello 1
☎ 0743 223 055 ⏱ Mon.–Fri. 10–7, Sat.–Sun. 10–8, late Jun. to mid-Sep.; Mon.–Fri. 10–12 and 3–7, Sat.–Sun. 10–7, mid-Mar. to early Jun. and mid-Sep. to Oct., Mon.–Fri. 2:30–5, Sat.–Sun. 10–7, Nov. to mid-Mar. 🎫 $$

Duomo ✉ Piazza del Duomo ☎ 0743 44307 ⏱ Daily 8–12:30 and 3–7, Apr.–Nov.; 8–12:30 and 3–5:30, rest of year (until 7 p.m. Mar.–Oct.) 🎫 Free

Sant' Eufemia and Museo Diocesano ✉ Via Aurelio Saffi 13 ☎ 0743 231 022 ⏱ Tue.–Fri. 10–1 and 3–6, Sat.–Sun. 10–6, Mar.–Oct.; Wed.–Fri. 11–1 and 2:30–5:30, Sat.–Sun. 11–5, rest of year 🎫 $

Sant'Ansano ✉ Via Brignone ☎ 0743 40305 ⏱ Daily 10–12:30 and 3–7, Apr.–Oct.; 10–12:30 and 3–5:30, rest of year 🎫 Free

San Pietro ✉ Via Giro del Ponte, on east side of N3 outside town ☎ 0743 44882 ⏱ Daily 9:30–11 and 3:30–6:30 🎫 Free

Todi

Once an important Etruscan outpost, ancient Todi is situated on a great bluff above the Tiber river. It reached its heyday in the 13th century, when the superb ensemble of buildings around the main square, the Piazza del Popolo, were constructed. Here you'll find the lovely Romanesque-Gothic Duomo (Cathedral). The interior has a lovely carved choir, but it's the pink facade and great rose window that draw the eye. The square has some fine medieval palaces, particularly the Palazzo dei

The Palazzo Ducale, in Urbino, was once home to the powerful dukes of Montefeltro

Priori and the Palazzo del Capitano, which houses Todi's superb museum and art gallery. San Fortunato, a huge 13th-century church, is nearby; from here you can walk through public gardens to reach Santa Maria della Consolazione, one of the best Renaissance churches in Italy.

✚ C1

Tourist information ✉ Piazza Umberto I 5 ☎ 075 894 3933 ✉ Piazza del Popolo, 38–39 ☎ 075 8956227/8942526; www.conoscerelumbria. regioneumbria.eu ⏰ Daily 10–1 and 4–7, Apr.–Oct.; Mon.–Sat. 10–1 and 3–5, Sun.10–1, rest of year

Duomo ✉ Piazza del Popolo ☎ 075 894 3041 ⏰ Daily 8:30–12:30 and 3–7, Apr.–Sep.; 8:30–12:30 and 2–5:30/6:30, rest of year 🖐 Church free; Museum $

Museo-Pinacoteca e Museo della Città ✉ Palazzo del Capitano, Piazza del Popolo 29/30 ☎ 075 894 4148 ⏰ Tue.–Sun. 10–1:30 and 3–6, Apr.–Oct.; 10:30–1 and 2:30–5, rest of year 🖐 $; combined ticket with San Fortunato tower $$

San Fortunato ✉ Piazza Umberto 1 ⏰ Tue.–Sun. 10:30–1 and 3–6, Apr.–Oct. 🖐 Church free; Tower $; combined ticket with Museo-Pinacoteca $$

Santa Maria della Consolazione ✉ Viale della Consolazione ⏰ Mon. and Wed.–Sun. 9–1 and 2:30–6, Apr.–Oct.; Mon. and Wed.–Sun. 10–12:30 and 2:30–6, rest of year 🖐 Free

Trevi

Trevi is perched high on a cone-shaped hill. Wend your way up through the

olive groves (which produce some of Umbria's best oil) and spend a couple of hours wandering around an unspoiled hill town. You'll find narrow streets, intricately paved with patterned cobblestones, and an unhurried small-town atmosphere. Like many towns in Umbria, there are some treasures, notably an art gallery, the Pinacoteca Comunale, and the adjoining museum which is devoted to olives (Museo della Civiltà dell'Ulivo).

✚ D1

Tourist information ✉ Piazza Mazzini 6 ☎ 0742 332 269; www.treviturismo.it ⏰ Daily 9–1 and 3:30–6 or 7

Pinacoteca Comunale ✉ Largo Don Bosco 14 ☎ 0742 381 628 ⏰ Fri.–Sun. 10–12:30 and 2:30–5 🖐 $ ℹ Ticket includes admission to the Museo della Civiltà (same opening hours as Pinacoteca Comunale)

Urbino

Nowhere outside Tuscany did the Renaissance flower as vividly as in beautiful Urbino, the Marche's most stately and distinguished small city. The birthplace of Raphael, Urbino flourished in the 15th century under the rule of Duke Federico da Montefeltro to become one of Europe's most sophisticated and enlightened courts.

This university city is dominated by Duke Federico's 1465 Palazzo Ducale, still among central Italy's most sublime buildings. Federico hired some of the greatest Renaissance artists and architects to construct and decorate his palace. The Galleria Nazionale delle Marche is housed in elegant rooms around the central courtyard. Its two outstanding treasures are Piero della Francesco's *Madonna di Senigallia* and his tiny *Flagellation*, both in Federico's private apartments, where you also can admire the stunning wood inlay in the study. His portrait hangs nearby, while Luciano Laurana's *View of an Ideal City* encapsulates the Renaissance ideal.

Other masterpieces in the collection include Titian's *Resurrection* and Raphael's *La Muta*. Away from the palazzo, Urbino has a large 18th-century Duomo (Cathedral), while Raphael devotees can visit the artist's birthplace. It's worth the climb to the Fortezza Albornoz gardens for views over the city, then pause for a drink in the Piazza della Repubblica.

➕ D3

Tourist information ✉ Via Puccinotti 33 ☎ 0722 309 602; www.urbinoculturaturismo.it Ⓖ Mon.–Sat. 9–1 and 3–6, Sun. 9–1

Palazzo Ducale, Galleria Nazionale delle Marche
✉ Piazza Duca Federico ☎ 0722 322 625
Ⓖ Tue.–Sun. 8:30–7:15, Mon. 8:30–2 🖉 $$
Duomo ✉ Piazza Rinascimento Ⓖ Daily 7:30–1 and 2–8 🖉 Church free; Museum $
Casa Natale di Raffaello ✉ Via Raffaello 57
☎ 0722 320 105 Ⓖ Mon.–Sat. 10–1 and 3–6, Sun. 10–1 🖉 $

The Valnerina

If you're looking for mountainous country, steep gorges and rushing rivers, delectable villages and imposing sights, this is the place. Bustling Terni marks the start of the Valnerina; from Terni the scenic SS209 follows the valley floor.

Your first stop should be the Cascate delle Marmore, a 545-foot waterfall created by the Romans in 271 BC. The falls now feed a hydroelectric plant, but at full power are truly dramatic. Farther up the valley stands the abbey of San Pietro in Valle. The location is breathtaking, and the abbey church has

some of Umbria's most important 12th-century frescoes. Pause at the medieval village of Scheggino, with its trout-filled canals and warren of alleyways. The hills on either side become steeper and the valley narrows, with tiny hamlets clinging to the slopes.
➕ D1

Volterra

Imposing and isolated, Volterra stands on a plateau surrounded by balze (cliffs), which have steadily eroded over thousands of years. This ancient settlement has plenty of evidence of Etruscan and Roman occupation in the shape of walls, gates and a theater. It also has one of the most comprehensive Etruscan museums in central Italy, the Museo Etrusco Guarnacci. The town's heart is Piazza dei Priori; on this square stands the town hall, built in the first half of the 13th century, and other impressive medieval palaces. Behind the square is the black-and-white striped 12th-century Duomo (Cathedral).

The Pinacoteca Comunale has a pleasing collection of Sienese and Florentine paintings; Domenico Ghirlandhaio's and Luca Signorelli's serene Madonnas make a sublime contrast to the angular forms and acidic colors of Rosso Fiorentino's superlative Deposition. This part of Tuscany is mining country, and you'll see alabaster carvings for sale in many of the local workshops.
➕ B2

Tourist information ✉ Piazza dei Priori 20
☎ 0588 87257; www.volterratur.it
Ⓖ Daily 9–1 and 2–7, Apr.–Oct.; 10–1 and 2–6, rest of year
Museo Etrusco Guarnacci ✉ Via Don Minzoni 15
☎ 0588 86347 Ⓖ Daily 9–7, mid-Mar. to Oct.; 8:30–1:45, rest of year 🖉 $$$ (includes Pinacoteca and Museo d'Arte Sacra)
Duomo ✉ Piazza San Giovanni Ⓖ Daily 8–12:30 and 3–5 🖉 Free
Pinacoteca Comunale ✉ Via dei Sarti 1
☎ 0588 87580 Ⓖ Daily 9–7, mid-Mar. to Oct.; 9–1:30, rest of year 🖉 $$$ (combined ticket)

Siena's Palio

The Siena Palio is no mere tourist attraction; this spectacular bareback horse race, dating from medieval times, is a real Sienese festival.

The Palio is named after the victory pallium, a banner embroidered with the image of the Blessed Virgin. The contest is between the city's wards, the *contrade*. The race runs on July 2 and August 16, each occasion preceded by weeks of preparation, bets and pageantry. The 17 wards each have their own church, museum and social center. Allegiance to your native *contrade* is absolute; children are baptized in the *contrade* fountain, and each neighborhood holds an annual parade. Ten neighborhoods take part in the Palio; they are chosen by lot, as are the horses. The jockeys are protected before the race for fear of bribes or worse. Each group has its traditional enemies and allies, and the pre-race weeks are filled with intrigue as alliances are forged and broken.

The days before the race are filled with processions and trial races. On race day the horses are blessed in the church. It's considered the best of luck if the horse defecates during the service. In the late afternoon a stunning procession, the *corteo storico*, takes place in the *campo* (town square), with drummers, flag-throwers and costumed captains and grooms. Huge bets are placed, and once the race starts anything goes. Ninety seconds of incredible excitement follow as the horses gallop three times around the square, which has a temporary surface of sand and mattresses to protect the most dangerous corners. The winning horse, with or without the jockey, is handed the Palio and mobbed by its jubilant supporters. Parties and parades go on all night and into the following weeks; the *contrade* hold street banquets as they relive every moment of the day.

You can watch the procession and race from the campo, which means standing for at least two hours prior to the race, and up to six hours if you want to be near the rails, with no exit once the barriers are closed. There are seats in the windows of the houses overlooking the campo; these are sold out for months before the race and should be booked a year ahead. (Contact Palio Viaggi at Piazza la Lizza 12 ☎ 0577 280 828; www.palioviaggi.it.)

Siena's exciting Palio is run twice each year, on July 2 and August 16, in the Campo

Tuscany, Umbria and the Marche

Drive
Renaissance Tuscany

Duration 2.5 to 3 hours

Start this drive in Monteriggioni, a medieval walled town lying just off the Siena–Florence *raccordo* (link road).
You can walk from one end of Monteriggioni to the other in five minutes, as the town consists of little more than a spacious square with an old church, two dozen houses, two excellent restaurants and a hotel, all encircled by impressive walls punctuated by towers. Beneath the walls are vegetable gardens and tiny pretty streets. Built by the Sienese in 1213 as a border outpost againt Florence, Monteriggioni was immortalized by Dante in *The Inferno*, where he refers to its towers as giants in an abyss; the verse is inscribed over the town's main gateway.
From Monteriggioni, take either the SS2 or the Siena–Florence *raccordo* to Siena (see page 110). If you are not going to visit Siena, then take the *tangenziale* (bypass) to avoid the city; watch for the exit back to the SS2, signposted Roma.
The SS2 follows the route of the Cassia, one of the great Roman consular roads that fanned out all over the Roman Empire; the road is still known by this name.
About 17 miles (28 kilometers) south, the Cassia skirts Buonconvento, which is well worth a stop.
Buonconvento was another of Siena's key outposts; today it's a bustling small town with some lovely old buildings

and a fascinating museum of local farming and country life, which also displays some lovely Sienese paintings.
Turn left into the hills at Buonconvento, following the signs through woods and past cypresses to the Abbazia di Monte Oliveto Maggiore.
The abbey of Monte Oliveto is set in the Crete Senesi, the strange landscape of clay landslips and escarpments that characterizes this part of Tuscany. The abbey was founded in the early 1300s by a branch of the Benedictines and soon became one of Italy's most powerful religious foundations, falling from influence in the 19th century. Monks still live here, restoring books and producing wine and olive oil.
   The main artistic attraction is the Chiostro Grande (Great Cloister), which has scenes of the life of St. Benedict. The frescoes were started by Luca Signorelli, who completed nine panels before handing the job over to Il Sodoma, who painted the other 27. These paintings are full of life – look for the birds and animals. The monastery also has a lofty church with some wonderful inlaid choir stalls and a fine Renaissance library.

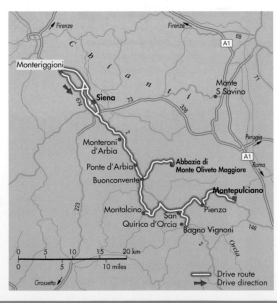

Looking out over Siena, with the prominent Church of Santa Maria dei Servi in the distance

Return to Buonconvento and head south to follow the SS2 for about a mile (2 kilometers) before branching right to Montalcino (see page 104).
As this road climbs to approach the town, you'll pass wineries advertising the famous Brunello wine.
Leave Montalcino by the main road back to the SS2, a lovely stretch through vineyards, olive groves and wide views over southern Tuscany. Turn right on the S2 and continue for 3.5 miles (6 kilometers) before turning left at San Quirico d'Orcia onto the SS146 heading toward Pienza (see page 107) and Montepulciano (see page 105).
You could stay on the SS2 south for 3 miles (5 kilometers) before making a detour to Bagno Vignoni, one of

Tuscany's most memorable hamlets. It's built around a hot spring, well known since Roman times. The central square is a huge Renaissance piscina, or bath, overlooked by a charming loggia. It's best seen in cool weather, when wisps of steam rise from the gently bubbling waters.

Buonconvento
Museo della Mezzadria Senese ✉ Via Soccini 18 ☎ 0577 807 190 or 0577 809 075 🕐 Tue.–Sun. 10–1 and 3–6, Apr.–Oct.; Tue.–Fri. 10–1, Sat.–Sun. 10–1 and 3–5, rest of year. Closed two weeks in Aug. 🎟 $$
Abbazia di Monte Oliveto Maggiore ✉ Monte Oliveto Maggiore ☎ 0577 707 611; www.monteolivetomaggiore.it 🕐 Daily 9:15–noon and 3:15–6, Apr.–Sep.; 9:15–noon and 3:15–5, rest of year 🎟 Free

Central Italy

Opposite: A detail of the Fontana dei Quattro Fiumi (fountain) in Piazza Navona, Rome

Central Italy

Central Italy

Three regions bridge the gap between northern and southern Italy – Lazio, the Abruzzo and Molise. Rome and its attractions tend to overshadow the rest of the Lazio region, with its gentle landscape and quiet towns. Across the Apennines lies the Abruzzo, one of the least known areas of Italy, a region of rugged mountainous scenery and villages and medieval walled towns where tourists are still a novelty. Abruzzo's smaller neighbor, Molise, offers more remote rolling hill country and economically has much more in common with the southern part of the country rather than with central Italy. All three have long coastlines, mostly undiscovered by international visitors.

Lazio

Until the 1860s, Lazio was part of the Papal States, the territory held by the Vatican. During the process of Italian unification, Rome – with its historical connotations of centralized power – became the symbol of the new united Italy and therefore the obvious choice as the country's new capital. In fact, Rome had to wait until 1870 to join the united Italy, the last but symbolically most important part of the Italian peninsula to do so. Like other areas that were once part of the Papal States, Lazio was traditionally poor and had little sense of identity and few historic towns. The area's economy has made major strides

in recent years, with the development of new industrial areas to the south of Rome. Of course, on the negative side, this brings with it pollution as well as urban growth that eats into the surrounding countryside.

The countryside itself varies from the gentle rolling hills of the north to steep mountains south and east of Rome. Lake Bolsena in the north attracts many visitors, as does Lazio's coastline, which is more attractive south of Rome.

Abruzzo and Molise

Abruzzo and Molise were one region until 1963. Since then, the Abruzzo has forged ahead at the expense of Molise – the contrast between the two on every level is startling. They are both sparsely populated, mountainous areas prone to

A classically inspired summer house in the gardens of Rome's Villa Borghese

earthquakes, with a tradition of standing outside the mainstream of Italian affairs. Over the last 40 years, Abruzzo has emerged from poverty, developing the tourist potential of its national park's mountain wilderness and expanding a string of lucrative resorts along its sandy coastline. Despite this, huge areas are still remote and unspoiled, and you'll find a true sense of pride and regional identity manifested in local festivals, crafts and costumes. The landscape, a wilderness of upland plains, remote valleys and high peaks, is superb.

Molise is poor, disorganized and undeveloped, and ranks fairly low on the tourist trail. More than 40 percent of the terrain is covered by mountains and industrial cities. If you're heading south to Apulia (Puglia), you'll pass through Termoli, a small fishing port and attractive beach resort.

A Sense of the South

When traveling into central Italy from the north or from Rome itself, you'll at once sense an almost indefinable

Le Cento Fontane (The Hundred Fountains) in the grounds of the Villa d'Este, Tivoli, near Rome

difference and grasp why this central area is viewed as "southern" by northern Italians. Towns are not as stylish or prosperous, villages are not so spic-and-span. There's more remote countryside and less cultivated land. The pace seems slower and more laid-back, though the people can still be noisy and ebullient. In some parts of the mountainous areas, the high-tech world seems to have barely impinged and the arrival of foreigners may still cause comment.

The tourist infrastructure is not as good as, perhaps, that in Tuscany and Umbria, with fewer hotels of international standard. This area is well-served by *autostrade* (freeways); the A24/25, which cuts through the

Apennines east of Rome to penetrate the Abruzzo, is one of Italy's finest and most scenic. Good roads run down both the west and east coasts, and the whole of Lazio is easy to explore. In Abruzzo and Molise, the roads in remoter areas are often steep, winding and narrow.

Highlights

Rome is going to be your number one stop in this part of Italy, and you should set aside four or five days to explore the city. It makes sense to do most of your exploring into Lazio from a Roman base; Tivoli, the Castelli Romani, Ostia Antica and Tarquinia are all potential day trips from Rome via public transportation. If you're heading farther afield, a rental car

which is the best time to visit the Abruzzo mountains if you're interested in fresh air and exercise. Avoid Rome in July and August, when the city is crammed with tourists but Romans themselves are on vacation, leaving many stores and restaurants closed. Fall, with its soft light and shaded, golden colors, can be a magical time to visit the region.

The People

The inhabitants of this central area are notably different from other northern Italian folk. More than 50 percent of the population of the area live in Rome. However, to the north of the city, many of the rural towns and villages are still experiencing a degree of depopulation, leaving many areas without a replenishing and available workforce.

Romans have always had a reputation for surliness and impatience with visitors, so it pays to go out of your way to charm them by using a few key Italian phrases said with a winning smile. If you're exploring remoter areas, you'll find that few people speak English. This all adds to the delight, and there are few places in Italy where you'll get a better sense of traditional attitudes.

may be better. Abruzzo National Park and the Gran Sasso are good choices. If you're looking for a few days of relaxation, there are charming, tranquil resorts south of Rome and all along the Abruzzo coast to the east.

When To Go

If you're planning to spend most of your time in Rome, there's much to be said for a winter trip, when the city is less crowded and the stifling heat won't be a problem. Late November and December can be wet, but January and February are generally crisp and dry, with surprisingly warm midday sun. Spring comes early to Rome, making April and May lovely months to enjoy the city. Crowds and heat build in summer,

The Roman amphitheater at Ostia Antica

Rome

The vibrant capital of Italy provides magic and frustration in almost equal measure. Packed with art, steeped in history and humming with life, this most beautiful of cities will ensnare you with its charms, even if its traffic, never-ending noise and confusion sometimes make you wonder why you came. A heady mixture of classical, medieval, Renaissance and baroque sights fills the streets and squares. Golden light filters through pine trees to ancient stones; fountains splash quietly in sun-dappled piazzas. But traffic also roars up polluted streets, crowds push and shove, and heat levels and noise can

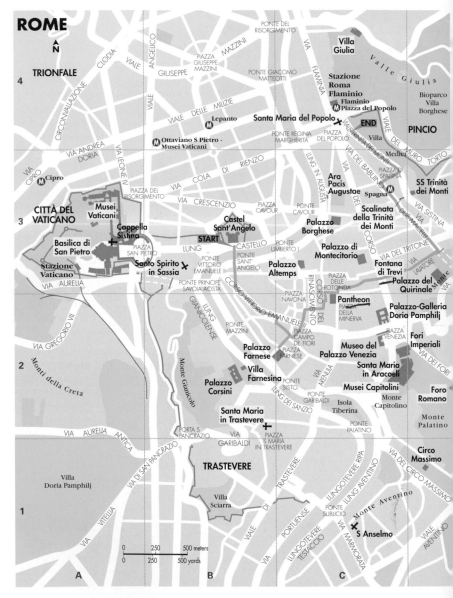

be intense. Accept this mixture and put aside your preconceptions. Rome (Roma) is a living city, not a museum, and therein lies its enchantment.

Getting Your Bearings

It shouldn't take you long to realize that Rome, laid out and built long before the automobile age, is not a huge city in terms of area. It lies on either side of the Tiber (Tevere) river and sprawls across seven hills. The Vatican, St. Peter's and the Trastevere quarter (with its excellent restaurants) lie on the west bank of the river; everything else you'll want to see is to the east.

This eastern part is roughly bisected by Via del Corso, which runs from Piazza del Popolo to Piazza Venezia and is dominated by the vast "wedding cake" of the Victor Emmanuel Monument. South of the monument are the Forum, the Colosseum and the heart of classical Rome. Between the Corso and the Tiber river lies the *centro storico* (historical center), a mix of medieval streets, Renaissance palaces and beguiling squares. East of the Corso there are more fine buildings and palaces, Rome's most elegant shopping streets, verdant parks, splendid scenic vistas and the elegant Via Vittorio Veneto, home to the American Embassy in addition to some of the city's most fashionable hotels.

Sightseeing

There are hotels scattered all over the city, but bear in mind that nowhere you choose to stay is going to be quiet. The *centro storico* is perhaps the best place to base yourself for its proximity to just about everything, and has a good selection of hotels. The only area to avoid is around the Stazione Termini train station.

To start your visit, spend a couple of hours on an organized tour. Several companies offer "get on and off" options, with tickets valid all day. Once oriented, it's important to prioritize. There's no way you're going to be able to see everything, so decide what's important to you and see it properly. Big sights such as the Vatican and the Forum are best tackled early in the day while you're fresh, and be sure to rest for a couple of hours during the midday heat. Most people directly involved with tourism speak English and are generally helpful, although you may not get quite

Basilica di San Pietro stands on the traditional site where St. Peter the Apostle was crucified and buried

such an enthusiastic response from city dwellers going about their business.

You shouldn't miss St. Peter's Basilica, the interesting Vatican museums or other classical sights such as the Roman Forum and the majestic Colosseum.

Add to these a couple of other major museums and churches and you'll be busy for at least three days. In addition, there's a wealth of delights ranging from ancient churches and idiosyncratic museums to lovely green parks, elegant shops and jolly markets. Rome hosts splendid temporary exhibitions and shows; pick up a copy of the monthly *Un Ospite a Roma* (*Roman Guest,* also online at www.unospitearoma.it) from your hotel to find what's happening.

Culinary Pleasures
Like all Italians, Romans like to eat out regularly, so choose a restaurant patronized by locals to enjoy some Roman specialties. There's an excellent choice of places to eat in Trastevere and in some of the old streets around Piazza Navona and the Pantheon, while more obviously upscale choices can be found nearer Via Vittorio Veneto. Roman

cooking can often feature organ meats, tripe and brains, but there are many other dishes to choose, such as the delicious *saltimbocca alla Romana* – veal cooked with prosciutto and sage – that are more appetizing.

Do sample the mixed vegetable antipasti, often found in family-run restaurants, and pasta dishes such as spicy *rigatoni all'amatriciana,* or the delicious and familiar spaghetti alla carbonara with bacon and egg. Artichokes, often eaten deep-fried or raw, are a great Roman specialty.

Food-to-go includes fabulous pizza by the slice, an ideal and tasty quick lunch. As everywhere in Italy, ice cream is absolutely wonderful, with a great range of flavors available. Local wines come from the Castelli Romani, the hills outside Rome, but you'll find wines and liqueurs from all over Italy, as well as international brands.

Retail Therapy
Shop till you drop in hedonistic Rome, where elegant women devote most of their lives to the art. The trendiest stores cluster around Via Condotti and Via

A detail from *Testa di Apostolo*, by Melozzo da Forlí, in the Musei Vaticani (Vatican Museums)

Frattina near Piazza di Spagna, where you'll find the top names in fashion, lingerie, leather and jewelry, as well as luxury housewares. Prices are lower, but quality and style are still good along Via del Corso and Via Nazionale. Fans of department stores should try La Rinascente, Coin, Upim or Standa. There are souvenir shops all over the city, but if you're looking for religious mementos, buy them in the shops in the vicinity of St. Peter's. Try to take in a typical food market; the daily one in the Campo dei Fiori is great for color and atmosphere.

Peace and Quiet

Rome has its parks and gardens, and you'll occasionally stumble across a grassy square complete with benches to rest your weary feet. To escape the traffic's roar, head for the Galleria Borghese (see page 130), the Botanical Gardens in Trastevere or the Colle Oppio near the Colosseum. Best of all, eat a picnic on Palatine Hill.

Entertainment

Dinner and a stroll may be all you're after, but there's plenty of entertainment too – *Un Ospite a Roma* will fill you in. Opera is a superb summer option, when performances are held outdoors. Several theaters show films in their original language, and there's also live rock and jazz and nightclubs for dancing.

Mosaics

Rome's oldest churches are rich in mosaics. They serve as reminders of the early Christian church and the last days of the Roman Empire, when faith went hand in hand with Byzantine skill. Mosaics are composed of tiny pieces of polychrome stone, marble and gilding, shaped so that they will lock together on a vault or curved roof. They are built to create pictures and images of Christ and the saints and are usually set against a gold background and filled with charming details of plants, birds and animals. To see them at their best, visit the churches of Santa Prassede, Santa Costanza, San Clemente (see page 132), Santa Maria in Trastevere (see page 132) and Santa Pudenzia, where the mosaics were created between the fourth and ninth centuries.

Essential Information

Tourist Information

☎ 060608; www.turismoroma.it
- Via Leopardi 24 ⊕ Daily 9:30–7
- Ciampino airport: Arrivals hall
  ⊕ Daily 9–6:30
- Fiumicino airport: Arrivals hall, Terminal 3
  ⊕ Daily 9–7:30
- Ostia Lido: Lungomare Paolo Toscanelli
  ⊕ Daily 9:30–7
- Castel Sant'Angelo: Piazza Pia
  ⊕ Daily 9:30–7
- Fori Visitor Center, Via dei Fori Imperiali
  ⊕ Daily 9:30–7
- Minghetti: Via Marco Minghetti
  ⊕ Daily 9:30–7
- Navona: Piazza delle Cinque Lune
  ⊕ Daily 9:30–7
- Nazionale: Via Nazionale near Palazzo delle
  Esposizioni ⊕ Daily 9:30–7
- Sonnino: Piazza Sidney Sonnino
  ⊕ Daily 9:30–7
- Termini: Termini Railway Station
  Inside station at Binario 24 (Platform 24)
  ⊕ Daily 9:30–7

Urban Transportation

Public transportation – orange buses and trams and a two-line subway system – can be slow. Bus tickets must be purchased before boarding; find them at automatic machines or shops and newsstands displaying an ATAC sticker. They are valid for any number of bus journeys plus one subway trip within a 75-minute period and must be validated when you board at the rear of the vehicle. The *biglietto integrato* (BIG) is valid for a day's unlimited travel on buses, trams, the subway and suburban rail service. A weekly pass, the *carta integrata settimanale* (CIS), is valid for

buses and the subway only. Taxis are yellow or white and can be picked up from a stand indicated by a blue-and-white sign; they do not stop on the street. You can call a taxi from Radio Taxis (☎ 06 3570). The meter will start running immediately after your call. Be sure the meter is at zero if you pick up a taxi at a stand. Do not get into private taxis.

Airport Information

Rome has two airports, Leonardo da Vinci (☎ 06 65951; www.adr.it), at Fiumicino to the west of the city, and Ciampino (☎ 06 65951; www.adr.it/ciampino), south of Rome. You are most likely to arrive at Leonardo da Vinci. It is easy to get to and from Leonardo da Vinci by train from Stazione Termini; there are daily departures every 30 to 60 minutes between 6:37 a.m. and 11:37 p.m. Trains also run from the airport to Fara Sabina and Tiburtina suburban railroad stations; if you use these you will have to get a connection. There is a nightly bus service between the airport and Stazione Termini. To reach Rome from Ciampino, take the Terravision shuttlebus (☎ 06 9761 0632; www.terravision.eu; timed to meet certain flight arrivals) or subway line A to Anagnina and connect with the COTRAL bus service (www.cotralspa.it), which runs daily from about 6:50 a.m. to 11:40 p.m. (€4 one way). A taxi will cost around €40 from Fiumicino to central Rome.

Climate – average highs and lows for the month

Jan.	Feb.	Mar.	Apr.	May	Jun.	Jul.	Aug.	Sep.	Oct.	Nov.	Dec.
13°C	14°C	16°C	19°C	23°C	27°C	31°C	31°C	27°C	23°C	18°C	14°C
55°F	57°F	61°C	66°F	73°F	81°F	88°F	88°F	81°F	73°F	64°F	57°F
3°C	4°C	7°C	8°C	12°C	15°C	18°C	18°C	14°C	11°C	9°C	5°C
37°F	39°F	45°F	46°F	54°F	59°F	64°F	64°F	57°F	52°F	48°F	41°F

Rome Sights

> **Key to symbols**
>
> ✚ map coordinates refer to the Rome map on pages 124–125 👖 admission charge: $$$ more than €7, $$ €4–€7, $ less than €4
> See page 5 for complete key to symbols

Basilica di San Pietro

The present Basilica di San Pietro (St. Peter's Basilica), the heart of the Catholic Church worldwide, stands on the site of the saint's burial place. It was built between 1506 and 1626. The principal architects were Donato Bramante and Giovanni Bernini, working to Michelangelo's concepts; the soaring dome is his creation. The sweeping colonnades, fountains and triumphant facade are a fitting prelude to the vast interior, dominated by Bernini's great high altar *baldicchino* and its spiraling columns. Don't miss Michelangelo's sublime *Pietà*, the bronze statue of St. Peter with his right foot worn away by caresses, and the crypt where numerous popes are buried around the tomb of St. Peter.

✚ A3 ✉ Piazza San Pietro, Città di Vaticano ☎ 06 6998 3731; www.vatican.va ⏰ Basilica: daily 7–7, Apr.–Sep.; 7–6, rest of year. Closed during religious services. Dome: daily 8–6, Apr.–Oct.; 8–4:45, rest of year ⓜ Ottaviano 🚌 23, 64, 81, 492 👖 Basilica free; $$ for elevator to terrace and steps to Dome ℹ Dress code: no shorts, short skirts or bare shoulders

Colosseo

Every modern public stadium's design ultimately copies that of the Colosseo (Colosseum), a massive structure dating from AD 72. Its tiers of seats held 55,000 people, while the "backstage" facilities allowed the arena to be flooded. Shows here featured gladiators, slaves and animals often fighting to the death; few Christians were martyred here. The Colosseum served as a source of building material during the Middle Ages, hence the missing sections.

✚ D2 ✉ Piazza del Colosseo, Via dei Fori Imperiale

The Foro Romano viewed from the Palatine Hill

☎ 06 0608; www.pierreci.it ⏰ Daily 9 a.m to 1 hour before sunset ⓜ Colosseo 🚌 3, 60, 81, 84, 85, 87, 117, 175, 186, 271, 571, 810, 850 👖 $$$ (two-day ticket also valid for Palatino and Foro Romano); ground floor free

Fontana di Trevi

You'll hear the Fontana di Trevi (Trevi Fountain) before you see it. Tucked into a tiny piazza amid a warren of narrow streets, it's a wonderful array of figures, tritons and horses set against an architectural backdrop. The latest in a series of fountains here since Roman times, Trevi dates from 1732 and gets its name from the three streets – *tre vie* – that converge here.

✚ D3 ✉ Piazza Fontana di Trevi ⓜ Spagna or Barbarini 🚌 52, 53, 71, 95 and all services to Via del Tritone

Foro Romano

The Foro Romano (Roman Forum), today a jumble of fallen columns and tumbling walls, was the heart of the Roman Empire and contained all the most important political, religious and municipal buildings. Time and imagination are needed to puzzle it out, but be sure to track down the House of the Vestal Virgins, home to the guardians of the sacred flame, and the second-century Temple of Antoninus and Faustinus (AD 141). Other

Central Italy

highlights include the fine Arch of Septimius Severus, and the Palatine Hill. Once covered with grand palaces, today the ruins of the Palatine lie among oleanders and cypresses.

✠ D2 ✉ Largo Romolo e Remo 1 ☎ 06 3996 7700 ◉ Daily 8:30–7:15, Apr.–Aug.; 8:30–4:30, Nov. to mid-Feb.; 8:30–5, mid-Feb. to mid-Mar.; 8:30–5:30, mid-Mar. to last Sun. in Mar.; 8:30–7, Sep.; 8:30–6:30, Oct. ⓠ Colosseo ⊟ 40, 60, 63, 70, 75, 81, 85, 87, 95, 117, 160, 170, 186, 175, 271, 571, 628, 716, 810, 850 ▨ $$$ (two-day ticket also valid for the Colosseum and Palatino) ❚ English audio guide

Galleria Borghese

Built in 1613 by Cardinal Scipione Borghese as a summer retreat, the Villa Borghese is now a museum housing superb art collections. The cardinal's favorite sculptor was Giovanni Bernini, whose works dominate; the *David* is said to be a self-portrait, and there's an *Apollo and Daphne*, full of flight and panic. Don't miss Antonio Canova's *Pauline Borghese*, a likeness of Napoleon's sister. The paintings also are spectacular, with treasures by Raphael, Titian's sensuous *Sacred and Profane Love* and Caravaggio's famous *Boy with a Fruit Basket*.

✠ D4 ✉ Villa Borghese, Piazzale Scipione Borghese 5 ☎ 06 3997 7800/32810; www.galleriaborghese.it ◉ Tue.–Sun. 8:30–7:30 ⓠ Spagna ⊟ 5, 19, 52, 53, 56, 57, 116, 319, 490, 495, 910 ❚❚ Restaurant in museum ▨ $$$ (booking fee) ❚ Advance booking necessary (☎ 06 32810; www.ticketeria.it)

Musei Capitolini

Occupying two palaces on Piazza del Campidoglio, the Capitoline Museums boast outstanding Greek and Roman sculptures. Start in the magnificent Palazzo dei Conservatori, home to the superb second-century bronze equestrian statue of Marcus Aurelius and other famous bronzes, as well as an art gallery. A tunnel connects this to the Palazzo Nuovo, home to some of the world's greatest classical sculpture.

✠ C2 ✉ Piazza del Campidoglio 1 ☎ 06 0608; www.museicapitolini.org ◉ Tue.–Sun. 9–8 ⓠ Colosseo ⊟ 44, 46, 62, 80, 160 ▨ $$

Musei Vaticani

Allow plenty of time to enjoy the 1,400 rooms that make up the Musei Vaticani (Vatican Museums). You can follow one of the color-coded routes to the museum's highlights, the Cappella Sistina (Sistine Chapel) and the Stanze di Raffaello (Raphael Rooms). The walls and ceiling of the lofty Sistine Chapel are entirely frescoed, most notably by Michelangelo. His extraordinary creation scenes from the Old Testament cover the rear wall of the chapel and were painted from 1508 to 1512; they show more than 300 figures and include his extraordinarily powerful *Last Judgment*. The Raphael Rooms provide a balance to the huge energy of the Sistine. Elsewhere you'll find classical sculpture, paintings and much more (there's even a piece of moon rock presented by the U.S. government), while the richness of the building itself is an added bonus.

✠ A3 ✉ Viale Vaticano, Città del Vaticano ☎ 06 698 846 76 or 06 698 3145; www.vatican.va ◉ Mon.–Sat. 9–6 (last ticket 4), last Sun. of month 9–2 (last ticket 12:30). Closed major religious holidays ⓠ Ottaviano, Cipro-Musei Vaticani ⊟ 49 to front of museums; 32, 81, 982 to Piazza del Risorgimento; or 492, 990 to Via Leone IV (both five minutes' walk) ▨ $$$; free last Sun. of month ❚ English audio guide available

Museo d'Arte Contemporanea Roma

An imaginative old brewery conversion houses the Rome Museum of Contemporary Art (Museo d'Arte Contemporaneo di Roma – MACRO), a new contemporary art space. The original building was extended with a 107,500-square foot space capable of housing large multimedia installations.

The permanent collection concentrates on Italian modern artists working from the 1960s onward, while the changing exhibitions highlight the work of contemporary Italian and international artists. MACRO works with MACRO Future, another stunning space in the Mattatoio, a former slaughterhouse, in Testaccio, Rome's most vibrant late-night area.

➕ E4 ✉ Via Nizza 131 (corner of via Cagliari) ☎ 06 6710 70400; www.macro.roma.museum ⏰ Tue.– Sun. 11–11 🚍 38, 90 💵 $$$

Palazzo Altemps

A beautifully restored 15th- through 16th-century palazzo houses Cardinal Ludovisi's wonderful classical sculpture collection, augmented by pieces from other private collectors. The building is a joy in itself; charming rooms with high vaulted ceilings surround a frescoed loggia above a beautiful, traditional inner courtyard. Be sure not to miss the famous sculpture *Dying Gaul* and the tender Greek *Aphrodite Rising from the Waves*, dating from the fifth century BC.

The museum is best visited just as darkness begins to fall, when the statues are beautifully lit by spotlights.

➕ C3 ✉ Piazza Sant'Apollinare 46 ☎ 06 3996 7700; www.archeoroma.beniculturali.it ⏰ Tue.–Sun. 9–7:45 🚍 C3, 30, 70, 81, 87, 116, 130, 186, 492, 628 💵 $$; combined ticket with Palazzo Massimo and some other sights $$$ 🛈 English audio guide available

Palazzo Massimo alle Terme

The Museo Nazionale Romano (National Roman Museum), in the 19th-century Palazzo Massimo, is the showcase for a breathtaking collection of sculptures, bronzes, mosaics and frescoes dating from Roman times.

The artifacts are arranged in order to explain different themes running through Roman history from the Republican era up to the fifth century. You'll find superlative busts and bronze figures alongside Roman copies of the best of ancient Greek sculpture. Highlights include the *Discus Thrower*, a languid *Apollo and a* sensuous *Sleeping Hermaphrodite*. The third floor is devoted to frescoes and mosaics; the first-century BC garden paintings from the dining room of Livia's villa could grace any modern house.

➕ E3 ✉ Piazza dei Cinquecento 67, Largo di Villa Peretti 1 ☎ 06 3996 7700 ⏰ Tue.–Sun. 9–7:45

🚇 Termini, Repubblica 🚍 C2, H, 16, 36, 38, 40, 90, 92, 105 🍴 Café 💵 $$ 🛈 English audio guide available

Pantheon

The greatest surviving complete Roman building, the Pantheon was erected from AD 119 to 128. This superbly engineered building gives a vivid impression of the grandeur of ancient Rome. Built as a temple, it survived the fall of Rome due to its conversion in AD 609 to a Christian church. The stately portico leads to a huge dome; here you'll find the tombs of Raphael and two Italian kings.

➕ C2 ✉ Piazza della Rotunda ☎ 06 6830 0230 ⏰ Mon.–Sat. 8:30–7:30, Sun. 9–6:30, holidays 9–1 🚇 Spagna 🚍 64, 70, 81, 86, 87, 90, 119, 170 💵 Free

Piazza Navona

The shape of the Piazza Navona follows the lines of the Roman racetrack that once occupied this site. Today's piazza was rebuilt in 1644 by Pope Innocent X, who commissioned its fountains from Bernini. The central one, known as the Fountain of the Four Rivers, shows the Nile, Ganges, Danube and the Plate. The Nile's head is veiled, as the source had yet to be discovered. Francesco Borromini's baroque church of Sant'Agnese stands on the west side.

➕ B3 ✉ Piazza Navona 🚍 30, 56, 60

The Pantheon, or Church of Santa Maria ad Martyres

San Clemente

No other church gives a better sense of Rome's layers of history than the church of San Clemente. This 12th-century basilica has columns, a marble choir and fine pulpit, with Byzantine mosaics in the apse above. Beneath lies a fourth-century church with eighth-century frescoes, while lower still are the remains of streets and a Mithraic temple.

✚ E2 ✉ Via Labicana 95 ☎ 06 774 0021; www.basilicasanclemente.com 🕓 Mon.–Sat. 9–12:30 and 3–6, Sun. noon–6 🚇 Colosseo 🚌 3, 85, 87, 117, 186, 571, 810, 850 🎟 Church free; Excavations $$

Santa Maria Maggiore

Mass has been said daily in Santa Maria Maggiore (St. Mary the Major) since the fifth century, when it was built on a site marked by a summer snow, as predicted by the Virgin when she appeared before the reigning pope. Much has been added over the years, but it retains fifth-century mosaics in the nave, while those in the apse date from the 13th-century. The ceiling is said to be gilded with the first gold from the New World.

✚ E2 ✉ Piazza di Santa Maria Maggiore 42 ☎ 06 6988 6800 🕓 Daily 7–7 or 8 p.m., Apr.–Sep.; 7–6:30 or 7, rest of year 🚇 Termini, Cavour 🚌 5, 16, 70, 71, 75, 84, 105, 360, 590 🍴 Agata e Romeo, see page 208 🎟 Church free; Museum $$; Loggia frescoes $

Santa Maria in Trastevere

If you're exploring Trastevere, make a point of visiting the church of Santa Maria in Trastevere. An 18th-century portico fronts the mosaic facade of this ancient church; the nave columns once supported classical buildings. The Byzantine-style 12th-century mosaics in the apse show the glorification of the Virgin Mary.

✚ B2 ✉ Piazza di Santa Maria in Trastevere ☎ 06 581 9443 🕓 Daily 7:30–8 🚌 44, 75, 161, 170 🎟 Free

Scalinata di Trinità dei Monti

The elegant Scalinata di Trinità dei Monti (Spanish Steps) curve gracefully up from the Piazza di Spagna to the church of Trinità dei Monti, a focal point for Rome's most fashionable shopping area. Built in 1723, the steps got their name from the piazza, which once housed the Spanish embassy. The poet Keats died in lodgings overlooking the steps in 1821; the building now houses a small museum devoted to Keats and Shelley. The piazza's fountain, built in 1627, resembles a sunken boat.

✚ C3 ✉ Piazza di Spagna 26 ☎ 06 678 4235; www.keats-shelley-house.org 🕓 Museo Keats–Shelley: Mon.–Fri. 10–1 and 2–6, Sat. 11–2 and 3–6 🚇 Spagna 🚌 116, 117, 119 🎟 $

Via Appia Antica

A section of the Via Appia Antica (Old Appian Way) still survives just outside the city. It's one of the many roads that fanned out to all corners of the Roman Empire. Built in the fourth century BC to link Rome and Brindisi, today it's a picturesque cobbled way, shaded by pines and lined with tombs and monuments. It was here that St. Paul marched on his way to prison, and Spartacus and his slaves were executed in 71 BC. Nearby you can visit two sets of catacombs.

✚ Off map E1 ✉ Via Appia Antica 136 ☎ 06 785 0350; www.catacombe.org 🕓 Catacombs: San Sebastiano Mon.–Sat. 10–5. Hours may vary 🚌 118, 714 🎟 Catacombs $$

Villa Giulia

The beautiful Villa Giulia houses one of Italy's great museums devoted to the enigmatic Etruscans. The collection includes the Castellani exhibits, with striking Minoan jewelry, fine Greek vases and seventh-century BC gold and silver from the Barbarini tombs. Most touching of all is the Sarcofago degli Sposi, a sixth-century BC sarcophagus containing what appears to be a married couple reclining on a banqueting couch.

✚ C4 ✉ Piazzale di Villa Giulia 9 ☎ 06 322 6571; (online booking at www.ticketaria.it) 🕓 Tue.–Sun. 8:30–7:30 🚇 Flaminio 🚌 19, 30, 52, 926 🎟 $$ 🛈 English audio guide available

The Vatican

Until Italian unification, the papacy held territory, known as the Papal States, throughout central Italy. In 1870 these lands became part of the new united Italy, and Pope Pius IX retreated to the Vatican as a virtual prisoner. As supreme head of Catholics worldwide, the pontiff clearly needed his own independent sovereign territory to retain his spiritual authority, and in 1929 the Treaty of the Lateran was signed with Mussolini. This established the Vatican State (Città del Vaticano), an area covering 110 acres around the Basilica of St. Peter and the Vatican Palace, today the world's smallest state.

The Vatican Today

The pope is Europe's sole remaining absolute monarch, with complete power over this tiny state. In April 2005, 78-year-old Cardinal Joseph Ratzinger of Germany was elected pope following the death earlier in the month of Pope John Paul II who had reigned for 26 years. The new pope, who took the name Pope Benedict XVI, is well known for his conservative views and dislike of liberal reform. Even so, he is a popular choice among the faithful and was greeted by the cheers of tens of thousands of followers when he stepped onto the balcony of St. Peter's Basilica to give his first blessing, proclaiming that he was but "a simple, humble worker." Latin is still the official language in the Vatican, which has all the appurtenances of an independent state including a daily newspaper and a broadcasting service.

The Pope's Army

The Pope and the Vatican itself are defended by the Swiss Guard, a 90-strong brigade drawn from Switzerland's four Catholic cantons since 1506. Young men aged 19 to 25 sign up for two to 20 years; their duties are largely ceremonial, but they are highly trained for all contingencies. They normally wear a picturesque navy-blue uniform. Their instantly recognizable red-, yellow- and blue-striped dress uniform, said to have been designed by Michelangelo, is reserved for state occasions. The Agenti di Vigilanza, formed in 1816, augment the Swiss Guard.

Seeing the Pope

When he is in Rome, the Pope traditionally gives a midday Sunday blessing from the window of his rooms overlooking the piazza. Since the 1970s, weekly audiences have been held in the Aula Paolo VI (Paul VI Hall). Up to 7,000 people attend these moving occasions; tickets are free and available from the Prefetura della Casa Pontifica, in the right-hand colonnade of the Piazza San Pietro.

The impressive nave of St. Peter's Basilica

Walk
The Best of Rome

Refer to route marked on city
map on pages 124–125

This walk takes you from Papal
Rome through medieval Rome to
some of the city's Renaissance
splendors. You could spend a whole
day walking the route, stopping for
museum visits along the way and
lunching at one of the cozy
restaurants near the Pantheon.

Start at the Castel Sant'Angelo.

The Castel Sant'Angelo was built by the
Emperor Hadrian in AD 130 as a
mausoleum; it got its present name
when Pope Gregory the Great had a
vision of an angel on its summit in
AD 590. Beginning in the ninth century,
it was a papal fortress; it was linked in
1277 to the Vatican by a passage. After
spells as a prison and barracks it became
a museum in 1933.

Cross the Ponte Sant'Angelo and walk
straight across the Piazza Ponte
Sant'Angelo into Via Banco Santo Spirito.
Continue left to Largo Tassoni, then turn left
onto the busy Corso Vittorio Emanuele II.
Continue for five blocks, then cross the
corso and turn right down Via Sora, then left
onto Via del Pellegrino. This will bring you
to the Campo dei Fiori.

One of the city's most alluring squares,
the Campo dei Fiori stood at the heart of
medieval Rome, surrounded by private
palaces, inns and brothels. The statue in
the center is the philosopher Giordano
Bruno, who was burned here for heresy
in the 17th century. The square has a
daily fruit, vegetable and fish market.
Neighborhood stores abound in the
surrounding streets, and it's the perfect
place to experience local life and have a
cappuccino.

**Turn right down Via Farnesi Gallo to Piazza
Farnese, one block south.**

Piazza Farnese is dominated by the
Palazzo Farnese, a Renaissance
architectural masterpiece partly
designed by Michelangelo and begun in
1516. It's now the French Embassy. The
beautiful baths forming the fountains are
Roman and came from the ruins of the
Baths of Caracalla.

**Retrace your steps to the Campo dei Fiori,
cross the square and head down Via dei
Baullari back to Corso Vittorio Emanuele.
Cross the corso and walk past the church of
San Pantaleo and down Via Cuccagna into
Piazza Navona (see page 131). After visiting
the piazza, go back to where you entered it,
face the square and turn right to reach
Corso del Rinascimento. Cross the road and
head up Via Sediari. Turn left at the end
onto Via della Scrofa, then take the second
road on the right to reach the Piazza della
Rotonda and the Pantheon (see page 131).
With your back to the Pantheon, turn right
and walk along Via dei Pastini and Via di
Pietro to Via del Corso; this section is
marked with brown pedestrian signs to
the Fontana di Trevi (see page 129).**

The Castel Sant'Angelo, or Mausoleum of Hadrian

Via del Corso runs from the Piazza del Popolo to the Piazza Venezia, bisecting the northern half of the city. Partially pedestrian-only, it's a favorite shopping street with a good variety of clothes, shoes and accessories.

Cross Via del Corso and follow Via della Muratte (and the brown signs) to the Fontana di Trevi. Keep the fountain on your left and head up Via Lavatore and Via delle Scuderie, with the bulk of the Palazzo del Quirinale on your right, then branch left to Via del Tritone with the Quirinale behind you.

The Palazzo del Quirinale is home to the president of Italy; it was built in the 16th and 17th centuries as the papal residence. Opposite the palace are the 18th-century Scuderie (Papal Stables),

restored and converted in 2000 to an exhibition hall.

Cross Via del Tritone and head straight down Via Due Macelli to the Piazza di Spagna. Climb the Scalinata di Trinità dei Monti (Spanish Steps, see page 132) on your right and turn left at the top of the steps. Follow Viale della Trinità dei Monti all the way along, keeping the Giardini della Villa Borghese on your right, until you reach Piazzale Napoleone.

You'll pass the Villa Medici on your right, a gracious 16th-century villa that houses the French Academy. From the Piazzale Napoleone you could visit the Museo Etrusco at the Villa Giulia (see page 132), the Galleria Borghese (see page 130) or simply take a break and sit and enjoy the tranquility of the park.

Beautiful flowers adorn the Spanish Steps in front of the Church of Trinità dei Monti during spring

Regional Sights

Key to symbols
➕ map coordinates refer to the region map on pages 120–121 🖐 admission charge: $$$ more than €7, $$ €4–€7, $ less than €4
See page 5 for complete key to symbols

Gran Sasso d'Italia

The highest peak on the Italian peninsula is the 9,554-foot Gran Sasso d'Italia (Etna on Sicily and many Alpine summits are higher). It rises above the Campo Imperatore, a huge upland plain. This is snowcapped mountain scenery at its best, and the area attracts hikers and climbers, although motorists also can enjoy some inspiring vistas.

The best access point is the tiny settlement of Fonte Cerreto, where a cable car runs up to the Albergo-Rifugio Campo Imperatore. It was here that Mussolini was imprisoned after the Italian surrender in 1943, only to be lifted out in a daring aerial raid by an ace German pilot dispatched by Hitler.

From the Rifugio, trails lead higher into the massif. Take number 10 to Monte della Scindarella (7,326 feet) for a taste of the area, a two-hour hike. You could drive farther across the rock-strewn landscape of the Campo Imperatore to explore some of the semi-deserted villages that fringe it; Castel del Monte, crowned with a ruined castle and church, and the abandoned settlement of Rocca Calascio, with its crumbling castle, make interesting stops.
➕ C3
Tourist information ✉ Via del Convento, Assergi
☎ 0862 62521 🕐 Mon.–Sat. 10–1 and 3–6, Sun. 10–6, Apr.–Oct. ✉ Via del Convento, L'Aquila
☎ 0862 60 521; www.gransassolagapark.it
🔢 For information on hiking in the Gran Sasso massif contact the Italian Alpine Club on www.cailaquila.it, www.cai.it or www.parks.it

Opposite: A tiny hamlet in the Gran Sasso d'Italia
Right: A chapel near the abandoned village of Rocca Calascio

L'Aquila

L'Aquila is the regional capital of the Abruzzo, and has always been a relatively undeveloped town, little known to outsiders. All this changed at 3.32 a.m. on April 6, 2009, when one of the worst earthquakes in Italy's recent history ravaged the town and many of its surrounding villages. It killed 297 people, injured many hundreds and left over 65,000 homeless. L'Aquila was declared off limits and the inhabitants rehoused as far as 20 miles away.

Reconstruction is proceeding and certain areas have been repaired but the city has effectively ceased to function and is expected to remain out of bounds for the foreseeable future.
➕ C2

Molise

Part of the Abruzzo until 1963, Molise is Italy's newest region, an undeveloped area that has more in common with its neighbors to the south than those to the north. Forty percent of Molise is mountainous; these mountains offer great hiking, particularly around the lakes, woods and high plains of the Matese chain.

From Boiano you can hike up Monte Gallinola, a two-hour climb that culminates in a coast-to-coast view across the whole Italian peninsula.

Molise's main centers are Isernia and Campobasso, sprawling modern cities surrounded by factories. To taste the best of the region, head for the rolling countryside or the coastal resort of Termoli, with its long sandy beach and medieval heart. Attractions in Molise include Saepinum, Italy's best-preserved example of a Roman provincial town.

➕ D1–E1

Campobasso tourist information ✉ Piazza della Vittoria 14 ☎ 0874 415 662 🕐 Mon.–Sat. 8–2

Isernia tourist information ✉ Palazzo della Regione (6th floor), Via Farinacci 9 ☎ 0865 3992; www.iserniaturismo.it 🕐 Mon.–Sat. 8–2

Saepinum ✉ Altilla, 2 miles from Sepino 🕐 Site always open

Montecassino

Scene of one of World War II's most bitterly fought battles, the Benedictine Abbey of Montecassino was founded in AD 529 by St. Benedict; legend maintains he was led to this impregnable spot by three ravens. It quickly became one of the most important monasteries in Europe, sending monks far and wide to disseminate Benedictine ideals. Its strategic mountaintop position between Rome and Naples made it a target over the centuries for repeated attacks, and the abbey has been rebuilt many times.

During World War II the abbey became the German regional headquarters and was besieged by the Allies for more than six months. It was completely destroyed by Allied bombs in May 1944. Its destruction, although vital to the Allies' cause, has created controversy ever since. The old monastery complex has been faithfully rebuilt and still looms impressively over the valley. The views from the central cloister are as exceptional as ever. The area around and to the south of Montecassino is scattered with much-visited war cemeteries.

➕ D1

Abbazia di Montecassino ✉ Via Montecassino ☎ 0776 311 529; www.montecassino.it 🕐 Daily 8:30–12:30 and 3:30–6:30, May–Sep.; 8:30–12:30 and 3:30–5:30, rest of year. Closed during services ✋ $

Ninfa

Ninfa is an enchanting spot, a romantic and semi-wild garden planted amid the ruins of a medieval village. The ancient settlement dates from at least Roman times, reaching its heyday in the 13th century when Pope Boniface VIII, a member of the Caetani dynasty, bought the town as a gift for his nephew. Although conflict and malaria led to the town's ruin, the Caetani continued to

The impressive bulk of the Abbey of Montecassino, scene of bitter fighting in World War II

take an interest and began planting roses against the ruined walls during picnics here in the 1920s. The garden gradually developed and in 1977, when the last Caetani died, it was entrusted to a charitable foundation.

➕ B1

🕿 www.fondazionecaetani.org 🕐 First Sat.–Sun. of the month, Apr.–Oct.; also third Sun. of the month Apr.–Jun. Hours are 9–noon and 2:30–6, Apr.–Jun.; 9–noon and 3–6:30, Jul.–Sep.; 9–noon and 2:30–4, Oct.

🖐 $$$

Parco Nazionale d'Abruzzo

The vast 99,000 acres of the Parco Nazionale d'Abruzzo (Abruzzo National Park) make up one of Europe's great wilderness areas. If you love the great outdoors, this is a place you must try to visit. Once a royal hunting reserve, the park was established in 1917 and consists of a jumble of Apennine mountain massifs, with the Sangro Valley cutting through its heart. Here lie the villages of Pescasseroli, Opi and others, where you can pick up information on hiking and viewing wildlife; there are more than 150 well-marked trails of different standards. You'll likely see a subspecies of chamois (a type of antelope) native to the Abruzzo. Wolves are harder to spot, though some are kept in reserves at Civitella Alfedena's Museo del Lupo. Rarest of all is the Apennine brown bear; there may be between 50 and 80 in the park and numbers are increasing. Spring and fall are probably the best times to explore: spring flowers are stunningly beautiful, while fall sees mountain slopes glowing with colors.

➕ D2–D1

Information office ✉ Via Colli dell'Oro, Pescasseroli 🕿 0863 911 3221; www.parcoabruzzo.it 🕐 Daily 10–7, Jul.–Aug.; 10–5, rest of year ❶ There are smaller summer-only offices at Opi, Barrea and Civitella Alfedena and elsewhere

Tarquinia

It's hard to imagine that 5,000 years ago unassuming Tarquinia boasted a population of more than 100,000 and was the most important of the 12 Etruscan cities. Today's town retains its medieval walls and the 12th-century Romanesque church of Santa Maria di Castello, but most visitors are drawn here by the Etruscan tombs and the superlative Museo Nazionale Tarquiniense (National Tarquinian Museum), which is housed in the 15th-century Palazzo Vitelleschi. This museum has a significant collection of treasures discovered in the Etruscan necropolis that stands to the east of town. There are sarcophagi, detailed ceramics and delicate gold jewelry, although pride of place must be given to the beautiful pair of winged terra-cotta horses, a breathtakingly sophisticated piece of sculpture. The necropolis itself, just outside town, is an underground honeycomb of tomb chambers, many of which have been opened so you can admire the colorful wall paintings that adorn them. Steps lead down into the earth to allow you to see these lively 5,000-year-old paintings. Excavation of the tombs continues today.

➕ A2

Tourist information ✉ Barriera San Giusto 🕿 0766 849 282 🕐 Daily 9–1 and 4–7

Santa Maria di Castello ✉ Piazza Santa Maria di Castello 🕐 Fri.–Sun. 10:30–12:30 and 3–6

Museo Nazionale Tarquiniense ✉ Palazzo Vitelleschi, Piazza Cavour 1 🕿 0766 856 036 🕐 Tue.–Sun. 8:30–7:30. Closed Jan. 1, May 1 and Dec. 25 🖐 $$ ❶ Ticket also is valid for the necropoli in the Zona Archeologica

Zona Archeologica "Monterozzi Necropolis" ✉ Via Ripagretta 🕿 0766 856 308 🕐 Tue.–Sun. 8:30–7:30, Apr.–Oct.; 8:30–2, rest of year (ticket office closes 12:30 p.m.). Closed Jan. 1, May 1 and Dec. 25 🖐 $$ (combined ticket with museum) ❶ The tombs are opened in rotation to help conserve the paintings, and there is no way of knowing in advance which will be open on any particular day

Tivoli

The main attractions of Tivoli, a small town in a lovely wooded location some 18 miles from Rome, are the Villa d'Este and the vast classical site of the Villa Adriana (Hadrian's Villa). Both of these attractions are usually crowded with day-trippers from Rome, so come early to appreciate them at their best. The Villa d'Este, built in 1550 and now rather shabby, has superb gardens with terraces, cascades and fountains; wherever you are in its shady green coolness, you'll hear the refreshing splash of falling water. The two superb Bernini fountains, the elegant Fontana di Biccierone and the Fontana dei Draghi, are the most splendid, but make sure you don't miss the breathtaking Viale delle Cento Fontane (Avenue of a Hundred Fountains).

Outside town are the ruins of the Villa Adriana (Hadrian's Villa), built by the emperor in AD 125 as a retirement home. The villa was designed to incorporate copies of buildings he had seen on his travels. This fascinating place is vast, rambling, green and romantic.

Sunlight sparkling on pretty fountains dazzles the eye in the gardens of the Villa d'Este at Tivoli

+ B2

Tourist information ✉ Piazzale Nazioni Unite
☎ 0774 313 536 ⏲ Tue.–Sun. 10–1 and 4–6
Villa d'Este ✉ Piazza Trento ☎ 199 766 166;
www.villadestetivoli.info ⏲ Tue.–Sun. 8:30 a.m.–one hour before sunset (ticket office closes an hour earlier)
🍴 Refreshments available in gardens 🖐 $$
Villa Adriana ✉ Via di Villa Adriana 204 ☎ 0774 530 203; www.villa-adriana.net ⏲ Daily 9–6, May–Aug.; 9–5:50, Mar., Apr., Sep. and Oct.; 9–3:30, rest of year. Last ticket 90 minutes before closing 🍴 Refreshments available at villa site 🖐 $$$

Viterbo

Capital of northern Lazio, Viterbo's heyday was in medieval times, when it was a favored place for different popes to escape troubles in Rome. Their legacy is a collection of grand palaces and fine churches still enclosed by intact city walls. The entire city has an intensely medieval atmosphere, which is best appreciated by exploring the San Pellegrino neighborhood, a tight mass of hilly streets dotted with towers and elevated medieval walkways. At the heart of the city, Piazza del Plebiscito is a fine square surrounded by 15th- and 16th-century buildings. The decorative lions, which you'll see examples of all over the city, are Viterbo's symbol.

From Piazza del Plebiscito, head to Piazza San Lorenzo to see the 13th-century Palazzo dei Papi (Papal Palace); its Gothic loggia overlooks the green gorge cutting into the city's center. The Duomo (Cathedral) stands opposite the palace, an austere and serene Romanesque church of great beauty. The city's Museo Civico is mainly devoted to exhibits from the surrounding area, including Etruscan artifacts.

+ B3

Tourist information ✉ Via Ciscenzi 4 ☎ 0761 325 992; www.viterboonline.com or www.comune.viterbo.it
⏲ Tue.–Sun. 10–7, mid-Aug. to early Sep.; 10–1 and 3–7, Jul. to mid-Aug. and Sep.; 10–1 and 3:30–7, Jun.; 10–1 and 3–6, Apr.–May and Oct.; 10–1 and 3–5, rest of year
Duomo ✉ Piazza San Lorenzo ☎ 0761 325 462
⏲ Daily 9–12:30 and 3:30–6 🖐 $$
Museo Civico ✉ Piazza F. Crispi ☎ 0761 340 810
⏲ Tue.–Sun. 9–7, Apr.–Oct.; 9–6, rest of year 🖐 $

The Etruscans

While traveling in Lazio and other parts of central Italy, you'll come across frequent signs of the Etruscans in the shape of monuments, tombs and museums. Who were these enigmatic and mysterious people?

The Etruscans stepped into history's limelight around the fifth century BC. They were a people probably made up of indigenous tribes and seafarers from Asia Minor. Inhabiting an area of central Italy called Etruria and stretching from modern Tuscany down to Rome, they formed a confederacy of 12 cities, building towns, passing laws and trading overseas. They were a lively and imaginative people with sophisticated cultural, political and social systems. That much is clear, but little else of their everyday life is known. This is explained by two factors. First, the Romans so admired them that they absorbed much of Etruscan culture as they rose to power. By the third century BC, the Romans had virtually assimilated all of Etruria, together with much of its language, customs and religious beliefs. Secondly, the Etruscans built their cities of wood, not stone, and nothing remains.

We also know that the Etruscans were deeply religious, firmly believing in an afterlife and burying their dead, as did the Egyptians, with all they would need for the future. Their tombs (*necropoli*), unlike their wooden cities, were permanent, made either of stone or carved out of the soft tufa rock found all over ancient Etruria. Wonderful finds have been made in these tombs and, from these, historians have learned much about the Etruscan way of life. The artifacts from the tombs are preserved in on-site museums, although the finest have gone to the Vatican Museums (see page 130) and the Villa Giulia (see page 132) in Rome.

You can explore different Etruscan sites all over central Italy, but the most interesting can be found in Lazio. Tarquinia (see page 139) has some wonderful painted tombs. Orvieto, in Umbria (see page 106), has fascinating streets carved from tufa, while in Sutri a 6,000-seat amphitheater is carved from the living rock. Cerveteri, north of Rome, is literally a "city of the dead," complete with streets, houses and piazzas. There are more than 5,000 tombs here, although only around 50 or so have been systematically excavated.

A bronze statue of the she-wolf suckling Romulus and Remus stands in Piazza del Campidoglio

Drive
The Coast to the Alban Hills

Duration: 4.5 to 5 hours

Start this drive in San Felice Circeo, a honey-colored coastal village with a good beach, an hour's drive south from Rome.

From San Felice, you have access to the Parco Nazionale del Circeo (Monte Circeo National Park), named after the limestone headland of Monte Circeo, which looms above the town. Monte Circeo was reputedly the home of the sorceress Circe, who lured Ulysses with her guiles and siren song. You can drive to the summit for wonderful coastal views. The park, the smallest of Italy's national parks, was established in 1934 to preserve some of the natural beauty of the neighboring marsh and wetland area, as well as to preserve the woodlands and wonderful flora of Monte Circeo itself. It's of special interest to bird enthusiasts,

as the lakes and lagoons provide marvelous habitats for many varieties of waterfowl. With luck you'll spot herons, storks and fish hawks.

Continue north along the coast to Anzio (follow signs to Sabaudia).

North of Monte Circeo, the road hugs the coast for more than 20 miles (32 kilometers), then makes a brief detour inland before hitting the sea again at Nettuno. There's a big, peaceful and beautifully tended World War II cemetery at Nettuno where nearly 8,000 American GIs are buried, killed at the Anzio landings in 1944.

At Anzio, take the SS207 (signposted Aprilia) and continue for 20 miles (33 kilometers) to Aprilia, then Pavona. Turn right and then follow signs to Castel Gandolfo.

Castel Gandolfo, set high above Lago Albano (Lake Albano) in the Alban Hills, is best known as the pope's summer retreat. Several pontiffs have come here to escape the broiling heat of the Roman summer. It's a pleasant little town, dominated by the Papal Palace, in whose courtyard the pope traditionally gives a Sunday blessing when he's in residence. Below the town, the picturesque lake is tempting, where you can have a swim or eat at one of the many lakeside restaurants.

Follow signs to Frattocchie, then branch right on an unnamed road across country to the junction with the SS215 and follow the signs to Frascati.

Frascati is another of the Alban hill towns; it's the nearest to Rome, and therefore often packed with day-trippers and Romans who flock there to eat Sunday lunch. It's attractive and picturesque, dominated by the bulk of the

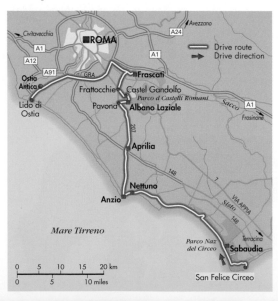

Ostia Antica's excellent amphitheater, built around 12 BC, could hold up to 4,000 spectators

majestic Villa Aldobrandi, which was built in 1598. The villa's gardens today are romantically overgrown. The spectacular fountains are often switched off, but if the gardens are open it's worth going in for the sweeping views from the terrace in front of the house. White wine has been made in Frascati since Roman times, and it is well known outside Italy. There are plenty of places where you can sample this light and clean-tasting wine and some growers offer tours.

Rejoin the SS215, this time following signs to the Grande Raccordo Annullare (GRA), Rome's ring road, and turn left. Continue on the GRA for 11 miles (18 kilometers), then exit on the SS8 to Lido di Ostia, Ostia Antica and the coastline.

Lido di Ostia is a relatively modern town, with some very art nouveau houses built on the waterfront. Its popularity with day-tripping Romans makes it uncomfortably crowded in summer and during fine weekends. For a break from the crowds, take in some of the sedate beaches about 5 miles (8 kilometres) to the south in Tor Vaianica, but make time to explore the real treasure of this area, the archeological site of Ostia Antica. You'll learn far more here, in far greater peace, than moving with the crowds in the Forum in Rome itself. The site is huge, dotted with grass-covered mounds and umbrella pines. You could wander for hours, but if time is short, head for the Piazzale di Corporazione, the ancient city's commercial center. Ruined shops and offices still line it, and the mosaics in front indicate each building's purpose – ropemakers, grain merchants and chandlers. You can explore private houses (the Casa di Diana with its central courtyard is among the best), walk the streets and visit the Thermopolium, an ancient café. Pride of place goes to the vast 4,000-seat amphitheater, which is used for open-air concerts in summer. There are also the remains of the Forum, and the Baths of Neptune, with their splendid mosaics.

Parco Nazionale del Circeo information office
✉ Via Carlo Alberti 107, Sabaudia ☎ 0773 512 240; www.parks.it 🕐 Daily 9–1 and 2:30–5

Frascati tourist information ✉ Piazza G. Marconi 1 ☎ 06 942 0331 🕐 Mon.–Sat. 8–2. Hours may vary

Ostia Antica ✉ Via Romanogli 717, Ostia ☎ 06 5635 8099; www.ostia-antica-org 🕐 Daily 9–7:30, Apr.–Sep.; 8:30–6, Oct. and Mar.; 8:30–5, Nov.–Feb. Last ticket one hour before closing 🎫 $$

The South

Opposite: Clear blue seas and craggy hills add to the appeal of Ravello

The South

Southern Italy – the Mezzogiorno – starts south of Rome and includes four very diverse regions: Campania, with its breathtakingly beautiful coastline; the mountainous inland areas of Calabria and Basilicata; the empty flatlands along the Ionian coast; and the hills and seaboard of Puglia (Apulia). Its chief city is Naples, one of the most vibrant, frustrating but ultimately bewitching cities in Italy. Spiritually a million miles from the dynamic north, Italy's south, remote and relatively little explored, provides a balance to the northern regions and the Renaissance perfection of the central areas.

Echoes of the Past

Invaders have poured into the south for more than 2,500 years. Greek, Arab, Norman, German and Spanish each systematically bled the region. However, these successive waves of invasion left behind a superb artistic legacy of temples, churches and palaces. They established a genetic mark on the population and incorporated the rhythms of their own speech in local dialects, and brought echoes of their tastes to the intense flavors of southern cuisine. Their absolutist regimes also bequeathed the very elements that kept the south one of the most economically depressed areas of Western Europe.

Today

Southern Italy is still poor. This is partly the result of centuries of foreign neglect, but it's also due to a policy of industrializing the north, while using the south as a labor pool to fuel this industry. After World War II, millions of southerners moved north to find work. The south was increasingly depopulated and its industry and infrastructure undeveloped. The north–south divide is very real and will be apparent if you've explored northern and central Italy.

Despite massive central government and European Union investment in the country in recent years, the southern standard of living still lags far behind the rest of Italy. Organized crime and corruption still exist, although things are improving and the average visitor certainly won't be affected. You will notice the dilapidation and grime of many southern towns, while away from the tourist areas you'll have to bear in mind that you're traveling in the poorer half of the "two Italys." Persevere; the rewards are tremendous and you'll see a facet of Italy that relatively few visitors experience.

Passionate People

Southern Italians may come across as passionate and volatile. Seemingly huge altercations may be simply an everyday exchange of news or views. Watch the hand gestures to get some idea of the level of feeling – ill will evaporates as

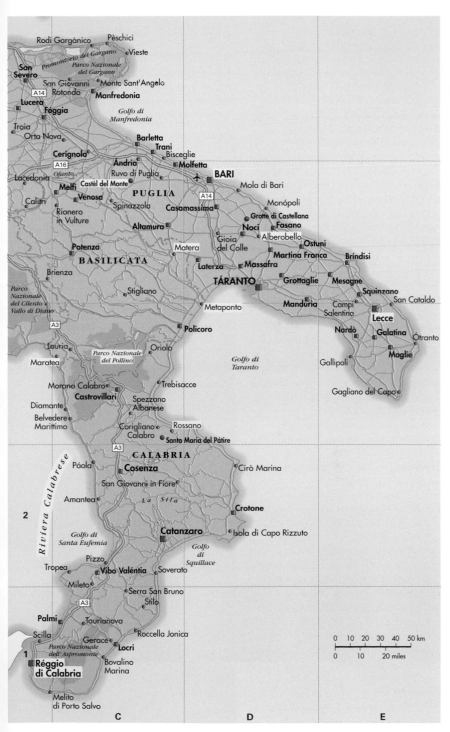

Rodi Gargànico
Pèschici
Vieste
San Severo
Promontorio del Gargano
Parco Nazionale del Gargano
San Giovanni
Monte Sant'Angelo
A14
Rotondo
Manfredonia
Lucèra
Fòggia
Golfo di Manfredonia
Troia
Orta Nova
Barletta
Trani
Cerignola
Bisceglie
A16
Àndria
Molfetta
Lacedonia
Ofanto
Ruvo di Puglia
BARI
Melfi
Castèl del Monte
Mola di Bari
Calitri
Venosa
PUGLIA
A14
Monópoli
Rionero in Vulture
Spinazzola
Casamassima
Grotte di Castellana
Altamura
Noci
Fasano
Potenza
Gioia del Colle
Alberobello
Ostuni
Matera
Martina Franca
Brindisi
BASILICATA
Laterza
Massafra
Brienza
Stigliano
TÁRANTO
Grottaglie
Mesagne
Parco Nazionale del Cilento e Vallo di Diano
Metaponto
Manduria
Campi Salentina
Squinzano
San Cataldo
A3
Policoro
Lecce
Lauria
Oriolo
Golfo di Taranto
Nardò
Galatina
Òtranto
Maratea
Parco Nazionale del Pollino
Gallipoli
Maglie
Morano Calabro
Trebisacce
Gagliano del Capo
Castrovillari
Spezzano Albanese
Diamante
Belvedere Marittimo
Corigliano Calabro
Rossano
Santa Maria del Pátire
A3
CALABRIA
Riviera Calabrese
Páola
Cosenza
Cirò Marina
San Giovanni in Fiore
Amantea
La Sila
2
Crotone
Golfo di Santa Eufemia
Catanzaro
Isola di Capo Rizzuto
Pizzo
Golfo di Squillace
Tropea
Vibo Valéntia
Soverato
Mileto
Serra San Bruno
A3
Stilo
Palmi
Tauriranova
Scilla
Roccella Jonica
Gerace
Parco Nazionale dell'Aspromonte
Locri
Réggio di Calabria
Bovalino Marina
Melito di Porto Salvo

C   D   E

0 10 20 30 40 50 km
0   10   20 miles

fast as it flares up. Likewise, the cool welcome you may first encounter can turn quickly to overwhelming warmth and friendliness. Spontaneous and open, southerners react quickly, their hearts often ruling their heads.

People tend to be smaller and darker complected than in the north, although red and blonde hair and blue eyes are the genetic legacy of northern occupation. Society is still male-dominated, particularly in remote areas where it's rare even to see women on the streets. In some rural regions many people still work on the land, and you may still see traditional agricultural methods in use.

What to See and Do

With some notable exceptions, the south is less rich in artistic treasures than central and northern Italy. You'll want to visit the classical sites of Pompeii, Paestum and Metaponto, and the ancient city center of Bari, with its Arabic echoes. Apulian towns such as Alberobello and Lecce are interesting, but it's the southern coast that many visitors will remember.

South of Naples stretches one of Europe's most stunning coastlines, where you could happily spend a week exploring the pretty villages and soaking up the sun. If you prefer less chic surroundings, head farther south and east to the quaint little resorts along the Ionian Sea coast and within Calabria. Apulia's long beaches and the cliffs of the Gargano strike a happy balance between rural charm and good facilities. Wilderness lovers will find the south's interior everything they could hope for, with great hiking in wonderful mountain scenery. Explore the Sila and Pollino inland areas, where you'll find upland meadows and forests reminiscent of northern landscapes.

When to Go

As in the rest of Italy, the best time to visit the south of the country is in spring, early summer or fall. Spring reveals the country at its greenest and most beautiful, clothed in colorful wild flowers; by May and June it's already heating up and can be warm enough to enjoy the stunning beaches. September and October can be idyllic, with velvet-warm seas and balmy evenings.

July and August are months to be avoided if at all possible; the south has a true Mediterranean climate, and temperatures can climb well into the 90s. These also are the Italian holiday months when coastal resorts are at their most crowded, and the cities empty of their residents. Many hotels outside the main centers are closed throughout the winter months, when daylight hours are short and the weather tends to be wet and windy.

Houses line the hills above the harbor at Conca Verde, southwest along the coast from Sorrento

Naples

Vibrant Naples (Napoli), the capital of southern Italy, is very different from the dynamic, work-driven north. Ramshackle and confusing, in places, Naples can sometimes feel alien and intimidating, but most visitors are quickly won over by its exuberance, way of life and people.

Come to Naples with an open mind, remembering you'll find a big, sprawling city that suffered huge damage in World War II. Indiscriminate construction has wrecked some of the loveliest outlying areas. Concentrate instead on the superb monuments, churches, museums, galleries and the welcoming charm of the people. In no other major Italian city will you find such friendliness.

Getting Around

The horrific traffic makes all transportation excruciatingly slow, so it's best to tackle central Naples on foot. Sites are grouped together in different areas, so take a bus or cable car to reach them and then walk. Wandering around is an essential part of the Naples experience, but stick to well-frequented areas. Avoid the back streets, the docks and railroad station. Take great care crossing streets; Neapolitan drivers ignore pedestrian crossings, and scooter users appear to come out of nowhere and often use the sidewalk. One of the best ways to appreciate the beauty of Naples' coastal setting is from the sea; you could combine this with a boat trip to Sorrento (see page 164) or the islands of Capri (see page 157) and Ischia.

Essential Information

Tourist Information
■ Piazza del Gesù 7 ☎ 081 551 2701
■ Via San Carlo 9 ☎ 081 402 394;
www.inaples.it ☻ Hours very variable

Urban Transportation
It's best to walk in traffic-clogged Naples. Longer distances can be covered by subway, bus and cable car. The two types of Giranapoli tickets are valid for 90 minutes or all day; they are interchangeable between the systems and are sold at tobacconists or newsstands. Validate tickets at each system in the special machines. The Circumvesuviana railway (☎ 081 772 111; www.vesuviana.it) runs every half-hour from Corso Garibaldi to Sorrento, an hour's trip. You also can travel to Sorrento by ferry or hydrofoil (www.caremar.it, www.alilauro.it or www.snav.it) from either

Mergellina or the Molo Beverello docks. The same companies also serve Capri, Ischia and the other islands. There are taxi stands throughout the city, or phone Taxi Napoli (☎ 081 556 4444), Taxi Free (☎ 081 551 5151), Conrazio 5–70 (☎ 081 570 7070) or Partenope (☎ 081 556 0202).

Airport Information
Naples Capodichino Airport (☎ 848 888 777; from cell phones or abroad 081 751 5471 for flight information; www.gesac.it), with internal and European flights, is 4 miles northwest of the city center. Airport "Alibus" (www.anm.it) buses leave every 20 minutes (6:30 a.m.–11:30 p.m.) and take 30 minutes to get to Piazza Garibaldi. The local ANM city bus number 35, which leaves every 30 minutes takes 30–45 minutes (www.anm.it).

Climate – average highs and lows for the month

Jan.	Feb.	Mar.	Apr.	May	Jun.	Jul.	Aug.	Sep.	Oct.	Nov.	Dec.
12°C	13°C	15°C	18°C	22°C	26°C	29°C	29°C	26°C	22°C	17°C	13°C
54°F	55°F	59°F	64°F	72°F	79°F	84°F	84°F	79°F	72°F	63°F	55°F
4°C	5°C	7°C	9°C	13°C	17°C	19°C	19°C	17°C	13°C	8°C	5°C
39°F	41°F	45°F	48°F	55°F	63°F	66°F	66°F	63°F	55°F	46°F	41°F

Mediterranean Flavors

Neapolitan cooking ranks among Italy's best, with intense flavors and a strong emphasis on fresh fish and seafood, as well as local fruits and vegetables. It is home to the thin, crisp pizza, baked in wood-fired ovens, favored by many over the deep-pan crust variety found elsewhere. Cakes and pastries, stuffed with *crema* and dripping with liqueurs, come from a *pasticceria*, where you'll often find glorious mounds of ice cream in sumptuous flavors – best in the summer when it's made with luscious, seasonal fruit. Local wines to try are Lacryma Christi (Christ's Tears) and Greco di Tufo. And be sure to sample Limoncello, a lemon-flavored liqueur.

Shopping and Entertainment

Head for the Via Toledo and the Via Chiaia for chic designer outlets, copious leather goods, knitwear and accessories; this area also is home to department stores such as la Rinascente and Coin, while the Vomero district has shopping centers at Galleria Vanvitelli and Galleria Scartelli. The San Biagio neighborhood is the place to find coral jewelry and cameo brooches, as well as beautiful traditional nativity figures.

If you are a fan of opera and classical music, try to take in a performance at the San Carlo opera house in the city. Traditional music is easy to find everywhere, and many restaurants feature evening serenades.

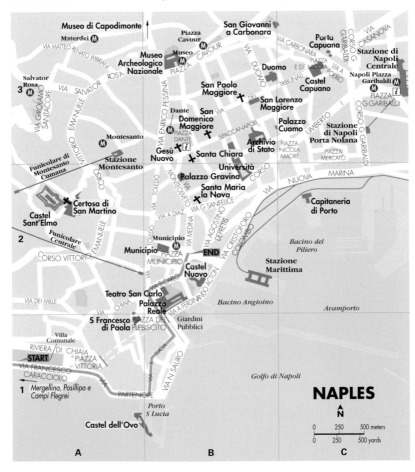

Naples Sights

Key to symbols

🔢 map coordinates refer to the Naples map on page 151 🎫 admission charge: $$$ more than €6, $$ €3–€6, $ less than €3

See page 5 for complete key to symbols

Castel Nuovo

The Castel Nuovo (New Castle), with its five massive chess-piece towers, dominates the waterfront and can be seen for miles. First built in 1282, it was enlarged in the 15th century and was later the residence of the Aragonese monarchs. Today it's the home of the Naples city council. A magnificent Renaissance gateway opens onto the central courtyard, which is surrounded by buildings housing the Museo Civico (Civic Museum), the Gothic Sala dei Baroni (Baron's Hall) and the Cappella Palatina (Palatine Chapel), a surviving part of a 13th-century building.

Nearby is the huge and imposing Palazzo Reale, a grandiose structure built in 1602 with a flamboyant but strangely, and disappointingly, dull interior. The famous San Carlo, Italy's largest opera house, is east of the castle.

🔢 B2 ✉ Piazza Municipio ☎ 081 795 5877 🕐 Mon.–Sat. 9–7 🚌 C25, R2, R3; tram 1 🎫 $$

Castel dell'Ovo

Encircled by the sea, Castel dell'Ovo (Egg Castle) is on a small island joined to the mainland by a causeway. It is Naples' oldest castle and was built between the ninth and 16th centuries. The castle's unusual name is derived from the story that it was built on top of an egg placed here in Roman times; legend has it that if the egg broke, Naples would fall. Run-down and dilapidated by the 1970s, the castle has now been extensively restored and is often used for cultural events.

🔢 A1 ✉ Borgo Marinari ☎ 081 240 0055 🕐 Mon.–Sat. 9–6, Sun. 10–2 🍴 La Cantinella, see page 210 🚌 4, 140, 601, R3 🎫 Free

Certosa di San Martino

The hilltop complex of the Certosa di San Martino (St. Martin's Charterhouse) was mainly constructed between the 16th and 18th centuries. Explore the Chiostro Grande (Main Cloister), the sumptuous baroque church and the lavish Quarto del Priore (Prior's Quarters). Don't miss the exhibition of *presepi* (Nativity figures), a collection of figures, animals and everyday objects fashioned for 19th-century nativity scenes, the highlight here. Walk through the monastery to the planted terrace at the back; it commands a sweeping view of the city and Bay of Naples.

🔢 A2 ✉ Piazzale San Martino 5 ☎ 081 558 6408; www.polomusealenapoli.beniculturali.it 🕐 Thu.–Tue. 8:30–7:30. Hours and prices may vary 🚌 Take funicular Montesanto, Centrale or Chiai to Vomero 🚌 V1 🎫 $$$

Mergellina

This waterfront area west of the city is a popular place to eat. The harbor is the focal point of the traditional fishermen's quarter, and it's a delightful place to stroll. Fishing boats and island ferries still leave from the little harbor.

🔢 Off map A1 ✉ Via Mergellina 🍴 Don Salvatore, see page 210 🚌 Mergellina 🚌 C4, C16, R3

Museo Archeologico Nazionale

The Museo Archeologico (Archeological Museum) houses one of the world's most important collections of classical sculpture, mosaics, gems, glass and silver. Buy an English-language guide before your tour. The first floor is devoted mainly to sculpture, much from the 17th-century Farnese collections that were largely discovered in Rome. Dating from about 200 BC, this is the world's largest classical sculptural group to have survived. The stars are the *Farnese Hercules* and the *Farnese Bull*. Many rooms have finds from Pompei and Herculaneum; don't miss the fresco of Flora scattering spring flowers, and a mosaic of a fierce but friendly dog from a Pompeian front door.

⊞ B3 ✉ Piazza Museo 19 ☎ 081 442 2149; http://
museoarcheologiconazionale.campaniabeniculturali.it
🕓 Wed.–Mon. 9–7:30 🚇 Museo 🚌 57, 63, R4
🍴 $$$ ℹ️ English-language guidebooks are available
at the museum shop

Museo di Capodimonte

Built in 1738 as the Bourbon King
Charles III's palace and surrounded by a
wooded park, Capodimonte has been
restored and rearranged. You can
wander freely through the opulent royal
apartments on your way to the majolica
and porcelain collection, much of it
made by the Capodimonte factory and
painted with local scenes. Upstairs is a
collection of paintings spanning the
15th to 17th centuries, with an emphasis
on Renaissance works. Some rooms are
often closed, but with luck you'll get to
see Botticelli's *Madonna*, Umbrian
paintings by Perugino and Pinturicchio,
and some sensitive portraits of Pope
Paul III by Titian. There's a Raphael
portrait of Pope Leo X, contrasting with
Sebastiano del Piombo's worldly
interpretation of Pope Clement VII.

⊞ Off map B3 ✉ Parco di Capodimonte, Via Miano 2
☎ 081 749 9111 or toll free in Italy 848 800 288;
www.pierreci.it or www.polomusealenapoli.
beniculturali.it 🕓 Museum: Thu.–Tue. 8:30–7:30. Park:
daily 8 a.m.–1 hour before dusk 🚇 Colli Aminei/train
line 2 to Via Cavour then 🚌 C63 or R4 🍴 $$$; Park
free ℹ️ English-language audio guide is available

Santa Chiara

This entire area teems with life, noise
and confusion. By contrast, the
Franciscan church of Santa Chiara is
simple and austere. Rebuilt after a fire in
1943, it contains tombs and offers access
to a 15th-century cloister. This was
transformed in the 18th century by
making the center a garden surrounded
by majolica-tiled pillars, benches and
walls showing scenes of everyday life.

The church is a good starting point for
exploring Spaccanapoli (see below).

⊞ B3 ✉ Via Santa Chiara 49/c ☎ 081 552 6280;
www.monasterodisantachiara.eu 🕓 Church:
Mon.–Sat. 9:30–5:30, Sun. 10–2. Cloister and museum:
Mon.–Sat. 9:30–1, 2:30–5:30, Sun. 9:30–1 but hours
vary 🚌 In the pedestrian zone 🍴 Museum and
cloister $$; Church free

Spaccanapoli

Spaccanapoli is the name given to the
string of atmospheric streets slicing
through Naples' historic core, which
follow the line of the classical city's
main artery. Its length is lined with
monuments that trace the city's story –
medieval, Renaissance and baroque
palazzi, churches and civic buildings,
many superbly endowed with works of
art. There's no better place to get a taste
of the reality of this vibrant city.

⊞ B3 ✉ Via Benedetto Croce, Via San Biagio dei
Librai 🚌 In the pedestrian zone

Santa Chiara, one of the best-known churches in the city, stands at the center of historic Naples

Walk
Waterfront Naples

Refer to route marked on city map on page 151

This walk starts from the Villa Comunale and goes through the elegant neighborhood of Chiaia to Santa Lucia and on to Piazza Municipio.

Start on Via Francesco Caracciolo, a waterfront, pedestrian-only street west of the Castel dell'Ovo.
Via Francesco Caracciolo was built in the late 19th century; its broad elegance will help you to appreciate Naples' glorious location.
Walk east along Via Francesco Caracciolo's walkway with the green oasis of the Villa Comunale, Naples' central park, on your left.
The gardens, with steps down to the sea, were laid out in 1778 with parallel walks, trees, shrubs and statues; they were enlarged in the 19th century when the promenade was built. The gardens are always crowded on summer evenings and on the third weekend of every month, when an antiques market takes place in the villa. In the middle of the park stands the 19th-century building housing the Aquarium, a rather dreary collection of fish and marine life.
Walk along farther to Piazza Vittoria and continue beside the sea along Via Partenope, an upscale street lined with luxury hotels. To your right looms the Castel dell'Ovo (see page 152), which you'll pass on the right as the road swings around to reach the harbor of Santa Lucia.
There's a splendid fish market here in the mornings, while later in the day you can eat a delicious seafood lunch or dinner in one of the restaurants along the waterfront. Every Neapolitan song you've heard seems to feature this area, including the best-known of all, O Sole Mio. Ahead is the flamboyant fountain known as the Immacolatella.
Cross Via Partenope and turn left up Via Santa Lucia.
This area contains some of Naples' most elegant shops, where you'll find outlets for Italian and international designer names. Local stores specialize in more traditional Neapolitan products, such as coral necklaces, bracelets and earrings, and delicate cameo brooches.
Via Santa Lucia opens on Via Cesario Console, where you turn left to head up to sweeping Piazza del Plebiscito, with the Palazzo Reale to your right. Turn right onto Via San Carlo, which leads past San Carlo opera house and the Castel Nuovo (see page 152) to bustling Piazza Municipio, with the grandiose city hall at the top of the square.

The harborside near the massive bulk of the Castel dell'Ovo, Naples' oldest castle

Season by Season

There's no best time to visit Naples, although spring and fall are ideal for those who don't enjoy extremes. July and August can be hot, with temperatures well over 95 degrees Fahrenheit (35 degrees Celsius), while winter can be cold and wet. But whenever you visit, you'll find the calendar punctuated by a series of feasts and festivals.

Spring and Summer

Carnival generally falls in February. March 19, the feast of San Giuseppe, is the traditional date for changing to spring clothes, and Good Friday sees religious processions through the streets of many city neighborhoods. This time of grief is followed by the joyous celebrations of Easter Sunday and Monday, affectionately known as Pasquetta, when families head to the country for huge feasts.

The first Sunday in May is the first of two annual celebrations of San Gennaro, the patron saint of Naples, when his statue is carried through the streets from the cathedral. Many buildings and churches are opened in May, an inspired idea to encourage locals and visitors to rediscover historic Naples. The *Estate a Napoli* (Summer in Naples) festival, a series of arts events in and around the city, runs from July to September. July 16 is the feast of Madonna del Carmine; a fireworks display commemorates the saving of the church's belltower from fire by the Blessed Virgin Mary. August, the traditional vacation month throughout Italy, is Naples' quietest month, and many restaurants close.

Autumn and Winter

Autumn's biggest feast is on September 19, the feast of the miracle of the blood of San Gennaro. In front of huge crowds in the cathedral, accompanied by emotional scenes, a vial of the saint's normally solid blood liquifies. December 8, the feast of the Immaculate Conception, is the start of the Christmas season, when the first of the *presepi* (Nativity figures) are made. Christmas sees more feasting, while the days before January 1 are marked by fireworks and bagpipers. Children get presents on January 6, the Epiphany, when Befana, a benevolent witch, brings gifts to good children and "coal" (lumps of black candy) to bad children.

Costumed processions parade through Naples' streets on Good Friday

Regional Sights

> **Key to symbols**
> ✚ map coordinates refer to the region map on
> pages 146–147 🏛 admission charge: $$$ more
> than €6, $$ €3–€6, $ less than €3
> See page 5 for complete key to symbols

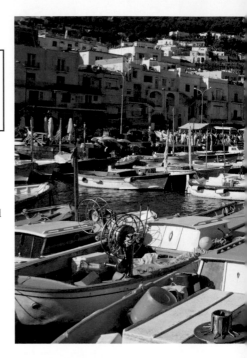

Alberobello

Driving inland south from Bari, you'll
start to notice round, stone buildings
with conical roofs topped with a stone
symbol; these structures are *trulli*, found
nowhere else in Europe except in this
area of Apulia. Scattered across the
landscape, there are more and more to
be seen as you approach Alberobello.
This little town, a UNESCO World
Heritage Site, has more than 1,400 *trulli*
in two different areas, the Rione Monti
and the Aia Piccola.

The Rione Monti, a series of *trulli*-
lined streets running down the hillside,
is tourist heaven. Most of the *trulli* have
been turned into craft shops, enabling
you to wander through the interiors and
even climb on their roofs, where you'll
find perfect photo opportunities
featuring a forest of these charming
structures. Aia Piccola is much more
authentic; here, the *trulli* are still
people's homes.

Nobody really knows the origin of this
architectural form, once thought to
have been a form of tax evasion on
permanent dwellings. The latest theories
link them with ancient Greece or even
Syria – Apulia was once part of Magna
Graecia – or they may even have been
introduced by the eastern monks or by
returning Crusaders.

✚ D4

Tourist information ✉ Associazione Turistica Pro
Loco Alberobello, Via Monte Nero ☎ 080 432 2822;
www.prolocoalberolbello.it ⏰ Daily 9–1 and 3–7

Alberobello's intriguing *trulli* are still lived in

Bari

Ancient Bari falls into two sections:
the grid-plan 19th-century town, with
its straight avenues and seafront

Vacation villas overlook the colorful waterfront of Marina Grande's harbor on Capri

promenade; and the old city, one of southern Italy's most vibrant warrens. Explore the narrow streets, where life surges around you: crowded one-room apartments opening to the street, women conducting animated conversations from balconies and roaring scooters.

Here you'll find the great Basilica di San Nicola (St. Nicholas), built between 1087 and 1180 and the prototype for many of Apulia's Romanesque churches. Behind the balanced facade lies a lofty, dim interior whose treasures include a 12th-century ciborio (altar canopy) and a superb episcopal throne. St. Nicholas is buried in the crypt. Each December the basilica is the focal point for the exuberant processions and festivities that celebrate the saint's feast. Nearby stands the more austere Cattedrale di San Sabino (St. Sabine's Cathedral), with a simple interior containing an eighth-century icon of the Virgin Mary, said to be a true likeness. Close by you'll find the huge 13th-century bulk of the

Castello (Castle), built by Frederick II, which stands on the site of a Roman fort. A word of caution: pay attention to what's going on around you and make sure your valuables are out of sight.

🔡 D4

Tourist information ✉ Piazza Aldo Moro 32/A
☎ 080 524 2361; www.pugliaturismo.com
🕐 Mon.–Fri. 8–2 (also 3–6 Tue. and Thu.)
Basilica di San Nicola ✉ Piazza San Nicola
☎ 080 573 7111; www.basilicasannicola.it 🕐 Daily
7:30–1 and 4–7:45 🎟 Free 🎉 Festivities with
processions, concerts and fireworks are held during
the week of Dec. 6
Cattedrale di San Sabino ✉ Piazza Odegitria
☎ 080 521 0605 🕐 Mon.–Sat. 8–12:30 and 4–7:30,
Sun. 8–12:30 and 5–8:30 🎟 Free
Castello ✉ Piazza Federico II di Svevia 2
☎ 080 528 6111 or 080 528 620 (information)
🕐 Thu.–Tue. 8:30–7:30 🎟 $

Capri

A favorite of Roman emperors, the tiny island of Capri has spectacular scenery and is surrounded by crystal waters,

A perfect example of flamboyant baroque architecture on Lecce's Basilica di Santa Croce

easily reached as a day trip from Naples. The two main settlements are Anacapri and Capri; their whitewashed houses and narrow, winding streets are packed with boutiques, cafés and restaurants. You can take a boat trip to the Grotta Azzurra (Blue Grotto), a spectacular sea cave filled with refracted turquoise light.

Another highlight is the beautiful Villa San Michele, in Anacapri. Built in the late 19th century by Swedish physician Axel Munthe, this dream-like villa with its peaceful green garden is filled with classical statues. You can enjoy some of the island's best views from its pergola.

Classical enthusiasts can walk to the ruins of Villa Jovis, emperor Tiberius' clifftop villa, from which he allegedly threw victims into the sea. Another stroll leads to a lookout above the Faraglioni, a cluster of offshore rocks jutting more than 360 feet out of the sea.

➕ A4

Tourist information ✉ Piazza Umberto I, Naples ☎ 081 837 0686; www.capritourism.com ⏱ Mon.–Sat. 8:30–8:30, Sun. 8:30–2:30, Apr.–Oct.; Mon.–Sat. 9–1 and 3:30–6:45, rest of year ✉ Via G. Orland 59, Anacapri ☎ 081 837 1524 ⏱ Daily 8:30–8:30, Jun.–Sep.; Mon.–Sat. 9–3, rest of year 🚢 Ferry operator: Caremar, from Molo Beverello, Naples (☎ Naples office 081 551 3882; www.caremar.it). Hydrofoil operators: Caremar, from Molo Beverello, Naples (☎ Naples office 081 551 3882; www.caremar.it); NLG, from Molo Beverello, Naples (☎ 081 552 7209; www.navlib.it); SNAV, from Mergellina, Naples (☎ 051 428 5555; www.snav.it)
Blue Grotto ☎ 081 837 0634 ⏱ Daily (weather permitting) 9 a.m.–1 hour before dusk 🚢 From Marina Grande 🎫 $$$
Villa San Michele ✉ Viale Axel Munthe 3, Anacapri ☎ 081 837 1401; www.villasanmichele.eu ⏱ Daily 9–6, May–Sep.; 9–3:30, Nov.–Feb.; 9–4:30, Mar.; 9–5, Apr. and Oct. 🎫 $$
Villa Jovis ✉ Via Tiberio ☎ 081 837 4549 ⏱ Daily 9 a.m.–1 hour before dusk, Feb.–Oct.; 9–3:15, rest of year 🎫 $

Castel del Monte

The gentle, rolling landscape behind the coast near Bari is dominated by the huge bulk of UNESCO World Heritage Site Castel del Monte. Built by the Sicily-based German emperor Frederick II in 1240, this mighty building soars up against the blue sky on a windswept, lonely hill. The octagonal castle is built around an octagonal courtyard and is flanked by eight towers, which also are octagonal. This mathematical precision is a mystery, as is the lack of defensive features normally associated with a medieval castle. Some scholars claim its proportions relate to the movement of the stars. Others think it may have been a pilgrim hostel or an imitation of a Jerusalem mosque. You can wander around the high, bare, interlinked rooms and look down to the courtyard through the windows and French doors on the upstairs floor. Windows also pierce the outer walls, giving panoramic views.

➕ C4

✉ 10 miles south of Andria ☎ 0883 569 997; www.casteldelmonte.beniculturali.it 🕐 Daily 10:15–7:45, Apr.–Sep.; 9–6:30, rest of year 🍴 Bar and restaurant outside gates 💲 $

Lecce

Elegant Lecce is packed with exuberant baroque architecture, the product of 17th-century mercantile money and the zeal of religious orders. Known as Leccese Baroque, the style is opulent and extravagant yet airy, with churches, palaces and houses all a riot of gamboling *putti* (cherubs), windswept saints and angels, curlicues, garlands and wreaths.

It's a joy to wander, but start with the Basilica di Santa Croce, the apotheosis of the style. It stands next to the wonderful Palazzo dei Celestini, whose restrained courtyard contrasts with its intricate facade. Both were designed by Giuseppe Zimbalo, who was responsible for many of Lecce's most successful buildings. From here, cross Piazza Oronzo, with its Roman amphitheater still used for concerts, and head up Corso Vittorio Emanuele II to Piazza del Duomo, a spacious and elegant square. Here the city's Duomo (Cathedral) is flanked by the lovely Seminario (Seminary) and Palazzo Vescovile (Bishop's Palace). Lecce's other treasures include more fine churches such as Santa Chiara, the Rosario, the Gesù and the Carmine, Charles V's vast 16th-century castle and the interesting Museo Provinciale.

➕ E3

Tourist information ✉ Via Monte San Michele 20 ☎ 0832 314 117; www.pugliaturismo.com 🕐 Daily 9–1 and 4–8, Jul.–Aug.; Mon.–Fri. 9–1 and 4–7, Sat. 9–1, rest of year

Basilica di Santa Croce ✉ Via Umberto I ☎ 0832 241 957; www.basilicasantacroce.eu 🕐 Daily 9–noon and 5–8, mid-Sep. to mid-Jul.; 8–1 and 4–6, rest of year 💵 Free

Duomo ✉ Piazza del Duomo ☎ 0832 308 557 🕐 Daily 7–noon and 4–7 💵 Free

Museo Provinciale ✉ Viale Gallipoli 28 ☎ 0832 307 415/683 503 🕐 Mon.–Sat. 9–1:30 and 2:30–7:30, Sun. 9–1:30 💵 Free

Maratea

Pretty Maratea is located on the Tyrrhenian Sea, where mountains drop to the water – and coves and beaches provide a contrast to the flat lands along the Ionian Sea. Maratea makes an ideal stopping point for a few nights if you're traveling south. The old village has a tangle of narrow streets, squares and stairways, with some fine old houses and churches. Below lies the port, along with attractive houses, shops and restaurants. A winding coastal road gives access to secluded beaches. High above on Monte San Biagio stands a huge statue of Christ the Redeemer (erected in 1965). You can drive up the mountain to visit the Santuario di San Biagio, built on the site of a pagan temple, and take in the superb views. The village of Fiumicello is pretty and full of activity in summer.

➕ C3

Tourist information ✉ Via Santavenere 144, Fiumicello ☎ 0973 876 983; www.aptbasilicata.it 🕐 Mon.–Sat. 9:30–1 and 4:30–8, Sun. 9:30–1

Limestone arch on the Gargano Peninsula, caused by the erosion of wind and water

Drive
The Undiscovered Gargano Peninsula

Duration: 7 to 9 hours

This drive will give you a chance to explore the incredible natural beauty of the Gargano peninsula, as well as take in a couple of its inland and coastal towns, including Monte Sant'Angelo. All the roads are steep, twisting and often vertiginous, so don't attempt the trip if you suffer from travel sickness. It would be a long drive to tackle in a day; both Vieste and Peschici are good places to take a break and spend the night, with excellent swimming and seafood as enticements.

The Gargano is the "spur" on the boot of Italy. It's a limestone plateau bordered on the north by beaches and lagoons and on the south by pine-clad cliffs and rocky coves. The interior is mountainous, with high grassy meadows, agricultural terraces where almonds, olives and grapevines are cultivated, and upland forests of oak and beech trees.

The indigenous flora and fauna of the region are outstanding. The area has been declared a national park in order to protect the last remaining stands of native ancient deciduous forest that once covered much of southern Europe. **Start your drive at Monte Sant'Angelo, reached via the SS89 from Manfredonia on the coast.**

Monte Sant'Angelo, one of the oldest Christian shrines in Europe, is dedicated to the Archangel Michael. Hordes of devout pilgrims have been traveling to the town since at least the fifth century to pray at the spot where Michael is said to have appeared. His sanctuary stands on the grotto where he was sighted; you approach via 11th-century bronze doors made in Constantinople. The town is worth exploring: It has some interesting streets of terraced medieval houses and a fine Norman castle.

Take the SS272 north of town into the valley. At the intersection, branch right onto the SS528. Follow this until you finally reach the Foresta Umbra visitor center.

This is an exceptionally varied and lovely stretch through woods and meadowland and past ancient terraces. The Foresta Umbra (Forest of Shadows) stretches right across the upland heart of the Gargano. Stands of forest like this, mainly beech and oak, once covered much of Apulia. It's a wonderful wildlife habitat, home to a wide variety of animals and birds. The woods are rich in wildflowers; spring crocus gives way to numerous different orchids, and in autumn the woodland floor is carpeted with drifts of cyclamen. The deep forest is inhabited by a variety of wildlife. You can learn more at the visitor center. From here, easy hikes lead into the woods past a little lake and picnic tables.

Turn right onto an unclassified road running northeast and with signs for Segheria il Mandrione and Vieste. After 15 miles (24 kilometers), turn right onto the SS89 and on to Vieste.

Still a small fishing port, Vieste is a relaxed town with superb beaches and a range of hotels and restaurants. Although it's not yet swamped by tourism, it can get very busy in summer, but the old center, with its narrow cobbled streets, castle and 11th-century cathedral, is well worth a stop. The coastline to the south is beautiful, with hidden beaches beneath high limestone cliffs and a series of watery caves

and grottoes around the Testa del Gargano headland. You can take a boat trip to view them or venture farther to the beautiful Tremiti Islands. Watch for the *trabuco* on Vieste's headland. This huge wooden structure, entwined with miles of ropes and winches, is used for catching mullet; the design is said to date from Phoenician times.

Explore the road south of Vieste along the coast before retracing your route and heading north on the SS89 to Peschici.

The winding road follows more lovely coast and sandy shoreline before you reach Peschici, a picturesque town tumbling down a headland to a sandy beach. Peschici dates from the 10th century, when it was built as a defense against Saracen raids, and the claustrophobic labyrinth of alleys has a distinctly Arabian feel. Boats also run from Rodi Garganico, farther along the coast, to the Tremiti Islands.

Vieste tourist information ✉ Piazza Kennedy 13 ☎ 0884 708 806/701 080; www.parcogargano.it or www.vieste.it 🕐 Mon.–Sat. 8:30–1 and 3:30–8, Sun. 8:30–1, Jun.–Sep.

Tremiti Islands Ferries ✉ Tickets from Agenzia Sol, Via Treppicioni 5, Vieste ☎ 0884 701 558; www.solvieste.it ✉ Daily departures from Jun. to Sep. Also from Navigazione Libera del Golfo, Corso Fazzini 33, Vieste; tel: 0884 707 489; www.navlib.it. (There are services from Termoli, Peschici and Rodi Garganico.)

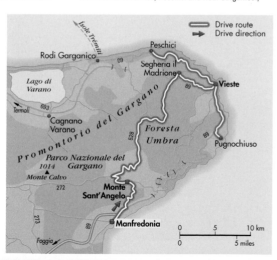

Matera

Matera, a UNESCO World Heritage Site, has been continuously inhabited since Paleolithic times, making it one of the world's oldest settlements. It's a provincial capital with an admirable dose of civic pride, and its *sassi* provide one of Europe's most bizarre urban features. *Sassi* are cave dwellings dug out of the sides of a ravine over the centuries. Many were inhabited until the 1960s, when the area was cleared and the people rehoused. Today, some *sassi* have been restored and people have moved back, living in very different conditions from some 40 years ago, when disease was rife. A road (Strada Panoramica dei Sassi) has been built through the *sassi* district, but to explore it thoroughly, you'll need to penetrate the maze of tiny streets. Be sure to see the *chiese rupestri* (rock-hewn churches), carved by monks from the eighth to the 13th centuries.

Leave time for the rest of the town, which centers around Piazza Vittorio Veneto, a lovely square. From here you can access both the *sassi* and the medieval *civita* area, whose winding streets lead to the 13th-century cathedral. Matera also boasts a superb archeological museum, housed in the old convent of Santa Chiara. Recently restored, the collection covers local finds from the Paleolithic age to the full flowering of Greek civilization in Magna Graecia.

🞤 C4

Tourist information ✉ Via Don Minzoni 11 ☎ 0835 334 413; www.aptbasilicata.it ⏱ Mon.–Thu. 9–1 and 4–6, Fri. 9–1 ❗ Apply at the tourist office for entry to churches in *sassi*. Guided tours in English can be pre-booked online at www.sassidimatera.it or by phone on 800 733 789 (inside Italy only).

Museo Nazionale Domenico Ridola ✉ Via Ridola 24 ☎ 0835 310 058 ⏱ Mon. 2–8, Tue.–Sun. 9–8 💷 $

Metaponto

Ancient Metapontum (Metaponto) was one of the greatest of the sixth-century BC Greek cities of Magna Graecia. It was a thriving metropolis packed with temples, theaters and public buildings.

Today Metaponto is a huge and confusing archeological site where you'll need a lot of imagination to visualize its heyday. Most evocative is the Tavole Paladine, a fifth-century BC temple that is dedicated to Hera and stands alone among flowery grass and oleanders. Metaponto's chief draw is the superb Museo Archeologico Nazionale (Archeological Museum), which

Matera's unique *sassi* (cave houses) are a must-see during any visit to southern Italy

traces the history of Metapontum from its native pre-Greek civilization to its decline after Romanization. The jewelry is lovely – look for the charming headdress of gilded leaves decorated with berries and crickets (third century BC), as well as the gold bracelets and earrings. The red-and-black figured vases are very fine, and careful study of their decoration will tell you much about everyday Greek life.

🔳 D3

Museo Archeologico Nazionale ✉ Via Aristea 21
☎ 0835 745 327 🕐 Tue.–Sun. 9–8, Mon. 2–8 💲 $

Parco Nazionale del Pollino

The Parco Nazionale del Pollino (Pollino National Park) is a massive 494,000-acre area of wild and unspoiled mountainous countryside in the southern Apennines. Its highest point is Monte Pollino at 7,400 feet.

The terrain varies from high mountain country through stony steppe and rich forests to gorges, river valleys, water meadows and dry river beds. The park's symbol is the Bosnian pine, a tree with scaled bark that grows on difficult terrain up to 6,000 feet; few exist elsewhere in Europe. Fascinating wildlife includes wolves, wild boar and otters; eagles, vultures and other raptors may be seen.

Twisting mountain roads link the scattered villages within the park, many of which are becoming popular as bases for hiking and climbing. The main villages are Terranova di Pollino, San Severino Lucano, Carbone, Latronico and Castelluccio.

Even if you don't have time to explore this wonderful area, you can get a taste of its scenic grandeur from the A3 *autostrada*; a spectacular section of this freeway skirts the park's eastern edge.

🔳 C3

Park information ✉ Complesso Monumentale, Santa Maria della Consolazione, Rotonda ☎ 097 366 9311; www.parcopollino.it or www.parks.it ✉ Visitor center, Morano Calabro ☎ 097 366 9311 🕐 Mon., Wed. and Fri. 8–noon, Tue. and Thu. 2:30–6:30

Reggio di Calabria

Calabria's capital, an ancient Greek foundation, faces Sicily across the Straits of Messina. It's the only city of any size this far south, with a vibrancy that belies its grim reputation. Repeatedly devastated by earthquakes, dogged by high unemployment and suffering from the octopus-like embrace of the Calabrian Mafia, physically it's a ramshackle and grubby city with a few redeeming features. But take time to stroll the superb seafront, with its Roman remains and tree-shaded garden, before heading down the main street, Corso Garibaldi, to Reggio's chief attraction, the Museo Nazionale. This wonderful collection includes material from all over Calabria and is well-presented, with plenty of English-language information. The highlights are the two antique male bronzes known as the *Bronzi di Riace*. These fifth-century BC sculptures were discovered underwater off the Ionian coast near Riace in 1972; after a lengthy restoration they were returned to Calabria in 1981. Naked, bearded and tautly muscled, these superb works are attributed to Phidias, the greatest sculptor of antiquity. On the top floor are canvases, primarily by southern Italian artists.

One of Reggio's fifth-century BC bronze sculptures known as the *Bronzi di Riace*

Reggio di Calabria has more shops and better bars than anywhere else in this region. It was also the home town of fashion designer Gianni Versace.

➕ B1

Tourist information ✉ Villa Genoese Zerbi, Via Zaleuco 16 ☎ 0965 331 360; http://turismo.reggiocal.it 🕐 Mon.–Sat. 8–7:30

Museo Nazionale della Magna Graecia ✉ Highlights are displayed temporarily at Palazzo Tommaso Campanella, via Cardinale Portanova ☎ 0965 880 111; www.bronzidiriace.org 🕐 Daily 9–7:30 💵 Free

Riviera Calabrese

The stretch of coast north from Reggio di Calabria is known as the Riviera Calabrese (Calabrian Riviera). It's a string of small resorts and coastal villages popular with Italian vacationers. Livery Tropea to the north is the prettiest, perched above golden beaches. On a clear day there are superb views of the Aeolian Islands and the cone of Stròmboli. Don't miss the church of Santa Maria dell'Isola, on a rocky massif near the sea, or the Norman cathedral, where you can see two unexploded American bombs dating from World War II. Farther south the coastline is more dramatic, with towering cliffs and views of Sicily. Tucked down at the shoreline lies Scilla, a picturesque village set around a castle, with a sandy beach that doubles as a fishing port at its foot. The northern end is dominated by a rock associated with the ancient Scylla of Homer's *Odyssey*, the lair of one of a pair of sea monsters. Charybdis, the other monster, in legend dwells across the Straits of Messina on Sicily.

➕ C1

Tropea tourist information ✉ Piazza Ercole, Tropea ☎ 0963 61 475; www.prolocotropea.eu 🕐 Daily 9–1 and 4–8, Jun.–Aug.; Mon.–Sat. 9–1 and 3–7, rest of year

Rossano

Modern Rossano is located on Calabria's east coast. It's a relaxed seaside resort with sandy beaches. Up a twisty road is old Rossano, a shabby and charming hillside town with elegant, if crumbling, 16th-century palaces and a spacious central square. From the eighth to 11th centuries Rossano was a great Byzantine center of scholarship and piety, and its greatest treasures date from this time. In the cathedral you can see a ninth-century Byzantine fresco of the Blessed Virgin Mary, while the tiny museum tucked behind contains the famous *Codex Purpureus Rossanensis* (Purple Codex). This is a sixth-century Greek manuscript written on reddish-purple parchment, from which it gets its name. The manuscript is illustrated with scenes from the gospels, and you can see how the *Last Supper* was originally depicted. From the museum, walk to ancient San Marco, a 10th-century Byzantine church, its triple-nave interior topped by five small cupolas. Few other buildings in southern Italy are so evocative.

➕ C3

Museo Diocesano ✉ Via Larga Dumo 5 ☎ 0983 525 263 🕐 Daily 9:30–1 and 4:30–8, Jul. to mid-Sep.; Tue.–Sat. 9:30–12:30 and 4–7, Sun. 10 noon and 4:30–6:30, rest of year. Hours may vary 💵 $$

Sorrento Peninsula and the Amalfi Coast

One of Europe's most beautiful coastal roads runs around the Sorrento peninsula south of Naples. Every twist and turn opens up another spectacular vista of sea and cliffs, while the string of villages it links are among the most attractive on all of Italy's coastline.

Castellammare di Stabia, nearest to Naples, is an ancient spa town; its springs still draw people to the therapeutic waters. Sorrento, a good jumping-off point for Capri (see page 157–158), is the first of the truly charming towns along the coast. Its pretty streets, beaches, bars and restaurants have been drawing visitors for the past 200 years.

From here the main road cuts inland and south to emerge on the Amalfi side of the peninsula. Positano, the first town of any size, is a pyramid of colorful

The popular tourist town of Sorrento overlooks the Bay of Naples, with views of Capri and Vesuvius

houses tumbling down the cliffs to a beach where sun worshipers share space with fishing boats. Tempting shops sell the town's famous brightly colored textiles. Bars and restaurants beckon, and boats sail to otherwise inaccessible swimming coves. To the east lies Praiano, where the cliff approaches are dotted with opulent private villas. Between here and Amalfi is the Grotta dello Smeraldo (Emerald Cave), a vividly green sea cave with stalagmites and stalactites. Amalfi, tucked between the mountains and the sea, is a cheerful small town whose only clue to its great past as a powerful maritime republic is the wonderful Duomo (Cathedral). Approached up a wide flight of steps, the cathedral was built in the 11th century, its bronze doors cast in Constantinople in 1066. Don't miss the 13th-century Chiostro del Paradiso (Cloister of Paradise), a peaceful enclave with whitewashed interlaced arches.

High above the coast east of Amalfi is Ravello, offering fine views of the coast.

The 11th-century cathedral has a pulpit donated by the Rufolo family, who also built the Villa Rufolo, where the courtyard and gardens inspired Richard Wagner's *Parsifal*. Find more gardens and views at the Villa Cimbrone.

Castellammare di Stabia 🕂 A4
Tourist information ✉ Piazza Matteoti 34–35 ☎ 081 871 1334; www.stabiatourism.it 🕔 Mon.–Sat. 9–1:30 and 4:30–7:30

Sorrento 🕂 A4
Tourist information ✉ Via Luigi de Maio 35 ☎ 081 807 4033; www.sorrentotourism.com 🕔 Mon.–Sat. 8:30–6:15, also Sun. 8:45–12:45 in Aug.

Positano 🕂 A4
Tourist information ✉ Via del Saracino 2–4 ☎ 089 875 067; www.aziendaturismopositano.it 🕔 Mon.–Sat. 8–2 and 3:30–8

Amalfi 🕂 A4
Tourist information ✉ Via delle Repubbliche Marinare 27 ☎ 089 871 107; www.amalfitouristoffice.it 🕔 Daily 8:30–1:30 and 3:30–7:30, Aug.; Mon.–Fri. 8:30–1:30 and 3:30–7:30, Sat. 8:30–1, rest of year
Duomo di Sant'Andrea ✉ Piazza Duomo ☎ 089 871 324 🕔 Daily 9:30–7, Jun.–Oct.; 9:30–5:15, rest of year. Chiostro del Paradiso: daily 9–7, Jun.–Oct.;

9–1 and 2:30–4:30, rest of year 🅟 Free to cathedral;
Museum and Cloister $
Grotta dello Smeraldo ✉ SS 163, 2.5 miles from
Amalfi Boats ☎ 089 873 190; www.coopsantandrea.it
🅒 Daily 9–4 🅟 $$$
Ravello ➕ A4
Tourist information ✉ Via Roma 18/bis ☎ 089 857
096; www.ravellotime.it 🅒 Mon.–Sat. 9–1 and 2–6,
Sun. 9–2
Duomo ✉ Off Piazza del Duomo ☎ 089 858 311
🅒 Duomo: daily 8:30–1 and 4–8. Museum: daily 9–1
and 3–7, Apr.–Oct.; Sat.–Sun. only, rest of year
🅟 Duomo free; Museum $
Villa Rufolo ✉ Piazza del Vescovado ☎ 089 857 621
🅒 Daily 9–8, May–Sep.; 9–4, Oct.–Apr. 🅟 $$
Villa Cimbrone ✉ Via Santa Chiara 26 ☎ 089 858
872; www.ravellotime.it 🅒 Daily 9 a.m.–1 hour before
dusk 🅟 $$

Vesuvius and Pompei

One of the world's best-known
volcanoes, Vesuvius (Vesuvio) rises to
4,200 feet above the Bay of Naples. It
has erupted more than 100 times since
the Roman era, the last in 1944. You get
an undisturbed view of the volcano from
the Circumvesuviana railroad. Buses run
up to within a half-hour's walk of the
volcano, which is worth it for the
spectacular views and odd wisps of
steam that come from the deep jumble
of reddish rocks that form the crater.

Vesuvius is infamous for its
devastating eruption in AD 79, when it
engulfed the city of Pompei (Pompeii)
and neighboring Herculaneum, burying
them under a thick layer of pumice and
volcanic ash. Pompeii remained buried
for more than 1,700 years, perfectly
preserved beneath a hard layer of
volcanic debris. Excavations started
about 1750 and the city gradually
emerged. Worth tracking down as you
explore the town are the forum, theaters,
covered market, bakery, laundry and
numerous taverns advertising bargain
prices on the walls outside.

The most interesting buildings are the
houses; some are wonderfully preserved
and still decorated with wall-paintings in
vivid reds and ochres. The House of the
Vetii, with its lovely garden and frescoed
dining room, is a highlight. Also notable
is the House of the Tragic Poet, whose
owners had a portrait mosaic of their
dog put up by the front door with *cave
canem* (beware of the dog) carefully
inscribed.

Other houses worth seeing are the
spacious House of the Faun; the House
of Menander, with its elegant bath; and
the Villa of the Mysteries. The villa lies
just outside Pompei's walls at the end of
the Via dei Sepolcri; its rich frescoes are
connected with the Dionysian cult.

Magnificent statues and artifacts were
found at Pompei, as were the bodies of
the town's inhabitants, unable to escape
and asphyxiated by the fumes; plaster
casts of these are scattered throughout
the city. Most of Pompei's artistic
treasures are now in the Museo
Archeologico Nazionale (see page 152).
Vesuvius ➕ A4 🅡 Circumvesuviana railroad to
Ercolano; then a bus stops close to the summit
Pompei ➕ A4 ☎ 081 857 5347; www.pompeiisites.
org 🅒 Daily 8:30–7:30, Apr.–Oct.; 8:30–5, rest of
year. Last admission 90 minutes before closing
🅡 Circumvesuviana or train to Pompei Scavi Station
🍴 Self-service restaurant and bar outside the forum
🅟 $$$ ❗ Note that areas within the site are often
closed for restoration work

Pompei's Forum, with Vesuvius in the background

Magna Graecia

Throughout southern Italy and Sicily, you'll see ruins of great Greek temples and cities and a spectacular array of Greek artistic treasures in archeological museums. Why are they here? Where did they come from?

Greek Arrivals
Greece is a mountainous country with little arable land. As its city-states grew in size and influence, they started to trade with parts of Italy and realized that colonization was feasible in this flat, fertile land. Greeks settled into the modern regions of Campania, Basilicata, Calabria and Sicily in the eighth century BC. They absorbed the cultures and populations of the indigenous tribes and established an efficient agricultural system. Grapes and olives were introduced, the colonies became successful, and cities such as Siracusa, Sybaris, Metapontum and Tarentum were soon richer and more sophisticated than those in Greece. The area was in every way Magna Graecia – "Greater Greece."

Decline
Like the city-states of mainland Greece, these colonies were split by internal rivalries and internecine war, uniting only when faced with the threat of outside invasion, sometimes from Greece itself. In 415 BC Siracusa and its allies trounced Athens in a great sea battle. The North African power of Carthage, founded by the Phoenicians, posed a continuous threat. The colonies allied in the third century BC against the growing might of Rome. In 400 BC the Romans razed Sybaris, and in 211 BC the sack of Siracusa marked the effective demise of Magna Graecia.

The Legacy
You can see archeological and historical traces of these city-states all over southern Italy and Sicily. On the mainland, head for the great temples of Paestum, Metapontum or the scattered ruins of Sybaris. Sicily is richest of all, with the theaters at Taormina and Siracusa and temples at Segesta, Selinunte and Agrigento. Smaller sites are everywhere, and even obscure museums have superb collections of stunning Greek vases and sculpture.

The Tempio della Concordia (Temple of Concord) in Agrigento, Sicily

Sicily and Sardinia

Opposite: The tiny green island of Isola Bella is connected to Taormina by a narrow, sand pathway

Sicily and Sardinia

Sicily (Sicilia), one of the Mediterranean's largest islands, is also one of its most beautiful, with rugged mountain scenery, plenty of woodlands, a diverse coastline, and rich agricultural land producing a host of crops that includes wheat, olives, vines and citrus fruits. The eastern half of the island is dominated by the graceful cone of Mount Etna, Europe's largest volcano, while the interior pushes north to the coast in the shape of the Monti Madonie. Beautiful beaches are found all around the island, with some internationally renowned and fashionable resorts on the east and north coasts, while the outlying islands are washed by some of the clearest waters in the Mediterranean.

Sardinia (Sardegna) is only a little farther from the African coast of Tunisia than it is from the Italian mainland. A trip here is feasible only if you have plenty of time.

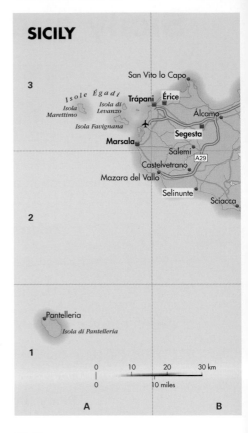

SICILY

Sicily's Past

A succession of foreign invaders ruled this island from the fifth century BC until the process of Italian unification began in Sicily in 1860. The ancient Greeks, Carthaginians, Romans, Arabs, Normans and the Spanish all left their marks. These conquerors drained Sicily economically dry, while their rule left a legacy of resentment, oppression and insularity – an ideal breeding ground for the corruption of organized crime. Marginalized for centuries from mainstream Italy, Sicilians still see themselves as a people apart, though this is more pronounced in rural areas, in contrast to the more sophisticated main urban centers. Since World War II, aid has poured in from the Italian government and the European Union, but poverty is still widespread.

Sicilians

Sicilian first and Italian second, the island's population is exuberant and outgoing. Tourism is important, and you'll find the people welcoming, although levels of accommodations and service may not be what you're used to. English is spoken in the main tourist centers and good hotels, but otherwise very few people speak English. In more remote areas it's rare to see women on the streets or working; society is still male-dominated. Some young men consider foreign girls fair game, a point for women traveling alone to bear in mind.

When To Visit Sicily

The best time to visit Sicily is the spring, when the island is carpeted in wildflowers and the temperature ideal.

SARDINIA

Spring arrives in late February. July and August can be unbearably hot, with the warm sirocco wind blowing in from Africa and little air-conditioning. Winters are mild on the coast, although there's snow in the interior and it can be wet and windy. Few tourists are around from November through February. Many coastal hotels are closed and daylight hours are short in winter.

What To See

You'll want to explore Sicily's diverse terrain, so renting a car is a good idea. Roads are generally uncrowded away from the towns, although the mountain roads can be very twisty. Sightseeing is a major attraction; Sicily has a wealth of ancient monuments, including some of the world's finest Greek archeological sites, and the museums are excellent.

Later architecture is a major draw; this includes Roman mosaics, Norman churches and elegant baroque towns. Many tourists simply enjoy a beach holiday, with delicious food, hot sun and a relaxed pace of life.

Visiting Sardinia

Sardinia's main attraction is its beautiful coastline and well-organized resorts, which attract the rich and famous from all over Europe. But there's more to Sardinia, including archeological traces of its first indigenous civilization, fine Romanesque churches built during the Pisan occupancy, fortresses erected by the Genoans, and towns that are more Spanish than Italian. The island is increasingly geared to international visitors, and accommodations and service are improving all the time. Spring, early summer and autumn are the best times to visit. If you want a beach vacation, summer is best for diving, sailing and windsurfing. Be sure to reserve well in advance, as Sardinia is a popular choice with mainland Italians.

Right: The Tempio dei Dioscuri (Temple of Castor and Pollux) in Agrigento's Valley of the Temples
Below: Detail of one of the statues on the Fontana Pretoria in Palermo

Palermo

Redolent with history and filled with artistic treasures, vibrant Palermo is like no other European city. Unemployment and crime levels are high, and visitors are frequently shocked by the noise, grime and decay. But despite the dirt and chaos, Palermo is full of wonderful things to see. Few other cities have so many rich churches, dating from 12th-century Norman to 17th-century baroque. There are good museums and galleries, a lively arts scene and excellent restaurants.

Discovering Palermo

Pick up a copy of the free monthly tourist information magazine *Palermo*, available from the tourist office. Printed in English, it's packed with useful tips to help make the city more accessible to newcomers, as well as arts, sports and entertainment listings.

After dark, avoid the back streets and the dock and market areas, and use taxis to travel around.Driving in Palermo is not recommended; traffic is chaotic, drivers are aggressive and parking spaces are almost impossible to find.

The historic core of Palermo is easily explored on foot. To investigate the tangled lanes, walking is the only way, as the streets are too narrow for buses. Taxis are inexpensive and horse-drawn carriages, *carrozze*, ply the main historic center; agree on a price before you start.

Shopping

Palermo has a good range of shops, including branches of nationwide department stores such as la Rinascente

Mondello

If the noise and dirt of Palermo start to get you down, head for Mondello, a charming resort that's virtually a city suburb. Located west of Palermo beneath the bulk of Monte Pellegrino, Mondello has sandy beaches, pleasant walkways, a tiny harbor, a huge range of souvenir and food stalls, and wonderful *gelaterie* (ice-cream shops). Restaurants line the waterfront, where you can eat the freshest fish and seafood before heading to the beach for a swim. Mondello buzzes at night, with cruising cars, an animated *passeggiata* (promenade) and lively outdoor discos.

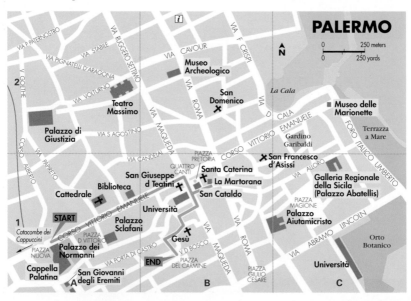

and Coin, and outlets for the big Italian designer names. Many stores cluster around Via Roma, Via Cavour and Viale della Libertà. Most tourists enjoy browsing in the Mercato delle Pulci (Flea Market), and visiting one of the food markets. Local crafts include ceramics, basketware and wrought iron, still made in the Via Cala and Via Calderai. Sculpted almond paste confectionery, called *frutta di Martorana*, is a real specialty.

Entertainment and Excursions

Palermo's city streets empty early and can feel threatening late at night, although things are much livelier in the newer areas. However, there's an excellent year-round choice of music, opera, theater, dance and open-air movies. The top venue is the beautifully restored Teatro Massimo. The other main theaters are the Politeama and the Golden; both stage classical concerts. Contact tourist information offices for full details. The quintessential Palermo entertainment is the puppet theater; you can see a performance at the Puppet Museum (see page 177) or search out the real thing at Opera dei Pupi. If time is short, take a city tour to see Palermo's high points.

Essential Information

Tourist Information
■ Piazza Castelnuovo 34 ☎ 091 605 8351; www.palermotourism.com ⊙ Mon.–Fri. 8:30–2 and 2:30–6:30
■ Aeroporto Falcone Borsellino ☎ 091 702 0273 ⊙ Mon.–Sat. 6 a.m.–midnight
■ Villa Igiea, Salita Belmonte ☎ 091 639 011; www.regione.sicilia.it ⊙ Mon.–Fri. 8:30–2 and 3–7
■ City tours: AMAT ☎ 848 800 817; www.amat.pa.it; CST ☎ 091 748 7234

Urban Transportation
You'll need to use buses to reach sights in the outlying areas; they are run by AMAT (☎ 199 240 800; www.amat.pa.it). Buy a single ticket (valid for 2 hours) or one valid all day; validate tickets in the machine at the back of the bus. Tickets are available at AMAT sales booths at the Stazione Centrale and Piazza Verdi, where you'll see the sign "Vendita Biglietti AMAT," as well as at tobacconists and newsstands. The circular routes served by minibuses, Linea Rossa (Red Line) and Linea Gialla (Yellow Line), cover the main sights. Taxis are inexpensive and can be hailed at stands, or you can call Autoradio Taxi (☎ 091 512 727, 513 311, 513 198; www.autoradiotaxi.it) or Radio Taxi Trinacria (☎ 091 225 455, 091 6878 or 225 460; www.radiotaxitrinacria.it).

Airport Information
Palermo Falcone Borsellino Airport (☎ info line 091 702 0273 or 091 702 0111; www.gesap.it), with national and international flights, is 19 miles west of the city center at Punta Raisa. There are no direct flights to and from the United States via Palermo or any other Sicilian airport. Buses Prestia e Comande (☎ 091 580 457; www.prestiaecomande.it) run into Palermo every 30 minutes daily from 5 a.m. until after the arrival of the last scheduled flight, a journey of 40 minutes. Buses also run three times daily to Agrigento. Taxis are available outside the airport.

Climate – average highs and lows for the month

Jan.	Feb.	Mar.	Apr.	May	Jun.	Jul.	Aug.	Sep.	Oct.	Nov.	Dec.
15°C	15°C	16°C	18°C	21°C	25°C	28°C	29°C	27°C	24°C	19°C	16°C
59°F	59°F	61°F	64°F	70°F	77°F	82°F	84°F	81°F	75°F	66°F	61°F
9°C	9°C	11°C	13°C	16°C	20°C	24°C	25°C	22°C	19°C	14°C	12°C
51°F	51°F	52°F	55°F	61°F	68°F	75°F	77°F	72°F	66°F	57°F	54°F

Palermo Sights

Key to symbols

⊞ map coordinates refer to the Palermo map on page 174 💰 admission charge: $$$ more than €6, $$ €3–€6, $ less than €3

See page 5 for complete key to symbols

Cappella Palatina

The huge Palazzo dei Normanni (Norman Palace), a ninth-century Arab structure enlarged in the 12th century by the Normans, houses Sicily's regional parliament. On the first floor you'll find Palermo's most beautiful artistic gem, the Cappella Palatina, built in the 1130s. The apses, nave and cupola are covered with iridescent mosaics showing scenes from the Old and New Testaments. The chapel is dominated by a majestic Christ Pantocrator (ruler of all). The marble floor dates from the same era, while the elaborate wooden ceiling is Arabic.

⊞ A1 ✉ Piazza Indipendenza ☎ 091 626 2833; www.ars.sicilia.it or www.federicosecondo.org 🕐 Mon.–Sat. 8:15–5:45, Sun. 11:15–1 (rest of palace complex Sun. 8:15–1) 🚌 Linea A, 104, 105, 108, 304, 309 💰 $$$: includes entrance to Sala di Reggero (Royal Apartments)

Catacombe dei Cappuccini

For hundreds of years, the Capuchin monks of the Convento dei Cappuccini (Capuchin Convent), on the western outskirts of Palermo, retained the right to place their own dead – and many lay people as well – in the corridors beneath the church. The bodies weren't buried in coffins; they were embalmed, dressed in clothes such as silks and top hats that were provided before death, then the bodies were installed in niches and placed in clear glass cases. It's a bizarre, grotesque collection, some contorted figures fixing you with a basilisk stare, others grinning, while the various states of decomposition can be very unnerving.

⊞ Off map A1 ✉ Piazza Cappuccini 1 ☎ 091 652 4156 🕐 Mon.–Sat. 9–1 and 3–5, Sun. 9–1 🚌 327 💰 $

Cattedrale

Palermo's Cattedrale (Cathedral) was founded in 1185 by English archbishop Roger of the Mill as a private power base. It wasn't finished for centuries, having been eclipsed by William II's magnificent cathedral at Monreale (see page 182).

The lovely triple-apsed eastern end and matching towers are pure Norman, as are numerous exterior carvings and details. The dome was added in the 18th century when the interior was given a neoclassic facelift. Be sure to see the huge sarcophagi in the chapels to the left of the entrance. Here lie Sicily's great Norman rulers – Frederick II, Henry VI and Roger II.

⊞ A1 ✉ Corso Vittorio Emanuele II ☎ 091 334 373; www.cattedrale.palermo.it 🕐 Daily 9–5:30 (7–7 for services). Treasury and crypt: 9:30–1:30 and 2:30–5:30. Closed during services 🚇 Linea Rossa 🚎 'A Cuccagna, see page 211 💰 Cathedral free; Treasury and crypt $

Galleria Regionale della Sicilia

Deep in the Kalsa district stands the imposing 15th-century Palazzo Abatellis, built from 1490 to 1495, which houses the Galleria Regionale Siciliana (Sicilian Regional Gallery), one of the greatest galleries in Italy. The collection ranges from sculpture and woodcarvings to

Exquisite mosaics in the church of La Martorana

frescoes, mosaics and paintings. Look for Francesco Laurana's serene, white marble bust of Eleanor of Aragon; paintings by Sicily's 15th-century master, Antonello da Messina; and some early 13th-century Madonnas. With their wide, dark eyes and long-fingered hands, these portraits clearly show the influence of Byzantine art.

✚ C1 ✉ Palazzo Abatellis, Via Alloro 4
☎ 091 623 0011 🕐 Tue.–Fri. 9–6, Sat.–Sun. 9–1
🚌 Linea A, 103, 105, 139 🎟 $$$

La Martorana

The Norman church of La Martorana was built by ruler Roger II's admiral; its name comes from the Spanish convent that later owned it. It's easy to ignore the baroque encrustations of the 16th-century remodeling inside and concentrate on the 12th-century mosaics rioting over the dome and surrounding columns. The figure of Christ is surrounded by angels with splendid wings, their golds and greens highlighted by the sunlight, while the Virgin Mary and Apostles occupy the side spaces.

✚ B1 ✉ Piazza Bellini 3 ☎ 091 616 1692
🕐 Mon.–Sat. 8:30–1 and 3:30–5:30, Sun. 8:30–1.
Closed during services 🚌 Linea A, 101, 102, 103, 104
🍴 'A Cuccagna, see page 211 🎟 Free

Museo Archeologico

A converted church and its cloisters house Palermo's Museo Archeologico Regionale (Regional Archeological Museum). This small collection is essential viewing if you're planning on visiting Sicily's classical sites. Here you'll see preserved wondrous fifth-century BC lion's-head waterspouts, *metopes* (stone carvings) and friezes from Selinunte temples, as well as artifacts from major Neolithic, Carthaginian, Greek and Roman Sicilian sites. A fierce bronze ram, a technical tour de force, comes from Siracusa; nearby you'll see Hercules grappling with a stag. Don't miss the fine Roman mosaics, excavated from the center of Palermo itself.

✚ B2 ✉ Via Bara all'Olivella 24 ☎ 091 611 6805
🕐 Closed for restoration at the time of writing
🚌 Linea A, 101, 102, 103, 104 🎟 $$

Museo delle Marionette

Puppet shows are a traditional Sicilian entertainment, usually centering on the exploits of the hero Orlando (Roland) and his struggles against the Saracens. The Museo delle Marionette (Puppet Museum) has Palermo's biggest collection of puppets, costumes and scenery. It also stages summer shows that are a great antidote to too much culture, even though it's unlikely you'll understand the rich dialect of the performers.

✚ C2 ✉ Piazzetta Antonio Pasqualetta 5 ☎ 091 328 060 🕐 Mon.–Sat. 9–1 and 2:30–6:30, Sun 10–1
🚌 Linea A, 103, 105, 139, 824 🎟 $$

San Cataldo

The ancient church of San Cataldo, with its red domes, stands amid palm trees in the heart of the city. Built in the 12th century, it was never decorated, and its peaceful, plain interior and detailed, marble mosaic floor exude a sense of spirituality often lacking in some of Palermo's more ornate and elaborate baroque churches.

✚ B1 ✉ Piazza Bellini 3 ☎ 091 637 5622 🕐 Daily 9:30–12:30 and 3–6 🚌 Linea A, 101, 102, 103, 104
🎟 $

San Giovanni degli Eremiti

To appreciate the weight of Palermo's Arab-Norman legacy, visit the deconsecrated church of San Giovanni degli Eremiti (St. John of the Hermits), founded by Roger II and built in 1132. There are distinct Arab overtones in the church's five domes; it was built around an earlier mosque, part of which is still visible. This is an evocative place set amid lemon trees, with a delightful 13th-century cloister; twin columns and pointed arches echo both Arab and Norman architectural styles.

✚ A1 ✉ Via dei Benedettini ☎ 091 651 5019
🕐 Mon.–Sat. 9–7, Sun. 9–1:30 🚌 103, 105 🎟 $$

Palermo's popular food markets are among the most exciting in the Mediterranean

Walk
From the Normans to a Vibrant Center

Refer to route marked on city map on page 174

This walk takes about 2 hours and offers you the chance to see some artistic treasures combined with a taste of Palermo's vibrant street life.

Start at the Porta Nuova (New Gate) at the west end of Corso Vittorio Emanuele II.
The New Gate was built in 1535 to commemorate Spanish ruler Charles V's Tunisian campaign; he stopped in Palermo on his way back to Spain, the only Spanish monarch to visit during the 400-year viceregal period.
Visit the Palazzo dei Normanni and the Cappella Palatina (see page 176), then walk east on Corso Vittorio Emanuele II to the left of the cathedral (see page 176). Continue to the Quattro Canti crossroads. Turn right onto Via Maqueda.
The Via Maqueda was constructed in the 16th century to run straight through the old quarters of the Albergheria and the Capo. This area has changed little over the past several hundred years. Behind Via Maqueda there's a warren of narrow streets, crumbling buildings and tiny

squares. You'll see evidence of World War II bomb damage, as well as derelict houses. Try to ignore them and concentrate instead on the vibrant street life and intense atmosphere. Fifty yards along Via Maqueda on the left you'll see the Piazza Pretoria. The large building is the Municipio (City Hall), and the huge 16th-century church is Santa Caterina. The square's central fountain was designed in the 1500s.
Adjacent to Piazza Pretoria and also on Via Maqueda, cross Piazza Bellini to visit the churches of La Martorana (see page 177) and San Cataldo (see page 177). Cross the road and turn right a little farther down Via Ponticello, a grubby and run-down street, to reach the glorious church of Il Gesù.
Built in 1564, this church is a Sicilian baroque extravaganza of marble, relief work and wood inlay, topped by a magnificent green-and-white dome.
Continue down Via Ponticello to lively Piazza Ballarò.
Piazza Ballarò, nearby Piazza del Carmine and the surrounding streets are home to a daily food market, something you shouldn't miss. Palermo markets are among the most raucous in the Mediterranean. The stalls are piled high with a bewildering variety of meat, fish, fruit and vegetables of excellent quality and freshness. You'll find a huge choice of ready-to-go food and tiny eating places where you can lunch on local specialties such as *arancini* (see opposite), raw sea urchins, or rolls filled with spleen and liver.

Cuisines of Palermo

Meals in Palermo and around Sicily will be a highlight; possibly no other region of Italy has been so influenced by the civilizations that have lived here. Each has left ingredients, flavors and cooking methods that together make up one of the most inventive cuisines in the Mediterranean.

Main Meals

Meals follow the standard Italian pattern of *antipasto, primo, secondo* and *dolce*, and portions are large. The emphasis is on fish, although inland you'll find flavorful meat and game dishes. Pasta dishes include *spaghetti alle vongole* with tiny clams and a hint of spicy *peperoncino* (chili); *pasta con le sarde*, with a piquant sardine sauce; and *spaghetti con le seppie*, with a rich black sauce derived from the ink sac of the cuttlefish. *Pasta alla Norma* with eggplant, tomatoes and melted cheese is a real Palermo specialty. The main course (*secondo*) is often plain grilled fish, so a squeeze of lemon is all it needs, or a delicate *fritto misto*, deep-fried prawns and *calamari*. Swordfish and tuna are particularly good. Vegetable dishes are superb; be sure to sample *caponata*, a traditional vegetable stew featuring eggplant, celery, olives and capers; *zucchine in agro-dolce*, an Arab-influenced sweet-sour dish; or anything that includes lime-green cauliflowers, a winter treat.

Delicious Snacks and Desserts

A slice of pizza in Palermo makes an excellent snack – paper-thin, crisp and blackened at the edges from a wood-fired oven. It's a revelation to those used to the Americanized version. *Arancini*, another Sicilian specialty, are rice balls stuffed with meat sauce and peas, coated with egg and breadcrumbs, then deep-fried. *Focaccia*, a bread snack with various toppings, also makes a quick lunch.

Sicilian desserts show the Arab legacy; heavy use is made of almonds and sugar, and you'll find trays of mouthwatering varieties in every *pasticcerria*. *Cannoli* and *cassata Siciliana* both use *ricotta* cheese, heavily sweetened and studded with candied fruits and chocolate, while Sicilian *gelato* (ice cream) is some of the world's best.

Local Drinks

Wines are straightforward and often served by the carafe. If you want something special, look for the red Corvo; Etna, made from grapes grown on volcanic soil; or Donnafugata, from outside Palermo. Settle your dinner with a glass of Sicilian *amaro* (bitters). *Averna*, found throughout Italy, is made in Sicily, as is Limoncello, a lemon-based liqueur produced on the east coast.

A typical selection of fresh fish and seafood

Sicily Sights

> **Key to symbols**
> ➕ map coordinates refer to the region map on pages 170–171 💷 admission charge: $$$ more than €6, $$ €3–€6, $ less than €3
> See page 5 for complete key to symbols

Agrigento

Agrigento's Greek temples and ruins once formed the Hellenistic city of Akragas, founded in the sixth century BC. The ancient city was spread along two ridges. Modern Agrigento stands on the higher ridge, with the temples known as the Valle dei Templi (Valley of the Temples) strung along the lower ridge a couple of miles down the hill. The site falls into two zones; head first for the eastern zone. Make your way along the path past the Tempio di Ercole (Temple of Hercules) to the superb Tempio della Concordia (Temple of Concord), built around 430 BC and converted to a Christian church in the sixth century, which explains why it is in such an excellent state of preservation.

Beyond the Temple of Concord stands the half-ruined Tempio di Giunone (Temple of Juno), its masonry still marked by the fire set by the Carthaginians in 406 BC. Farther down the hill you can explore the jumble of ruins that comprise the western zone. Here are the Tempio dei Dioscuri (the so-called Temple of Castor and Pollux) and the massive remains of the Tempio di Giove (Temple of Jupiter), the largest Doric temple ever to be built. It was supported by huge male figures – one still lies abandoned amid the ruins.

From the temples, return back up the hill to visit the Hellenistic-Roman Quarter, an excavated section of the original city, and the Museo Archeologico Regionale (Regional Archeological Museum), which has an excellent and varied collection. On the grounds you'll find the third-century BC, semicircular odeon and the lovely Norman San Nicola, a serene and solid church with a peaceful cloister.

Modern Agrigento is a mix of the medieval and baroque. Via Atanea runs through the heart of town, and off it old narrow alleys and steep stairs follow the Arabic layout past crumbling palaces to the vast cathedral, which stands at the town's highest point.
➕ C2

Tourist information ✉ Viale della Vittoria 225 ☎ 0922 401 352; www.regione.sicilia.it 🕐 Mon.–Sat. 8:30–1 and 3:30–7 (closes at 6 p.m. Nov.–Mar.)
Valle dei Templi ✉ Via dei Templi ☎ 091 26191; www.valleyofthetemples.com 🕐 Daily 8:30 a.m.–1

The ruins of the Temple of Juno Lacinia, also known as the Temple of Hera

hour before dusk 🍴 Bar at parking lot (summer only) 🖐 $$$ (combined ticket with Museo Archeologico) **Hellenistic-Roman Quarter** ✉ Via dei Templi 🕐 Daily 9 a.m.–1 hour before dusk 🖐 $ **Museo Archeologico Regionale** ✉ San Nicola, Via dei Templi ☎ 0922 401 565 🕐 Tue.–Sat. 9–7, Sun.–Mon. 9–1 🖐 $$$ (combined ticket with Valle dei Templi) ℹ There is no information in English on any of the exhibits

Catania

Catania, Sicily's second-largest city, is an ancient settlement crouching in the shadow of Mount Etna on the east coast. Catania makes a good base for visiting Etna, and has some good-value hotels and wholesome food outlets. Etna's eruptions and the 1693 earthquake have taken their toll, but there still remains a largely 18th-century city center with some fine baroque churches and monuments. The top sites include the Duomo (Cathedral), fronted by an elegant piazza; the 18th-century church of San Nicolò, Sicily's largest church; and the Museo Civico, housed in the Castello Ursino. Take care in this area, as the castle is in a grim neighborhood. On a lighter note, Catania also has one of Sicily's biggest and most exuberant food markets.

➕ D2 **Tourist information** ✉ Palazzo Minoriti, Via Etnea 63/65 ☎ 095 401 4070, office at airport 095 093 7023; www.turismo.catania.it 🕐 Mon.–Sat. 9–7, Sun. 10–2 **Duomo** ✉ Piazza del Duomo ☎ 095 320 044 🕐 Daily 7:30–noon and 4–7 🖐 Free **San Nicolò** ✉ Piazza Dante ☎ 095 715 9912 🕐 Tue.–Sun. 9–1, but times may vary 🖐 Free **Museo Civico** ✉ Castello Ursino, Piazza Frederico di Svevia ☎ 095 345 830 🕐 Mon.–Sat. 9–12:30 and 3–6 🖐 Free

Cefalù

Cefalù, on the northern coast, is an ancient port with a strong sense of identity. Its tangle of medieval streets was built in the shadow of a huge crag, and it offers good beaches, a lovely coastline and better-than-average shops and restaurants. Spend time exploring

the narrow alleys that lead down to the old port before wandering up Corso Ruggero to the palm-fringed Piazza del Duomo, dominated by the magnificent Duomo (Cathedral). Built by Norman ruler Roger II in 1131, this beautiful building is a fusion of Arab, Norman and Byzantine styles, the different architectural elements heavily influenced by the craftsmen who built it. As much fortress as cathedral, its twin towers and honey-colored facade soar above the historic town. The shadowy interior has surging columns and glittering gold mosaics, dominated by the huge image of Christ Pantocrator, his right hand raised in blessing.

For more artistic treasures, head for the Museo Mandralisca; its chief treasure is the fine *Portrait of an Unknown Man*, painted by Sicilian-born Antonello da Messina in 1465. Energetic visitors can climb the brooding outcrop above the town to enjoy fine views and the ruins of the fifth-century BC Temple of Diana. You also could use Cefalù as a suitable base for exploring the Madonie Mountains, a magnificent upland area with pretty villages, high peaks and good hiking.

➕ C3 **Tourist information** ✉ Corso Ruggero 77 ☎ 0921 421 050; www.comune.cefalu.pa.it 🕐 Mon.–Sat. 9–7:30 (also Sun. 9–1 in summer) 🚢 To Aeolian Islands **Duomo** ✉ Piazza del Duomo ☎ 0921 922 021 🕐 Daily 8–noon and 3:30–7 🖐 Free **Museo Mandralisca** ✉ Via Mandralisca 13 ☎ 0921 421 547; www.museomandralisca.it 🕐 Daily 9 a.m.–11 p.m., Aug.; 9–7, rest of year 🖐 $$

Enna

The ancient mountain stronghold of Enna stretches along a 3,068-foot-high ridge in the hills of inland Sicily. Just below the highest point stands the castle, built by Frederick II in the 14th century, a massive fortress with towers that offer magnificent views over Enna and the rugged interior landscape. From here Via Roma, the main street, runs down the ridge to Piazza Vittorio Emanuele, packed with crowds during the evening *passeggiata*. Enna's Duomo (Cathedral) partly dates from 1307, and you can see its treasures in the Museo Civico Alessi. The nearby Museo Archeologico has some fine Greek vases from the surrounding area. Spend time wandering along the promenade; from here hills stretch out in the distance, with the tumbling ochre-colored village of Calascibetta in the foreground.

🔂 D2

Tourist information ✉ Via Roma 411 ☎ 0935 528 228; www.ennaturismo.info ⏰ Mon.–Sat. 9–1 and 3:30–6:30

Duomo ✉ Piazza Mazzini, Via Roma ⏰ Daily 9–1 and 4–7 🎟 Free

Museo Civico Alessi ✉ Piazza Mazzini, Via Roma ☎ 0935 503 165 ⏰ Mon.–Sat. 9–7 🎟 $$

Museo Archeologico Varisano ✉ Piazza Mazzini, Via Roma ☎ 0935 528 127 ⏰ Daily 9 a.m.–1 hour before dusk 🎟 $

Erice

A twisting road winds up to Erice, a tiny hilltop town with sweeping views over its surroundings and the Isole Egadi (Egadi Islands) off the coast. It's easy to escape the throngs of summer visitors to wander through the pebbled streets and tiny piazzas, pausing to peek at the courtyards bright with flowering tubs. Erice was ancient Eryx; the temple of Aphrodite attracted worshippers from all over the Mediterranean. Succeeding waves of Carthaginian, Roman, Arab and Norman invaders settled here. Visitors can explore Roger II's Castello di Venere, built on the site of the ancient temple.

There are aged walls, towers and gates, some lovely churches, a 14th-century Duomo (Cathedral), a small museum and a wooded public garden, but your chief memories will be of winding alleyways and superb views. Have a drink in the Piazza Umberto, where you also can sample some of the almond-based sweetmeats, *dolci di badia*, for which the town is renowned.

Erice's Church of San Giuliano

🔂 B3

Tourist information ✉ Viale Conte Agistono Pepoli 11 ☎ 0923 869 388 ⏰ Mon.–Fri. 8:30–2

Castello di Venere ✉ Via Castello di Venere ⏰ Daily 8–6 🎟 Free

Duomo ✉ Piazza Matrice ⏰ Daily 10–noon and 3–6 🎟 Free

Museo Civico Antonio Cordici ✉ Piazza Umberto I ☎ 0923 386 9172 ⏰ Mon.–Fri. 8:30–1:30 (also Mon. and Thu. 2:30–5:30) 🎟 Free

Monreale

Above the slopes of the Conca d'Oro (Golden Shell) valley, some 5 miles from Palermo, stand the small town of Monreale and its Norman Duomo (Cathedral). Here you'll find the world's most extraordinary and accomplished Christian mosaics; the cathedral's ceilings and walls glitter with brilliant splendor. It was built from 1174 to 1184 by the Norman King William II as a direct challenge to Palermo's cathedral, which was erected at the same time by William's rival, the archbishop of Palermo. Completed in only 10 years, the result is an astonishingly homogenous building, its mosaics almost certainly the work of Greek and Byzantine craftsmen. The interior is dominated by the great Christ Pantocrator, while the Madonna and Child, angels and saints are ranked below. The side apses portray St. Peter and St. Paul and their martyrdoms, while the nave and aisles are covered with mosaics portraying scenes from the Old and New Testaments.

Outside the cathedral a side entrance leads to the superb Chiostro dei Benedettini (Cloisters), part of William's original Benedictine monastery. The elegant arcades are supported by 216 columns, with no two capitals the same.

➕ B3

Duomo ✉ Piazza del Duomo ☎ 091 640 4413 ◷ Mon.–Sat. 8–6, Sun. 8–10 and 3:30–5:30, May–Sep.; Mon.–Sat. 8–12:30 and 3:30–6, Sun. 8–10 and 3:30–5:30, rest of year 🅴 Take change for the coin-operated light switches and wear modest clothing **Chiostro dei Benedettini** ✉ Piazza Guglielmo il Buono ☎ 091 640 4403 ◷ Mon.–Sat. 9–noon and 5:30–7:30, Sun. 9–1:30 🅿 389 (from Piazza Independenza) 🎫 $$

Noto

In 1693 a severe earthquake devastated much of eastern Sicily, destroying churches and houses and wiping out entire communities. The little town of Noto was completely flattened, but remarkably, within weeks construction had started on what was to become one of Sicily's most beguiling baroque townscapes – a new town on a new site. Sicilian-Spanish aristocrat Giuseppe Lanza was in charge, and it was his vision that produced today's town.

Noto was deliberately designed so that the political and religious buildings stood apart from the residential streets. The Corso Vittorio Emanuele is the finest of the streets and is lined with graceful palazzi sporting sumptuously decorated facades. Vittorio Emanuele leads to the Piazza del Municipio, a harmonious tree-shaded square lined with beautiful buildings. It's also the site of the twin-towered cathedral, now much restored since the collapse of its

dome in 1996. West of the square is the eccentrically decorated Palazzo Villadorata, with galloping horses and plump cherubs. Spend time wandering the side streets, where you'll find architectural delights on all corners.

➕ D1

Tourist information ✉ Piazza XVI Maggio ☎ 0931 896 654 or 800 994 462; www.comune.noto.sr.it ◷ Mon.–Sat. 9–2 and 4–7, Apr.–Sep.; Mon.–Sat. 9–1, rest of year

Piazza Armerina and Villa Romana del Casale

The pleasant town of Piazza Armerina stands in the wooded hills of the southern interior, an attractive mixture of narrow streets and handsome squares with an elegant cathedral and some interesting churches and palaces. A few miles southwest of town is the hamlet of Casale where a wealthy Roman (possibly Maximianus Herculeus, co-emperor with Diocletian) built a grand villa in the depths of the country. The early fourth-century structure was probably designed as a hunting lodge, a theory borne out by the astounding mosaics that adorn every floor in the building. They show a wide variety of animals and birds, many native to Africa, which tie in with the African-Roman style of the compositions. Around the peristyle (courtyard) is a wide, decorated corridor featuring a lively hunting scene with tigers, elephants and sea creatures. The highlight, however (for some), is a walkway adorned with 10 bikini-clad girls engaged in sporting activities; the winner, with her triumphant smirk and decorous laurel wreath, is easy to spot. After extensive restoration, the Villa Romana del Casale is slowly reopening, but some areas may still be closed.

➕ D2

Tourist information ✉ Piazza Santa Rosalia ☎ 0935 680 201; www.comune.piazzaarmerina.en.it ◷ Mon.–Fri. 9–1 and 3–7 **Villa Romana del Casale** ☎ 0935 680 036; www.villaromanadelcasale.org ◷ Daily 9–6, Apr.–Oct.; 9–4, rest of year 🍽 Café/bar

Drive
The Slopes of Mount Etna

Duration: 5 to 6 hours

This drive takes you on a tour of 10,902-foot Mount Etna, with an opportunity to ascend as high as possible toward the summit of one of the world's largest and most active volcanoes. You'll drive through countryside graced with groves of citrus and fig trees, forests of chestnut and oak, and wonderful and ever-changing views of the mountain.

For all its grandeur, Mount Etna is little more than 60,000 years old – a mere stripling in geological terms. Its first recorded eruption was in 475 BC. Since then there have been 90 major eruptions, the worst in 1669, when a fissure opened on the mountain's flank and a stream of magma engulfed Catania, 25 miles (40 kilometers) away. Ash was thrown as far as 60 miles (100 kilometers), and in places the lava took seven years to cool completely. Since the early 1990s, Etna has erupted annually, often several times a year. In 1992 magma streams threatened villages. Between 2003 and 2011 there were more than 25 spectacular eruptions, both on the summit and flanks, all featuring lava fountains, magma, ash and explosions.

Start your drive at Taormina (see page 188) and take the SS114 south toward Catania. Turn right onto the SS120 (signposted Linguaglossa) at Fiumefreddo di Sicilia.

Linguaglossa is the main tourist center on Etna's northern slopes. In winter it's packed with skiers who base themselves here to use the lifts at Piano Provenzana, farther up the mountain. In summer it's a quiet and attractive town surrounded by pine forests.

Continue on the SS120 to Randazzo, well worth a stop.

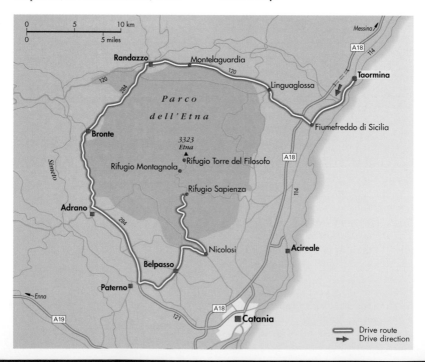

Mount Etna, on the east coast of Sicily, is one of the most active volcanoes in the world

As the crow flies, Randazzo is the town closest to Etna's summit and has been frequently threatened by lava flows, although never engulfed. The 1981 eruption came very close, and you can see the flow on the road near town. Built almost entirely of lava, Randazzo's gloomy medieval heart is, in fact, a reconstruction. The town was one of the main German defensive positions during World War II and was heavily bombed.

A short distance beyond Randazzo, fork left onto the SS284 toward Bronte.

The road climbs steadily from here, and you'll approach ever closer to the lava flows as you drive through woods of walnut and chestnut trees. Bronte was founded in 1535, and many of its churches date from this time. Today it's surrounded by pistachio-nut plantations; almost 85 percent of Italy's production comes from this vicinity.

Continue on the SS284 to Adrano; the road bypasses the town, but you can detour to visit it.

Founded by the Greeks, Adrano has a solid medieval castle and a clutch of churches (the nicest is the Chiesa Madre, next to the castle).

Continue on the SS284 to the major intersection with the SS121 at Paternò. Leave the main road here and take the unclassified road that climbs up Mount Etna, signposted Belpasso and Nicolosi.

Nicolosi, another winter ski resort,

marks the start of steeper roads leading up toward the summit. The road climbs up grassy slopes and through woods before emerging into the weird volcanic landscape. Here the slopes are dotted with spent craters and black-and-gray mounds of volcanic debris. The road ends at Rifugio Sapienza, 4,600 feet below the summit. There's a place here for overnight stays, as well as restaurants and shops.

You can continue to ascend Etna, either by walking on a rough track (six tough hours), or by taking an off-road vehicle. The cable car runs (weather permitting) as far as Rifugio Montagnola, from which jeeps and a guide take you as far as the Valle del Bove. Wear sturdy shoes or boots and glasses to keep the flying grit out of your eyes, and take plenty of warm and waterproof clothing. At this height you'll find yourself in a lunar landscape; no vegetation can compete with the black, gray and red lava. Farther up, the southeast crater of Etna smokes gently. At this altitude you may see gaseous explosions, rock showers and molten lava.

Nicolosi tourist information ☒ Piazza Vittorio Emanuel 323 ☎ 095 911 505 🕓 Mon.–Thu. 9–1 and 4–6, Fri. 9–1, Apr.–Oct.; Mon.and Thu. 9–1 and 4–6, Tue.–Wed., Fri. 9–1, rest of year

Etna Park Centre ☒ Via del Convento 45 ☎ 095 821 111; www.parcoetna.ct.it or www.parks.it

The remains of the ancient Greek Temple E, also known as the Temple of Hera, at Selinunte

Segesta

Standing alone on a windswept hillside, the luminous Greek temple of Segesta is probably the most evocative of all of Sicily's Hellenistic monuments. The city of Segesta flourished as early as the 12th century BC, became Greek in the fifth century BC and spent the following centuries fighting other Greek settlements and allying itself with Carthage. It was eventually overtaken by the city of Selinus to the south. All that remains is its glorious unfinished temple and hillside theater, although excavation work has been ongoing since 1987. From a distance the temple appears complete, its 36 columns, entablature and pediment all intact. Venture closer and you'll see the columns are unfluted and there's no interior *cella* (the area delineated by the outer columns), while the stone building studs have never been removed. The haunt of birds and lizards, it embodies the classical dream. On a hillside to the east stands the second-century BC theater, a graceful white shell hewn out of the bedrock, with breathtaking views to the sea.

🕂 B3

☎ 0924 952 356 🕐 Daily 9–5 🍴 Bar/cafeteria

🚍 Half-hourly shuttle bus service to theater in summer months 🎟 $$ ℹ Segesta stages classical Greek and Roman drama at the theater during the summer

Selinunte

The Greek city of Selinus (modern Selinunte), founded in the seventh century BC, reached its peak in the fifth century BC, the era from which the greatest of its temples date. Constantly at loggerheads with its northern neighbor Segesta, it was attacked by Segesta's ally Carthage, which sacked this powerful city in 250 BC. Selinus never really recovered; time and repeated earthquakes did the rest, and today it remains a vast jumble of ruins from which surviving temples soar. Nobody knows to which gods the temples were dedicated, so they are designated by letters. The site is huge, and you'll need comfortable shoes and stamina to explore it thoroughly. Pick up a plan from the tourist office outside the gates of the archeological park before you start. Temples E, F and G stand amid the wild parsley that gave Selinus its name. The reconstructed columns of E shine against the sky, with the sea behind them. A mile or so away and down by the sea lies the acropolis, as well as five additional temples, stretches of well-preserved streets and massive fifth-century BC walls. Climb to temple C at the highest point; from its 14 standing columns you can gaze over this once-mighty city to the sea.

➕ B2

Tourist information ✉ Entrance to Archeological Zone ☎ 0924 46277; www.selinunteservice.com 🕐 Mon.–Sat. 9 a.m.–1 hour before dusk, Sun. 9–noon and 3–1 hour before dusk

Parco Archeologico ☎ 0924 46 277 🕐 Mon.–Sat. 9–1 hour before dusk, Sun. 9–noon and 3–1 hour before dusk. Tickets are issued up to 2 hours before dusk

💶 $$$

Siracusa

Ancient Siracusa (Syracuse) grew up around the eighth century BC on a coastal island with two natural harbors. By the fifth century BC, it had grown to become the most powerful Greek settlement in the Mediterranean. Glorious centuries followed until Syracuse fell to Rome in 214 BC; it later became a prominent early Christian city, only to suffer successive waves of Arab, Norman and Spanish invaders. Much was destroyed in the 1693 earthquake; the subsequent rebuilding has shaped the existing glorious city. The main sights fall neatly into two areas: Ortigia, the old town on the island, linked for centuries to the mainland by a bridge; and the archeological zone, with its excavations and museum.

On Ortigia, head first to the Piazza del Duomo, an exquisite elongated square lined with graceful baroque buildings and dominated by the sumptuous facade of the Duomo (Cathedral). Its interior is unique; embedded in the walls you'll see massive columns, the remains of the original Greek temple around which the cathedral was built. No other building gives a better idea of the weight of Syracuse's history. Head next for the Galleria Regionale, housed in a Renaissance palace; highlights include Antonello da Messina's serene *Annunciation* and a vigorous Caravaggio showing the burial of St. Lucy, Syracuse's patron saint.

Other sights on Ortigia include the huge ruins of the Tempio di Apollo and the Fontana di Aretusa (Arethusa's Fountain), the spring that attracted the first citizens to Ortigia. North of the city center is the Parco Archeologico (Archeological Park); the highlight is the Teatro Greco (Greek Theater), the most complete theater in the ancient Greek world. This 15,000-seat auditorium is carved from living rock and has sublime views over the city and sea. Wander through the adjacent *latomia* (pits), the quarries that provided the building stone for the ancient city, now a verdant oasis of olive and lemon trees. Here is the oddly shaped cave known as the Orecchio di Dionisio (Dionysius' Ear), while nearby is the vast Roman amphitheater.

Outside the park, take in the Basilica di San Giovanni, from which there is access to an underground catacomb system where Christians were buried beginning around AD 200. Leave time for the splendid Museo Archeologico Regionale (Regional Archeological Museum), where English labels guide you through the superb, if daunting, collections. Don't miss the Venus Landolina, a decadent goddess rising from the sea. Also outstanding are some *kouroi*, athletes dating from the fifth century BC, unclothed as was the custom.

➕ E1

Tourist information ✉ Via Mirabella 29 (Ortigia) ☎ 0931 464 657; www.comune.siracusa.it 🕐 Mon.–Fri. 8:30–1:30 and 3:30–6:30, Sat. 8:30–1, May–Sep.; Mon.–Sat. 8:30–1:30 (times may be erratic), rest of year ✉ Via Roma 31 (Ortigia) ☎ 800 055 500; www.siracusadinverno.it 🕐 Mon.–Sat. 8:30–2 and 4:30–7:30, Sun. 8:30–2, May–Sep.; Mon.–Sat. 8:30–2 and 4:30–7 (times may be erratic), rest of year

Duomo ✉ Piazza del Duomo 🕐 Daily 8–6 (times may be erratic) 💶 Free

Galleria Regionale Palazzo Bellomo ✉ Via Capodieci 14 ☎ 0931 69 511 🕐 Tue.–Sat. 9–7, Sun. 9–1 💶 $$$

Parco Archeologico ✉ Viale Augusto-Largo Paradiso
☎ 0931 464 022 🕐 Tue.–Sat. 9–7, Sun. 9–1 🚌 4, 5,
12 from city center 🍴 Bars and cafeterias outside park
entrance 💲 $$

Basilica di San Giovanni ✉ Via San Giovanni
☎ 0931 69 966 🕐 Tue.–Sun. 9:30–12:30 and 2:30–4
🚌 4, 5, 12 from city center 💲 $$

Museo Archeologico Regionale ✉ Viale Teocrito 66
☎ 0931 464 022 🕐 Tue.–Sat. 9–7, Sun. 9–1 💲 $$

Taormina

Taormina draws visitors from all over
the world, attracted by its sublime
location, mild climate and excellent
facilities. There are more good hotels in
Taormina than anywhere else in Sicily,
plus elegant shops and some very good
restaurants. Taormina tumbles down
steep cliffs to a clutch of tiny beaches
and enchanting islets and headlands,
while to the southwest rises the graceful
sweep of smoldering Mount Etna, a
fitting backdrop for the town's lush
subtropical vegetation, palm trees and
cascades of bougainvillea. It's the ideal
spot for a stopover, a chance to unwind
and experience its charm after the tour
buses and day excursions have departed.

The main street, Corso Umberto I,
runs from one end of the walkable town
center to the other. It's lined with 15th-
to 19th-century palazzi and punctuated
by the cathedral, churches and piazzas.
Piazza IX Aprile, at the halfway point, is
a good place to pause at an outdoor café
and enjoy the splendid views of Etna
and the bay. Farther east, the Corso

leads to Via Teatro Greco, which offers
access to Taormina's main draw, a
Greco-Roman theater carved out of the
hillside with a superlative backdrop of
sea, coast and mountains. The theater
dates mainly from first-century Roman
adaptations of the original third-century
BC Greek construction, and you can
climb up and down the tiers of seats and
explore the backstage areas.

Down the hill below the theater, don't
miss the Villa Comunale (Giardino
Trevelyan), a lovely English-inspired
park above the sea. Taormina's beaches
lie far below the city center in outlying
Mazzarò; the best way to reach them is
to take the *funivia* (cable car) from Via
L Pirandello at the east end of town. For
the energetic, there are some good hikes
around town; you could walk up to the
medieval castle above Taormina or hike
to the tiny hill village of Castelmola.
✚ E2

Tourist information ✉ Palazzo Corvaja, Piazza Santa
Caterina ☎ 0942 23 243 🕐 Mon.–Sat. 8:30–2 and
4–7 (also Sun. 9–12:30, Apr.–Oct.)

Teatro Greco ✉ Via Teatro Greco ☎ 0942 23 220
🕐 Daily 9 a.m.–1 hour before dusk 💲 $$$
ℹ Contact the tourist office for details about Jul. and
Aug. festivals

Villa Comunale ✉ Via Bagnoli Croce 🕐 Daily
dawn–dusk ℹ Contact the tourist office for details
about summer events

Funivia ✉ Via L Pirandello ☎ 0942 23 906
🕐 Every 15 minutes Mon. 9 a.m.–1 a.m., Tue.–Sun.
8 a.m.–1 a.m, Jun.–Sep.; Tue.–Sun. 8 a.m.–8:15 p.m.,
Mon. 9–8:15, rest of year 💲 $$

The small island of Isola Bella, the Pearl of the Ionian Sea, lies just off Taormina

The Mafia

As a tourist in Sicily, you will remain untouched by the tentacles of the Mafia. But this mysterious criminal fraternity is inextricably linked with most aspects of everyday Sicilian life; its members are *uomini d'honore* (men of honor) who live by a code of silence *(omertà)*.

Beginnings
The Mafia goes back hundreds of years, when ex-bandits were recruited to "police" the interior, taking payments from colleagues and acting as middlemen between landowners and peasants. Bound together by ties of self-interest, they grew rich and powerful and established a semi-formal organization shrouded in secrecy. They filled the gap between Sicilians and authority, whether that authority came from the state, foreign rulers or absentee landowners. "Families" emerged, their members not always blood relations, headed by a *capo* (godfather). Each took its name from the village under its control and formed alliances with other families.

The 20th Century
During the 1930s, Mussolini was determined to break the power of the Mafia. Before the Sicilian landings in 1943, the Allies had only one source of intelligence and local support – the American Mafia, formed from among the thousands of Sicilians who had emigrated to America in the early 20th century. American *capi*, such as Lucky Luciano, provided the introductions in Sicily vitally needed for the invasion, but at the same time succeeded in ensuring the re-emergence of the Mafia as a powerful force in the postwar Allied military government. During the second half of the century, Mafia tentacles spread – into politics, construction, and arms and drug dealing. Immensely rich, the organization dealt brutally with anyone who stood in its way. In 1982 General della Chiesa was murdered, and in 1992 all Italy was greatly shocked by the killings of Giovanni Falcone, a respected magistrate, and that of Judge Paolo Borsellino.

The Future
Recent years have seen arrests of leading *capi*, while former Mafia members such as Tommaso Buscetta have fingered politicians, including Giulio Andreotti and prime minister Silvio Berlusconi. In March 2010 a huge undercover sting in northern Sicily culminated in the arrest of 19 suspected Mafia operatives. There is hope that as ordinary Sicilians' attitudes change, the change may finally defeat *la piovra* (the octopus).

Charlie "Lucky" Luciano (1897–1962) is considered as the father of organized crime in the U.S.

Sicily and Sardinia

Sardinia Sights

Key to symbols

➕ map coordinates refer to the region map on page 171 🎫 admission charge: $$$ more than €6, $$ €3–€6, $ less than €3

See page 5 for complete key to symbols

Cágliari

Sardinia's capital is in the southern part of the island. The hinterland is a bird-rich network of marshes and lakes, and in the foreground is the busy Golfo di Cágliari. Despite 250,000 residents, Cágliari's center is remarkably compact, the Castello district containing all the main sights. This historic area retains its defensive walls; they include the Torre del Elefante (Elephant's Tower), complete with a statue of an elephant on the facade, and the Torre di San Pancrazio (St. Pancras' Tower). Both were erected in 1305 by the Pisans after they captured the city from the Genoese. The best approach to the Castello today is through the Bastione San Remy; this Spanish-built defensive wall was transformed in the 20th century into a wide esplanade. Walk from here to Piazza Palazzo, Castello's main square. Here you'll find the Cattedrale (Cathedral), first built in the 12th century by the Pisans. The pulpits and lions guarding the entrance are Pisan, but the Romanesque-style facade was added in the 1930s. The interior contains the tombs of the princes of the House of Savoy.

Continue north and you'll come to the Cittadella dei Musei, a modern complex converted from an old arsenal, which now houses Cágliari's main museums. The pick of these is the Museo Archeologico (Archeological Museum), where there's plenty of information on the enigmatic Nuraghic culture. This indigenous civilization, traces of which you'll see all over the island, thrived between 1500 and 500 BC. The bronze votive statues depicting warriors, athletes, workers, animals and other subjects are the main source of information about this culture. The nearby Museo Cardu has a collection of Far Eastern art, mainly from Thailand, presented to the city in 1917 by a Cágliari native who worked at the Siamese (Thai) court. More appealing is the small Pinacoteca Nazionale (National Gallery), with Italian paintings dating mainly from the 15th and 16th centuries. Outside the Castello district, head for the church of San Saturnino. Recently restored, this is one of Sardinia's oldest Christian buildings, dating from the fifth century and enlarged in the 11th.

Across town you will find the second-century Anfiteatro Romano (Roman Amphitheater) and the Orto Botanico (Botanical Garden), a lovely green oasis filled with 500 varieties of trees, shrubs and tropical plants.

A mosaic of the Virgin Mary and Jesus decorates the Cathedral of Santa Maria in Cágliari

The old town of Castelsardo clusters around its imposing castle on a rocky promontory

➕ B1

Tourist information ✉ Piazza Matteotti 9 ☎ 070 669 255; www.sardegnaturismo.it or www.regione. sardegna.it 🕐 Mon.–Fri. 8:30–1:30 and 2–8, Sat.–Sun. 8:30–8 (times may vary)

Cattedrale ✉ Piazza Palazzo 4 ☎ 070 663 837; www.duomodicagliari.it 🕐 Mon.–Fri. 7:30–noon and 4–8, Sat.–Sun. 8–1 and 4:30–8:30 💵 Free

Museo Archeologico ✉ Cittadella dei Musei, Piazza Arsenale 1 ☎ 070 655 911 🕐 Tue.–Sun. 9–8 💵 $$

Museo Civico d'Arte Orientale Stefano Cardu ✉ Cittadella dei Musei ☎ 070 651 888 🕐 Tue.–Sun. 9–1 and 4–8, Jun.–Sep.; Tue.–Sun. 9–1 and 3:30–7:30, rest of year 💵 $$

Pinacoteca Nazionale ✉ Cittadella dei Musei ☎ 070 622 496 🕐 Tue.–Sun. 9–8 💵 $

San Saturnino ✉ Piazza San Cosimo ☎ 070 674 054 🕐 Mon.–Sat. 9–1 💵 Free

Orto Botanico ✉ Via Sant'Ignazio da Laconi 9–11 ☎ 070 675 3512 🕐 Daily 8–1:30 and 3–7, Apr.–Oct.; 8–1:30, rest of year 💵 $

Cala Gonone

Cala Gonone lies on one of Sardinia's loveliest stretches of mountainous coastline. This once secluded tiny village on the east coast has plenty of hotels, villas and restaurants. There's still a feeling of seclusion, though, and it's a good place to enjoy the beauty of the area. The macchia shrub-covered white cliffs are pitted with grottoes and sea caves, while tiny secluded coves offer lovely swimming. Boat trips visit the most scenic. Cala Luna and Cala Sisine are good choices, with wonderful views of the deep gorges that cut through the 3,000-foot-high mountains en route. Don't miss a trip to the Grotta del Bue Marino, one of the last refuges of the Mediterranean monk seal. The cave itself, a forest of stalactites and stalagmites, is astonishing.

➕ B2

Tourist information ✉ Viale Bue Marino 1/A ☎ 078 493 696; www.calagonone.com 🕐 Daily 9–7, Jun.–Sep.; 9–1 and 3–7, Apr., May and Oct.; Mon.–Fri. 9–1:30, rest of year

Castelsardo

Castelsardo occupies the hill around the castle built in the 13th and 14th centuries by the Genoese, who founded the town in 1102. Once known as Castelgenovese, the name changed in 1448 to Castelaragonese, after the Spanish conquerors, and then to Castelsardo in 1776.

Visitors come for the handicraft and souvenir shops lining the narrow streets – palm-leaf baskets are the local specialty. You can learn more about this traditional handicraft in the Museo dell'Intreccio (Museum of Wickerwork), which occupies the old castle. It's also worth the climb for the views from the terraces, with Corsica visible on a clear day. The town's Cattedrale (Cathedral) dates from the 17th century; inside you can see the Madonna degli Angeli (Madonna of the Angels), a 15th-century icon created by a local artist. If you're driving, you'll see a strange rock

formation outside town. This is the
Roccia dell'Elefante (Elephant Rock),
a bizarre formation wind-sculpted over
the years into the shape of an elephant.

🔁 A3

Tourist information ✉ Palazzo Eleonora d'Arborea, Via
Bastione 1 ☎ 079 470 220; www.comune.castelsardo.
ss.it 🕐 Mon.–Sat. 8–noon and 3–6, May–Sep.
ℹ The festival Lunissanti is on Easter Mon.

Museo dell'Intreccio ✉ Castello dei Doria, Via
Marconi ☎ 079 471 380 🕐 Daily 9 a.m.–midnight,
Jul.–Aug.; 9:30–1 and 3–9:30, Jun. and Sep.; 9:30–1
and 3–8:30, May; Mon. 9:30–1 and 3–7:30, Tue.–Sun.
9:30–1 and 3–6:30, Mar. and Oct.; Tue.–Sun. 9:30–1
and 3–5:30, rest of year 💶 $

Cattedrale di Sant'Antonio Abate ✉ Via Manganella
🕐 Mon.–Sat. 8–noon and 3–7. Closed Sun. during
services 💶 Free

Costa Smeralda

Until the early 1960s, the northeastern-
most corner of Sardinia was a lonely and
idyllic stretch of undiscovered coast. In
1962 the Consorzio Costa Smeralda
(Emerald Coast Consortium), headed by
the Aga Khan, was formed. Its plan was
to turn the area into the Mediterranean's
most fashionable playground, complete
with luxury hotels, opulent villas,
yachting marinas and excellent sporting
facilities. Money poured in, hotels,
restaurants and designer shops opened,
and the rich followed.

Today, the heart of the Emerald Coast
is Porto Cervo and Porto Rotondo, two
planned villages centered around
marinas, where you'll see some of the
world's most expensive yachts.
Construction is carried out using local
materials, and the buildings combine
different architectural elements found
all over the Mediterranean.

Each village is surrounded by
indigenous trees and draped in cascades
of flowering shrubs. Chic, wealthy and
tasteful, the development perfectly
fulfills its aim, but loses points on charm
and local color. If you plan to stay, it's
easy to fall into the sybaritic life and fill
your day with gentle strolling and
crowd-watching, while swimming and
perfecting your tan.

There's an excellent golf course and
a full summer program of sporting
events. For shoppers, the trendy
boutiques and designer showrooms of
Porto Cervo will be a draw, and there
are plenty of expensive and tempting
bars and restaurants. Not all of this
area is developed, however. You'll find
wonderful beaches and laid-back resorts
farther along the coast at places such as
Santa Teresa Gallura, a small 17th-
century town with an active fishing
fleet, Punta Falcone, Capo Testa and
La Marmorata.

Porto Cervo on the Costa Smeralda is a favorite destination for yacht owners

Off the northern coast lies the archipelago of La Maddalena, a group of about 60 islands with fabulous beaches, now a National Park and whale sanctuary. Giuseppe Garibaldi, who played a key role in Italy's unification, lived for many years on the island of Caprera and is buried there. Maddalena and Caprera are joined by a bridge, and a scenic road runs around Maddalena, with views of the other islands and Corsica to the north.

La Maddalena ✚ B3

Tourist information ✉ Via Principe di Napoli 16
☎ 0789 739 165; www.lamaddalenapark.net
🕐 Daily 8–8, May–Oct.; 9–1, rest of year

Gennargentu

The Monti del Gennargentu (Gennargentu Mountains) lie at the heart of Sardinia's rugged interior in the province of Nuoro. Now preserved within the Parco Nazionale del Gennargentu, the region contains Sardinia's highest peak, Punta La Marmora (6,052 feet), which rises above these lonely and unspoiled uplands. Small towns are located throughout the area; isolated and self-contained, these farming villages are home to generous people whose pattern of life has scarcely changed over hundreds of years. Feast days and festivals with traditional celebrations are the best places to see traditional dress being worn.

Driving is the only way to explore this fascinating area, basing yourself perhaps at Nuoro, an inland city situated on a plateau beneath Monte Ortobene. From here you can easily reach the wilderness park, which offers excellent hiking and is home to such wildlife as pine martens, wild boar, wild sheep (mouflon), griffon vultures and eagles. Bird enthusiasts may spot Sardinian partridges, red woodpeckers and buzzards flying above the strawberry trees and cork oak.

✚ B2

Nuoro tourist information ✉ Piazza Italia 7 ☎ 0784 238 878; www.parks.it or www.provincia.nuoro.it
🕐 Daily 9–7, Jun.–Sep.; Mon.–Fri. 9–1 and 2:30–5:30, rest of year

Giara di Gesturi

Strange basalt plateaus, known as *giare*, are found all over Sardinia. The Giara di Gesturi is one of the largest. It's an extensive plain more than 7 miles across, and its basalt outcrops, covered in maquis and wildflowers, appear amid huge forests of cork oaks. The plateau is home to a tiny native wild horse, once found all over the island.

Marshy areas form after rain, making the Giara a favorite feeding ground in spring for thousands of migratory birds.

Despite the development, quiet corners can still be found on the Costa Smeralda

To the southeast lies Su Nuraxi, the most extensive and oldest Nuraghic complex in Sardinia. Built by the indigenous population around 1500 BC, the site includes a fortress structure surrounded by living areas and defensive walls. It was probably inhabited by the Sards and later the Carthaginians for 2,000 years, until it was covered with earth around the time of the Roman conquest; a rainstorm exposed it in 1949. The excellently preserved buildings include a mill and a bakery.

✚ A2

Tourist information ✉ Piazza Matteotti 9, Cágliari ☎ 070 669 255; www.regione.sardegna.it ◉ Mon.–Fri. 8:30–1:30 and 2–8, Sat.–Sun. 8–8 (times may vary)

Su Nuraxi ✉ Half a mile east of Barumini ☎ 070 936 8128 ◉ Daily 9 a.m.–dusk 🍴 Bar and restaurant nearby 🎫 $$

Nora

Sardinia's most important archeological site is located 25 miles south of Cágliari, close to modern Pula, on a narrow spit of land swelling into the sea.

Nora was founded by the Phoenicians in the eighth century BC and later settled by the Carthaginians before becoming the Roman capital of Sardinia in AD 238. The city was abandoned around the third century, possibly because of some sort of natural disaster. Some parts are now submerged, and you can still see ruins beneath the water, but there are plenty of remains to be seen on dry land. The oldest ruin here is that of the Carthaginian Temple of Astarte.

Roman remains are plentiful; look for the fourth-century baths decorated with mosaics, the theater, the Forum, and the traces of streets and houses. Many finds from the site are in Cágliari's Archeological Museum (see page 190), including a Punic inscription with the first mention of the name "Sardinia;" other finds are in the museum in nearby Pula.

Close by is the Romanesque church of Sant'Efisio, the site of a famous spring

procession from Cágliari. The church backs up to a golden beach with crystal-clear waters; sadly, it can get horribly crowded in summer.

✚ A1

✉ 425 miles south of Cágliari ☎ 070 9200 9610 ◉ Daily 9 a.m.–dusk, Apr.–Oct.; 9–noon and 2–5, rest of year 🎫 $$ (combined ticket with Museo Civico Archeologico) ℹ Festival of Sant'Efisio May 1–4; commemorates the end of the plague in 1656. The saint's statue is carried through the streets of Cágliari, then taken to Nora on a cart drawn by oxen

Museo Civico Archeologico ✉ Corso Vittorio Emanuele II 67, Pula ☎ 070 920 9610 ◉ Tue.–Sun. 9–8, Mar.–Oct.; 9–5:30, rest of year 🎫 $

Porto Conte

Near the Spanish-influenced, old port town of Alghero are a series of beaches collectively known as the Porto Conte. Embraced by two rocky promontories, the beaches are part of the Riviera del Corallo (Coral Riviera). Much of the coral used in the jewelry on display in Alghero originates from here.

The northern promontory, Capo Caccia, rears up above the sea, with stunning views of Alghero to the south. The Capo is best known for the Grotta di Nettuno (Neptune's Grotto), a spectacular sea cave extending for more than a mile. Access is either by boat from Alghero, or by descending 654 steps from the Capo. The steps were built in 1954 and are aptly known as the Escala del Cabriol (Goat's Stairway). The caves, dramatically lit, have narrow corridors hung with stalactites and stalagmites.

The southern promontory of Porto Conte has good beaches and a fine Nuraghi site, the Nuraghi di Palmavera.

✚ A3

Alghero tourist information ✉ Piazza Portaterra 9 ☎ 079 979 054; www.alghero-turismo.it ◉ Mon.– Sat. 8–8, Sun. 10–1

Grotta di Nettuno ✉ Capa Caccia ◉ Daily 9–7, May–Sep.; 9–6, Apr. and Oct.; 9–3, rest of year 🚢 Ferries from Alghero: Linea Grotte Navisarda ☎ 079 950 603 or Line Grotte Attilio Regolo ☎ 368 353 6824 🎫 $$$

The Sardinian Coastline

The waters around Sardinia are among the clearest and cleanest in the Mediterranean, and the beaches attract tens of thousands of visitors who come to relax here and enjoy the sun and sea.

The Beaches

Around the island, beaches range from tiny hidden coves to glorious stretches of golden sands. The Costa Smeralda (Emerald Coast, see page 192) in the northeast is the most famous stretch, its granite cliffs and turquoise sea providing great diving, snorkeling and sailing. To the south, the Golfo di Orosei is a paradise for those seeking peace and quiet. Many of its idyllic coves, backed by limestone cliffs, are accessible only by boat or on foot. Poetto, outside Cágliari, provides a lively contrast. Its 4 miles of beaches are well stocked with restaurants and bars. Close to Piscinas, at Sardinia's southwestern corner, are 6 miles of sand dunes covered with tamarisk trees, juniper and maquis. Some dunes top 165 feet, the highest in Europe. North of here and south of Alghero, are more sandy beaches and clear sea, which give way to the dramatic cliffs to the north and south of Alghero. Windsurfers should head for the northern coast, with its guaranteed steady, strong breezes. Coastal cliffs provide an ideal nesting habitat for bird species. Herring gulls are everywhere, but also look for the rarer Audouin's gull and cormorants fishing from the rocks. It's not just seabirds that flock here: Peregrine falcons and kites also use the cliffs as nesting areas.

The Seas

Sardinia's clear azure waters are the least polluted in Italy, with some areas designated international marine reserves. This makes for wonderful diving into waters rich in flora and fauna. Coral grows from 90 to 300 feet down; the mainly red and white Sardinian coral is used for jewelry making, while the yellow and white gorgonian coral can grow to 3 feet in height. Divers will encounter neptune grass, while rocky crevasses make ideal homes for crustaceans and mollusks. If you're offshore, look for dolphins riding the waves off the northern coast. Sardinia's greatest marine success story is the re-establishment of the monk seal, once thought to be extinct, in the waters of Golfo di Orosei.

Many visitors are drawn to Sardinia purely for the beauty of its coastline

Hotels and Restaurants

Opposite: Cafés across the country make the perfect place for people-watching

Hotels and Restaurants

The hotels and restaurants in this book were selected by local specialists and include establishments in several price ranges. Since price is often the best indication of the level of facilities and quality of service, a three-tiered price guide appears at the beginning of the listings. Because variable rates will affect the amount of foreign currency that can be exchanged for dollars (and thus affect the cost of a room or a meal), price ranges are given in the local currency.

Although price ranges and operating times were accurate at press time, this information is always subject to change without notice. If you're interested in a particular establishment, it is advisable to call ahead to reserve. The larger and more expensive hotels and the better-known restaurants are more likely to have someone who speaks English on the staff, smaller establishments may not. In such cases it may be better to inquire by email rather than phone.

Many hotels are housed in historic properties

Facilities suitable for travelers with disabilities vary greatly, and you are strongly advised to contact an establishment directly to determine whether it will be able to meet your needs. Older buildings may not be adequately designed or equipped for visitors with limited or impaired mobility, although the situation is gradually improving.

Accommodations

Accommodations have been selected with two considerations in mind: a particularly attractive character or sense of local flavor, or a central location that is convenient for sightseeing. Remember that centrally located hotels fill up quickly, especially during busy summer vacation periods; make reservations well in advance. In-room bathrooms (sometimes referred to as "en-suite facilities") may not be available in smaller budget hotels.

Room rates for European hotels normally include a light breakfast of rolls or croissants and coffee (where this is not the case, the listing description notes that the rate is for "room only"). Some hotels offer a price for overnight accommodations that also includes an evening meal.

Eating Out

Listed restaurants range from upscale places suitable for an elegant evening out to small cafés where you can stop and take a leisurely break from a busy day of sightseeing. Some are close to attractions; where this is the case, there is a cross-reference under the attraction listing. Other possibilities for getting a bite to eat are the cafeterias and restaurants on the premises of museums and galleries.

In Italy, the different types of restaurants can be confusing. The terms *ristorante*, *osteria* and *trattoria* are on the whole fairly interchangable; *tavola calda* and *pizzeria* imply something a bit more humble.

KEY TO SYMBOLS

⊞	hotel
⊪	restaurant
⊠	address
☎	telephone number
⊘	days/times closed
⊜	nearest subway/mainline train station(s)
⊟	nearest bus/trolley-bus/tram route(s)
⊑	ferry
AX	American Express
CB	Carte Blanche
DC	Diners Club
MC	MasterCard
VI	VISA

Hotels
Price guide: double room with breakfast for two people
$ up to €115
$$ €115–€225
$$$ over €225

Restaurants
Price guide: dinner per person, excluding drinks
$ up to €30
$$ €30–€55
$$$ over €55

Room for Two

Italian hotels charge for the room, not for each person. The price, by law, is displayed on the back of the room door and may vary according to the season *(alta/bassa stagione)*. It may or may not include breakfast. Double beds are far more common than singles; they are generally queen or king size. Single rooms are generally in short supply and cost far more than half that of a double; you are paying for privacy, not space. Many hotels will put another bed in a double room if you request it; the charge for this must also be displayed.

ALBA

⊞ I Castelli $–$$
This modern, concrete and glass hotel has comfortable rooms, a gym and an excellent restaurant.
⊠ Corso Torino 14/1 ☎ 0173 361 978 AX, CB, DC, MC, VI

⊪ La Libera $$
The accent at this central restaurant is on local ingredients. Specialties include rabbit, homemade pasta and delicate pastry desserts.
⊠ Via Pertinace 24/A ☎ 0173 293 155 ⊘ Closed Mon. lunch and Sun. AX, DC, VI

AOSTA

⊞ Europe $$
Room prices vary widely at this traditional hotel, a few minutes' stroll from everything. The elegant rooms are quiet and comfortable.
⊠ Piazza Narbonne 8 ☎ 0165 236 363 AX, CB, DC, MC, VI

⊪ Vecchio Ristoro $$$
Once an old mill, this rustic-elegant restaurant offers a good range of seasonal local dishes. Try the *polenta* as a side dish or the delicious mushrooms if you're here in the fall.
⊠ Via Tourneuve 41 ☎ 0165 33 238 ⊘ Closed Sun. lunch, Mon. lunch and some weeks in Jun. and Nov. AX, DC, MC, VI

ASTI

⊪ Gener Neuv $$$
A well-established Asti institution where you're sure of a friendly welcome. Sample traditional dishes made with the freshest local ingredients. The decor is elegant yet rustic and the wine list formidable.
⊠ Lungo Tanaro dei Pescatori 4 ☎ 0141 557 270 ⊘ Closed Sun. dinner, Mon. and 3 weeks in Aug. AX, CB, DC, VI

⊞ Reale $
Next to the venue for Asti's Palio, this hotel is a favorite, with well-appointed rooms and friendly staff.
⊠ Piazza Alfieri 6 ☎ 0141 530 240 AX, CB, DC, MC, VI

BERGAMO

⊞ La Valletta $–$$
A pretty villa houses this intimate hotel set amid trees and meadows.
Rooms are comfortable with excellent bathrooms. Enjoy breakfast on the terrace.
⊠ Via Castagneta 19 ☎ 0352 42746 DC, MC, VI

⊪ Taverna del Colleoni-dell'Angelo $$–$$$
Housed in one of Bergamo's loveliest palaces, this is the place to enjoy sophisticated cooking. Choices include sturgeon, truffles and mushrooms in season, fabulous desserts and a great wine list. Tables outside for summer alfresco dining.
⊠ Piazza Vecchia 7 ☎ 035 232 596 ⊘ Closed Mon. and 2 weeks in Aug. AX, CB, DC, MC, VI

BOLOGNA

⊞ Al Cappello Rosso $$
This hotel has been in business since the 14th century and still offers a warm welcome, traditional service, and modern comfort and facilities. It's situated in the historic center.
⊠ Via de' Fusari 9 ☎ 051 261 891 AX, CB, DC, MC, VI

⊪ Pappagallo $$–$$$
You'll find classic Bolognese cooking at this restaurant in the heart of the old city. Housed in a 14th-century palazzo, the decor and service complement the food.
⊠ Piazza Mercanzia 3 ☎ 051 231 200 ⊘ Closed Sun., Sat. in Jul., and Aug. AX, CB, DC, MC, VI

COMO

⊪ Osteria l'Angolo del Silenzio $$
One of the oldest buildings in Como houses this pleasant restaurant offering good local cooking based on fish, mushrooms and game when in season. There's a good wine list.
⊠ Viale Lecco 25, Como ☎ 031 337 2157 ⊘ Closed Mon., Tue. lunch and 2 weeks in Jan. and Aug. AX, CB, DC, MC, VI

⊞ Terminus $$–$$$
This renovated lakeside hotel dates from the 19th century. Rooms with a view are preferable, but all are comfortable. Family run, and the restaurant is good.
⊠ Lungolario Trieste 14 ☎ 031 329 111 AX, DC, MC, VI

CREMONA

⊞ Delle Arti $$
Bedrooms in this high-tech designer hotel are large and comfortable and

KEY TO SYMBOLS

🏨	hotel
🍴	restaurant
✉	address
☎	telephone number
🕐	days/times closed
Ⓜ	nearest subway/mainline train station(s)
🚌	nearest bus/trolley-bus/tram route(s)
⛴	ferry
AX	American Express
CB	Carte Blanche
DC	Diners Club
MC	MasterCard
VI	VISA

Hotels

Price guide: double room with breakfast for two people

$ up to €115
$$ €115–€225
$$$ over €225

Restaurants

Price guide: dinner per person, excluding drinks

$ up to €30
$$ €30–€55
$$$ over €55

Wine and Water

Wine and water are the normal accompaniments to Italian meals, except with pizza, which calls for beer. Water is bottled mineral water, *aqua minerale*, and comes with bubbles, *gassata* or still, *naturale*; it is not expensive. The wine list in cheaper and mid-price restaurants normally has a reasonable selection of local wines, but it's rare to find wine from other Italian areas, let alone foreign wines. All establishments have both red and white carafe wine, *vino della casa*. This may be ordered in one-quarter, one-half or one-liter pitchers. You can order Coke and other soft drinks, although restaurants do not serve milk.

---

the emphasis is on clutter-free style and subdued lighting. The dining room is a showcase for modern and contemporary art. There is a pleasant garden courtyard, sauna, Turkish bath, Jacuzzi and gym.
✉ Via Bonomelli 8 ☎ 037 223 131 🕐 Closed Aug. and Dec. 23–31 AX, CB, DC, MC, VI

🍴 Osteria la Sosta $$

A welcoming restaurant that specializes in local dishes – don't miss the *mostarda di cremona*, the sweet mustard-spiked fruit that accompanies meat here.
✉ Via Sicardo 9 ☎ 0372 456 656 🕐 Closed Sun. evening, Mon. and 1 week in Feb. and 2 weeks in Aug. AX, CB, DC, MC, VI

FERRARA

🍴 Antica Trattoria il Cucco $

You'll find well-priced, seasonal, regional cooking here. Homemade pasta dishes, such as tagliatelle with prosciutto and peas *(piselli)* or pumpkin *(zucca)* ravioli are featured. Don't miss the *spumone*, a local ice-cream specialty for dessert.
✉ Via Volta Casotto 3 ☎ 053 276 0026 MC, VI

🏨 Ripa Grande $ $$

Housed in a Renaissance palazzo, the public rooms in this hotel are furnished with antiques and feature marble columns and tapestries. Bedrooms are more 21st-century, with Jacuzzi baths, wood flooring and elegant comfort. The restaurant is separately run.
✉ Via Ripa Grande 21 ☎ 053 276 5250 AX, DC, MC

GARDA

🏨 Gabbiano $

This excellent-value hotel overlooks the lake. Each comfortable room has a balcony, making it a superb summer choice for visitors who want to stay for three or more nights (minimum three nights).
✉ Via dei Cipressi 24 ☎ 0457 256 655 🕐 Closed Oct.–Mar. CB, MC, VI

🏨 Hotel du Lac e du Parc $$

This large hotel stands out among Lake Garda's numerous options for its park setting and a wide range of recreational options, including pool, sauna and tennis courts. Rooms are on a half-board basis, usually with a minimum three-night stay.

✉ Viale Rovereto 44 ☎ 0464 566 600 🕐 Closed Nov.–Mar. AX, CB, DC, MC, VI

GENOA

🏨 City Hotel $$–$$$

This modern hotel located in the heart of the city has pleasant bedrooms and good public rooms. It's popular with business people as a venue for meetings, so reservations are recommended.
✉ Via S. Sebastiano 6 ☎ 010 584 707 AX, CB, DC, MC, VI

🍴 Rina $$

Genoa's oldest established restaurant continues to please diners with fresh fish and other high-quality Ligurian dishes. The surroundings are pleasing and the service excellent.
✉ Mura delle Grazie 3/r ☎ 010 246 6475 🕐 Closed Mon. and Aug. AX, CB, DC, MC, VI

LEVANTO (CINQUE TERRE)

🍴 La Loggia $$

Conveniently located in the center of this coastal town, attractive La Loggia offers excellent seafood dishes and traditional northern Italian cuisine.
✉ Piazza del Popolo 7 ☎ 0187 808 107 🕐 Closed Wed. (except Jul.–Sep.) and mid-Feb. to mid-Mar. AX, DC, MC, VI

🏨 Stella Maris $$

This pretty hotel not far from the sea is housed in an 18th-century palazzo. The dining room and some bedrooms have frescoed ceilings and antique furniture. You can relax in the attractive garden.
✉ Via Marconi 4 ☎ 0187 808 258 🕐 Closed Feb. and Nov. AX, MC, VI

MANTOVA

🍴 Aquila Nigra $$$

A dining experience in this old palace with frescoed ceilings will be truly memorable. You can enjoy traditional dishes, which vary as the seasons change. Good wine list and professional service.
✉ Vicolo Bonacolsi 4 ☎ 0376 327 180 🕐 Closed Sun.–Mon. and some weeks in Aug.; open Sun. lunch Apr.–May, Sep.–Oct. CB, DC, MC, VI

🏨 Rechigi $$

At the heart of the old city, south of the church of Sant'Andrea. The rooms are elegant and the public spaces are hug with an interesting collection of modern art.

✉ Via Calvi 30 ☎ 0376 320 781 AX, DC, MC, VI

MILAN
🏠 Antica Locanda Leonardo $$
Set in a 19th-century building, this family-run hotel is close to Santa Maria delle Grazie. Rooms are comfortable and attractively decorated with antique furniture. There is a very pretty courtyard garden where breakfast is served.

✉ Corso Magenta 78 ☎ 02 4801 4197 ⓒ Conciliazione AX, DC, MC, VI

🏠 Lloyd $$
Located in the heart of the city and a short walk from the cathedral, this hotel has comfortable rooms kitted out with every convenience.

✉ Corso di Porta Romana 48 ☎ 02 5830 3332 ⓒ Closed 2 weeks in Aug., Dec. 22–Jan. 6 ⓒ Crocceta, Missori AX, CB, DC, MC, VI

🍴 Il Luogo di Aimo e Nadia $$$
One of the city's best restaurants where you can enjoy the finest of classic Milanese cuisine, using the best ingredients in dishes such as almond-crusted rack of lamb and veal tartare with tomatoes and ginger. Creativity, style and flavor are complemented with impeccable service, elegant surroundings and a superb wine list.

✉ Via Montecuccoli 6 ☎ 02 416 886 ⓒ Closed Sat. lunch, Sun., 3 weeks in Aug. and Jan. 1–7 ⓒ Bande Nere AX, CB, DC, MC, VI

🏠 Mennini $–$$
This central hotel, near the station, is primarily aimed at business travelers, but is worth considering for its clean-lined, understated rooms, complete with WiFi, and is excellent value for the money in this expensive city. You can expect a good breakfast buffet.

✉ Via Napo Torriani 14 ☎ 02 6690 951 ⓒ Closed Aug. and last week Dec. ⓒ Centrale F.S. AX, DC, VI

🍴 Al Mercante $$
A friendly atmosphere pervades this contemporary Milanese restaurant in a medieval square. Dine alfresco here in the summer.

✉ Piazza Mercanti 17 ☎ 02 805 2198 ⓒ Closed Sun. AX, DC, MC, VI

🍴 Savini $$$
This huge, bustling bistro (and more formal restaurant upstairs) is a Milanese institution, always busy and convivial. Rich in atmosphere and tradition, the food covers northern cooking at its best. Try the fixed-price menu for excellent value.

✉ Galleria Vittorio Emanuele II ☎ 02 7200 3433 ⓒ Bistro open daily. Restaurant closed Sat. lunch, Sun., 3 weeks in Aug. and Jan. 1–6 ⓒ Duomo AX, CB, DC, MC, VI

MODENA
🍴 Cucina del Museo $$
This pleasing restaurant, near the cathedral, offers both traditional Modenese and contemporary cuisine. Old favorites such as pumpkin ravioli and tortellini with butter and sage feature beside modern versions of classic dishes.

✉ Via Sant'Agostino 7 ☎ 059 217 4294 ⓒ Sun. p.m. and Mon., Aug., one week Dec. AX, DC, VI

🏠 Hotel Libertà $$
This is mainly a hotel for business people, but its location, moments from the Palazzo Ducale, also makes it an excellent base for sightseeing.

✉ Via Blasia 10 ☎ 059 222 365 AX, DC, MC, VI

MONTEROSSO
🏠 La Colonnina $$
There are beautiful views over the sea from the terraces and garden of this family-run hotel, which has spacious bedrooms and comfortable public areas. It does not have an onsite dining room.

✉ Via Zuecca 6 ☎ 0187 817 439 ⓒ Closed Dec.–Feb. AX, CB, DC, VI

🍴 Miky $$
This friendly, lively restaurant offers everything you'd expect – good pasta dishes, fresh fish, traditional specialties and pizza, which you can enjoy outside on a terrace overlooking the sea.

✉ Via Fegina 104 ☎ 0187 817 608 ⓒ Closed Tue. (except for a period in Aug.) and mid-Nov. to mid-Mar. AX, CB, MC, VI

PARMA
🍴 Al Tramezzo $$
Chef Alberto Rosselli is passionate about seasonal ingredients and this is reflected in the dishes served here. Parma's famous prosciutto, *capocollo*

and cheese are featured as well as a wonderful range of plates inspired by the area. Excellent wine list.

✉ Via del Bono 5\B ☎ 0521 487 906 ⓒ Closed Sun. and 2 weeks Jul. AX, CB, DC, MC, VI

🏠 Verdi $$
Parma's high standard of living is reflected in this elegant hotel overlooking the Parco Ducale. You'll be looked after impeccably. The building dates from the 19th century.

✉ Via Pasini 18 ☎ 0521 293 539 ⓒ Closed 2 weeks in Jul. and Dec. 23–Jan. 6 AX, CB, DC, MC, VI

PAVIA
🍴 Locanda Vecchia Pavia $$$
In a renovated mill, this restaurant continues to offer excellent traditional cuisine with creative variations. Reservations essential.

✉ Via al Monumento 5, Certosa di Pavia ☎ 0382 925 894 ⓒ Closed Mon., Tue. lunch, Apr.–Oct.; Sun. eve and Mon. Nov.–Mar.; Jan. 1–22 and Aug. 5–27 AX, CB, DC, MC, VI

🏠 Moderno $$
The four-star Moderno is Pavia's top hotel, but lies a little to the east of the historic center near the railroad station. Rooms are comfortable, if a little functional. The hotel restaurant, Bistrot Bartolini, offers a good range of local specialties.

✉ Viale Vittorio Emanuele 41 ☎ 0382 303 401 ⓒ Closed 2 weeks in Aug., 1 week Dec. AX, DC, MC, VI

PIACENZA
🍴 Antica Osteria del Teatro $$$
Food guides rate this among the top restaurants in Italy, an elegant place housed in a 15th-century palazzo. The menu has sophisticated interpretations of classic Emilian cooking and international dishes; service is attentive and professional.

✉ Via Verdi 16 ☎ 0523 323 777 ⓒ Closed Sun.–Mon., Jan. 1–10 and 3 weeks in Aug. AX, CB, DC, MC, VI

🏠 Grande Albergo Roma $$
Though aimed at business travelers, this newly renovated hotel has character, with well decorated bedrooms (all with WiFi) and the staff is welcoming. There is a fitness center and a good restaurant.

✉ Via Cittadella 14 ☎ 0523 323 201 AX, DC, MC, VI

KEY TO SYMBOLS

🏨	hotel
🍴	restaurant
✉	address
☎	telephone number
⊘	days/times closed
Ⓜ	nearest subway/mainline train station(s)
🚌	nearest bus/trolley-bus/tram route(s)
⛴	ferry
AX	American Express
CB	Carte Blanche
DC	Diners Club
MC	MasterCard
VI	VISA

Hotels
Price guide: double room with breakfast for two people
$ up to €115
$$ €115–€225
$$$ over €225

Restaurants
Price guide: dinner per person, excluding drinks
$ up to €30
$$ €30–€55
$$$ over €55

Showers or Tubs

Unless your hotel is extremely simple, there will be a private bathroom. It will contain a sink, flush toilet, bidet and bathtub or shower. In much of Italy, showers are far more common than tubs, due to the scarcity and expense of water. Italian showers are often not enclosed in stalls; instead, water drains directly through a hole in the center of the room. Water pressure is far below that in the United States. You will notice a cord in the bathroom; this is a legal requirement for emergencies and summons help when pulled.

PORTOFINO
🏨 Piccolo $$$
This charming hotel has access to a private beach. The pretty rooms have balconies facing the sea.
✉ Via Duca degli Abruzzi 31
☎ 0185 269 015 ⊘ Closed Nov.–Mar. AX, CB, DC, MC, VI

RAVENNA
🍴 Antica Trattoria al Gallo $$
You'll enjoy the uncomplicated excellence of the well-presented dishes here. The emphasis is on fresh local products, with vegetarian choices and a good wine list.
✉ Via Maggiore 87 ☎ 0544 213 775
⊘ Closed Sun. evening, Mon.–Tue., Easter and Dec. 20–Jan. 10 AX, CB, DC, MC, VI

🏨 Centrale Byron $
This good-value hotel is housed in an old palace only a short stroll from the heart of historic Ravenna and the main sights. The rooms have been modernized but still have a slightly faded old-fashioned appeal.
✉ Via IV Novembre 14
☎ 0544 212 225 ⊘ Closed during Christmas period AX, CB, DC, MC, VI

RIMINI
🏨 Ambasciatori $$ $$$
Room prices vary tremendously at this midsize hotel a few hundred yards from the sea. It has a pool, access to a private beach and a rooftop terrace.
✉ Viale Vespucci 22 ☎ 0541 55 561
AX, CB, DC, MC, VI

🍴 Osteria de Börg $$
This welcoming, rustic restaurant is in the old fishing quarter in Borg San Giuliano. Specialties include grilled meats and large platters of local salamis and cheeses. Pasta dishes are also very good. In warm weather there are tables outside. It's best to make a reservation.
✉ Via Forzieri 12 ☎ 0541 56 074
⊘ Closed lunch Jun.–Aug.
AX, MC, VI

STRESA
🏨 Astoria $$
This family-run hotel beside the lake has modern rooms, a pool and a pleasant terrace restaurant for summer dining.
✉ Corso Umberto 1° 31 ☎ 0323 32 566 ⊘ Closed mid-Oct. to Mar. 31
AX, CB, DC, MC, VI

🍴 Piemontese $$
A pretty and friendly restaurant with a pergola in the garden for summer dining. Sample the wide range of dishes on the *menú degustazione*. There is also a very good wine list.
✉ Via Mazzini 25 ☎ 0323 30 235
⊘ Closed Mon., and Dec.–Jan.
AX, CB, MC, VI

TURIN
🏨 Hotel Victoria $$–$$$
The rooms in this English country house-style hotel are spacious, all individually designed. There is a pleasant conservatory-style room for breakfast – or, in summer guests can sit in the garden under the gazebo.
✉ Via Nino Costa 4 ☎ 011 561 1909
AX, CB, DC, MC, VI

🍴 Sotto la Mole $$
This welcoming restaurant puts the accent both on local dishes and the Slow Food movement, where cooking is seasonal, regional and often uses organic produce. Local specialties such as artichoke flan or warm rabbit salad with nuts might be followed by chateaubriand steak or *osso buco* (oxtail with vegetables and rice).
✉ Via Montebello 9 ☎ 011 817 9398 ⊘ Closed Mon. and 2 weeks Jan. AX, CD, DC, MC, VI

AQUILEIA
🍴 Colombara $$
This restaurant, popular with local business people, is a good place to find local dishes, with the emphasis on fish. Its two dining rooms are classically styled and comfortable.
✉ Via S. Zilli 42 ☎ 0431 91513
⊘ Closed Mon. AX, CB, DC, MC, VI

🏨 Patriarchi $
This simple but comfortable hotel will give you a warm welcome and a real sense of personal service. There is also a good restaurant.
✉ Via Giulia Augusta 12 ☎ 0431 919 595 ⊘ Closed 2 weeks in Feb.
AX, CB, DC, MC, VI

ASOLO
🍴 Locanda Baggio $$
The accent is on fish in this pretty restaurant. You'll find Venetian specialties such as winter *radicchio di Treviso*, *pasta alle seppie* (black spaghetti with cuttle-fish ink) and *pasta e fagioli* (bean and pasta soup).

✉ Via Bassane 1 ☎ 0423 529 648
🕐 Closed Mon. and Tue. lunch
CB, DC, MC, VI

🏨 Villa Cipriani $$$
This world-class hotel is housed in a
16th-century villa with hill views.
Guests are cosmopolitan and often
famous, and the level of service
superb. The restaurant is almost as
famous as the hotel for local dishes
and Mediterranean cuisine.
✉ Via Canova 298 ☎ 0423 523 411
AX, CB, DC, MC, VI

BOLZANO
🏨 Greif $$–$$$
This historic central hotel has been
restored and retains several fine
period features alongside 33
redesigned rooms that vary between
modern and traditional in style.
Non-smoking rooms are available.
✉ Piazza Walther ☎ 047 131 8000
AX, DC, DC, MC, VI

🍴 Vögele $–$$
A series of cozy yet elegant rooms
makes up this traditional family-run
restaurant serving the best of
regional specialties. Try home-cured
speck (air-dried seasoned beef),
different types of *canederli*
(dumplings) and fine mountain
cheeses – food that's closer to
Austrian than Italian cuisine.
✉ Via Goethe 3 ☎ 047 197 3938
🕐 Closed Sun., Public Holidays
MC, VI

CIVIDALE DEL FRIULI
🏨 Locanda al Castello $$
The lovely Locanda al Castello was
converted from a convent. Verdant
grounds and superb views make up
for its location just outside the town.
There is an excellent restaurant.
✉ Via del Castello 12 ☎ 0432 733
242 🕐 Restaurant closed Wed.
AX, CB, DC, MC, VI

🍴 Osteria alla Terrazza $
This small family-owned trattoria in
the heart of town, has a great
atmosphere and a offers a good
choice of local dishes.
✉ Stretta C. Gallo 3 ☎ 0432 700 288
🕐 Closed Wed. MC, VI

MERANO
🏨 Meranerhof $$–$$$
This hotel opposite the thermal baths
has been run by the same family for
40 years. They pride themselves on

their welcome to regulars, families
and international visitors. There's a
garden with a heated pool.
✉ Via Manzoni 1 ☎ 0473 230 230
🕐 Closed mid-Jan. to mid-Mar.
AX, CB, DC, MC, VI

🍴 Sissi $$$
Chef Andrea Fenoglio's restaurant is
deservedly very popular. Signature
dishes include *anguilla affumicata e
mela Golden* (smoked eel with apple)
and *cappello del prete di vitello con
salsa al tartufo nero* (veal with black
truffles). There's an extensive wine
list. Reservations are essential.
✉ Via Gallilei 44 ☎ 0473 231 062
🕐 Closed Mon., Tue. lunch, 3 weeks
between Feb. and Mar. AX, MC, VI

PADUA
🍴 Antico Brolo $$
A 15th-century building houses this
elegant restaurant, serving
interesting local dishes with an
accent on fish. The wine cellar
houses a lively pizzeria, and there's
a pretty garden for outside dining.
✉ Corso Milano 22 ☎ 049 664 555
🕐 Closed Mon. lunch, 2 weeks in
Aug. AX, CB, MC, VI

🏨 Methis $$
The decor of each floor of this
boutique-style hotel is linked to one
of the elements – earth, air, fire and
water. Guest rooms are minimalist
and comfortable while the public
areas are elegantly contemporary.
There's a roof terrace with excellent
city views.
✉ Riviera Paleocapa 70 ☎ 049 8725
555 AX, DC, MC, VI

TREVISO
🍴 Antica Torre $$
In the heart of the *centro storico* in a
13th-century tower, this pleasant
restaurant serves up local dishes;
choices include risotto with scampi
and radicchio or a plate of cooked
and raw local ham. There is a good
wine list.
✉ Via Inferiore 55 ☎ 0422 583 694
🕐 Closed Sun., Mon. p.m., 2 weeks in
Jan. and 2 weeks in Aug. MC, VI

🏨 Carlton $$
This renovated hotel at the old city
walls has good-size rooms, pleasant
modern decor, ample bathrooms and
efficient service.
✉ Largo Porta Altinia 15 ☎ 0422
411 661 AX, CB, DC, MC, VI

TRIESTE
🍴 Antica Trattoria Suban $$
Founded in 1865, this restaurant is
still run by the Suban family, who
take the art of Trieste's central
European cooking style to great
heights with old recipes and
traditional flavors.
✉ Via Comici 2/d ☎ 040 54 368
🕐 Closed lunch, Mon.–Fri. all Tue.,
1 week in Jan. and 1 week in Aug.
AX, CB, DC, MC, VI

🏨 Grand Hotel Duchi d'Aosta $$–$$$
The style and atmosphere of this
well-run hotel exude restrained
elegance with modern comforts.
There is also the Thermarium
Magnum spa/wellness center.
✉ Piazza Unità d'Italia 2 ☎ 040 760
0011 AX, CB, DC, MC, VI

VENICE
🍴 Acquapazza $$
The outside tables at this reliable
restaurant, where the accent is firmly
on fish, sit on one of San Marco's
nicer *campi*. Starters include prawns
and rocket with a balsamic dressing,
a lemon-drizzle seafood platter and
fresh anchovies; follow with the
day's special catch or a fish risotto.
They also serve good, crisp pizza.
✉ Campo Sant'Angelo, 3808 San
Marco ☎ 041 277 0688 🕐 Closed
Mon. and Jan. 📅 1 AX, MC, VI

🏨 Ai Due Fanali $–$$
On a tranquil *campo* that overlooks
the Grand Canal, many of this
comfortable hotel's rooms have canal
views. Rooms are traditionally
furnished, and some are rather small,
though details include terra-cotta
and marble bathrooms. There's a roof
terrace for summer breakfasts.
✉ Campo San Simeon Grande, 946
Santa Croce ☎ 041 18 490 📅 1
AX, DC, MC, VI

🍴 Antiche Carampane $$$
This off-the-beaten-track restaurant
specializes in elegantly cooked and
served seafood and fish. The style is
a modern take on tradition, at its
best in dishes such as *spaghetti alla
granseola* (pasta with spider crab),
cassopipa (spaghetti with a spicy fish
sauce) or *branzino in salsa di peperoni*
(sea bass in a sweet pepper sauce).
✉ Ponte delle Tette, 1911 San Polo
☎ 041 524 0165 🕐 Closed Sun. and
Mon. lunch 📅 1, 2 AX, DC, MC, VI

KEY TO SYMBOLS

- 🏨 hotel
- 🍴 restaurant
- ✉ address
- ☎ telephone number
- ⊘ days/times closed
- Ⓜ nearest subway/mainline train station(s)
- 🚌 nearest bus/trolley-bus/tram route(s)
- ⛴ ferry
- AX American Express
- CB Carte Blanche
- DC Diners Club
- MC MasterCard
- VI VISA

Hotels
Price guide: double room with breakfast for two people
- $ up to €115
- $$ €115–€225
- $$$ over €225

Restaurants
Price guide: dinner per person, excluding drinks
- $ up to €30
- $$ €30–€55
- $$$ over €55

Coffee

Italian coffee, *caffè*, comes freshly made and very, very strong. It is perceived as a stimulant, not a drink, hence the tiny cups less than half full – a shot in the arm. For breakfast it is drunk with milk, either as a *cappuccino* or *caffè latte*. For the rest of the day, Italians drink an espresso, known in Italy as *un caffè*. It may have a drop of milk to make it *macchiato* (stained) or a shot of liquor for an extra kick, *caffè corretto*. Decaffeinated coffee is *caffè Hag*. To get anything remotely approaching American coffee, ask for *un caffè americano*, which will be weak and watery.

🍴 Bancogiro $$

Housed in a 16th-century building by the Rialto market, the Bancogiro is a laidback and welcoming restaurant that doubles as a bar serving *ciccheti*, Venetian snacks. The menu relies on local, seasonal ingredients prepared with a modern twist by chef Jacopo Scarso. The brick-vaulted interior is understated and elegant, the outside tables, beside the Grand Canal, make it one of Venice's best dining spots.
✉ Campo San Giacometto, 1220 San Polo ☎ 041 523 2061 ⛴ 1, 2 AX, DC, MC, VI

🏨 Ca' Maria Adele $$$

This hotel is the ultimate in taste and luxury. Its themed rooms are dripping in Murano glass and the trappings of luxury, while the unthemed rooms are elegantly decorated in sandy cream-colored brocades. The Moroccan-style roof terrace is perfect for chilling out over a glass of *prosecco*.
✉ Rio Terà di Catecumeni. Dorsoduro 111 ☎ 041 520 3078 ⛴ 1 AX, CB, DC, MC, VI

🏨 Locanda Antico Doge $$

This elegant palazzo hotel once belonged to the 14th-century Doge Marin Falier. The bedrooms are richly decorated with silk, brocades, damasks and gilt mirrors and almost all have views of the Canal Grande. The breakfast room is equally grand.
✉ Cannaregio 5643 ☎ 041 241 1570/74 ⛴ 1 AX, DC, MC, VI

🏨 Palazzo Stern $$–$$$

For a room with a view, check into the Stern. Outside, the breakfast terrace is set right on the water; inside, the interior has been restored to its extraordinary 19th-century Gothic-Moorish appearance. There's a rooftop Jacuzzi and charming public areas.
✉ Calle del Traghetto, 2792/A Dorsoduro ☎ 041 277 0869 ⛴ Ca'Rezzonico 1 AX, DC, MC, VI

🍴 Trattoria de Forni $$

More upscale than the name suggests, this historic "elegant-rustic" restaurant specializes in Venetian and classic Italian cuisine. Fish and shellfish feature – seafood risotto is a signature dish. You'll also find locally sourced meats as well as Venetian vegetable *pasticcio* (lasagne) and other excellent dishes.

✉ Calle dei Specchieri, San Marco 457/468 ☎ 041 523 2148 ⛴ 1 AX, DC, MC, VI

VERONA
🍴 Il Desco $$$

Verona's best restaurant has superb service, comfort, antique decor, a good wine list and attention to detail. The cooking is light and creative, using the best seasonal ingredients.
✉ Via Dietro S. Sebastiano 7 ☎ 045 595 358 ⊘ Closed Sun. and Mon., but open Mon. dinner Jul.–Aug. and Dec.; also closed Christmas to mid-Jan. and 2 weeks in Jun. AX, CB, DC, MC, VI

🏨 Torcolo $–$$

This is one of the most popular hotels in Verona, so make reservations. It's close to the Arena.
✉ Vicolo Listone 3 ☎ 045 800 7512 ⊘ Closed 2 weeks in Feb. AX, CB, MC, VI

VICENZA
🏨 Campo Marzio $$

Many of Vicenza's more comfortable hotels are outside the center; this is an exception, with good modern rooms and facilities and within an easy stroll of the cathedral.
✉ Viale Roma 21 ☎ 0444 545 700 AX, CB, DC, MC, VI

🍴 Tre Visi Vecchio Roma $$

It's worth eating here for the series of beautifully furnished 15th-century dining rooms alone. The food is local, with game, mushrooms and mouth-watering desserts.
✉ Corso Palladio 25 ☎ 0444 324 868 ⊘ Closed Sun. evening, Mon. and late Jan.–early Feb. AX, CB, DC, MC, VI

TUSCANY, UMBRIA AND THE MARCHE

AREZZO
🍴 Buca di San Francesco $$

Housed in a 14th-century palazzo with original Etruscan paving, this great restaurant follows three rules in its cooking – simplicity, flavor and fresh ingredients.
✉ Via San Francesco 1 ☎ 0575 23 271 ⊘ Closed Mon. p.m., Tue. and 2 weeks in Jul. AX, CB, DC, MC, VI

🏨 Continentale $–$$

This spacious and comfortable hotel is at the foot of the old center of

Arezzo. It has well-furnished rooms and a friendly, professional staff.
✉ Piazza Guido Monaco 7 ☎ 0575 20 251 AX, CB, DC, MC, VI

ASCOLI PICENO
🍴 Del Corso $$
Excellent value and local dishes are offered in this restaurant in the historic center. Housed in an ancient palazzo, the attractive dining room has stone walls and vaulted ceilings.
✉ Corso Mazzini 277 ☎ 0736 256 760 ◐ Closed Sun. dinner, Mon., week after Easter and mid-Aug. to early Sep. MC, VI

🏨 Palazzo Guidorocchi $–$$
This lovely 16th-century palazzo, set around an inner courtyard, has frescoed ceilings and big, comfortable rooms where 21st-century comfort goes hand in hand with traditional decor. The good restaurant is under separate management.
✉ Via Cesare Battisti 3 ☎ 0736 259 710 AX, DC, MC, VI

ASSISI
🏨 Albergo del Viaggiatore $
This little hotel is in the heart of Assisi's historic center. Step in from the street to a pretty reception area and a friendly welcome, before finding yourself in a room, which may be on the small side, with a rooftop view. Excellent value.
✉ Via Sant'Antonio 14 ☎ 075 816 297 AX, DC, MC, VI

🍴 Buca di San Francesco $$
Enjoy some of Assisi's most delicious pasta dishes and a wide variety of other local specialties in this excellent restaurant in a medieval building in the center of town.
✉ Via E. Brizi 1 ☎ 075 812 204 ◐ Closed Mon. and a period in Jul.
AX, CB, DC, MC, VI

FLORENCE
🏨 Brunelleschi $$$
Reserve ahead to stay in this comfortable hotel in the heart of Florence. A real sense of tradition and history.
✉ Piazza Sta. Elisabetta 3 ☎ 055 27 370 🚋 In the pedestrian zone; electric bus C2, C3 AX, CB, DC, MC, VI

🏨 Cestelli $
About two minutes' walk from the Ponte Vecchio this friendly little

place is one of the best deals in Florence, with immaculate rooms (five of the eight have bathrooms), and touches such as pretty chandeliers and pleasing fabrics. The owners strive to make your stay pleasant, making it a great deal. It's popular so book ahead.
✉ Borgo Ss Apostoli 25 ☎ 055 214 213 🚋 C1, C2 AX, MC

🍴 Enoteca Pinchiorri $$$
Considered one of the top five restaurants in Italy, this establishment is set in a 16th-century palazzo with a garden for summer dining. It serves outstanding and imaginative food, and the wine list includes some of the world's rarest.
✉ Via Ghibellina 87 ☎ 055 242 777 ◐ Closed Sun.–Mon., Tue.–Wed. lunch, and Aug. 🚋 14, 23 AX, CB, DC, MC, VI

🏨 Palazzo del Borgo Aprile $$
A peaceful hotel housed in a Medici palace with a quiet garden. The rooms have frescoed ceilings, old paintings and every modern amenity.
✉ Via della Scala 6 ☎ 055 216 237 🚋 All routes to Santa Maria Novella
AX, CB, MC, VI

🏨 Relais Santa Croce $$$
This elegant hotel blends tradition with cutting-edge design. Opulent furnishings, frescoed ceilings, Murano chandeliers and marbled walls feature in rooms that are all individually designed. Next door is Florence's only 3 Michelin-starred restaurant, the Enoteca Pinchiorri. The hotel restaurant offers innovative, seasonal regional menus.
✉ Via Ghibellina 87 ☎ 055 234 2230 🚋 14 AX, CB, DC, MC, VI

🍴 Trattoria al Trebbio $–$$
This neighborhood trattoria has been catering to locals and tourists alike for years. The food is Tuscan, with good *ribollita* (vegetable soup with bread), *bistecca* (Florentine T-bone steak) and bean dishes. Seasonal specials are good value; the wine list is short and strong on Chianti.
✉ Via delle Belle Donne 47 – 49r ☎ 055 287 089 ◐ Closed Sun., mid-Oct. to Mar. 🚋 C2, 4, 22, 36, 37
AX, DC, MC, VI

GREVE IN CHIANTI
🏨 Albergo del Chianti $
Small hotel on the main square, with

16 rooms of varying sizes. There's a good-sized pool on site.
✉ Piazza Matteotti 86 ☎ 055 853 763 AX, DC, MC, VI

🍴 Villa Sangiovese $$
It's worth driving the 4 miles to Panzano to find this panoramic garden terrace at the Hotel Villa Sangiovese. You can enjoy a typically Tuscan meal in the picturesque vineyard setting.
✉ Piazza Bucciarelli 5, Panzano ☎ 055 852 461 ◐ Closed Wed. and Dec. 25 through mid-Mar. MC, VI

GUBBIO
🏨 Gattapone $
This medieval building in the heart of old Gubbio has been tastefully converted into a comfortable hotel. Its antique furniture and pretty grounds are bonuses.
✉ Via Beni 11 ☎ 075 927 2489 ◐ Closed Jan. 8–Feb. 8
AX, CB, MC, VI

🍴 Taverna del Lupo $$
This big, busy restaurant offers delicious dishes, good service and a friendly and relaxed atmosphere.
✉ Via Ansidei 6 ☎ 075 927 4368 ◐ Closed Mon. (except Aug.–Sep.)
AX, CB, DC, MC, VI

LUCCA
🍴 Buca di Sant'Antonio $$–$$$
A series of cozy rooms gives this restaurant its special atmosphere. Superb food and service make it one of Tuscany's top establishments, where traditional dishes are served with a modern twist.
✉ Via della Cervia 1/5 ☎ 0583 55 881 ◐ Closed Sun. evening, Mon., Jan. 13–28 and 2 weeks in Jul.
AX, CB, DC, MC, VI

🏨 La Luna $$
One of the very few hotels within the city walls of Lucca. Comfortable rooms; within walking distance of the Piazza Anfiteatro.
✉ Via Fillungo, ang. (corner) Corte Compagni 12 ☎ 0583 493 634 ◐ Closed Jan. 7–Feb. 7 AX, CB, DC, MC, VI

MONTALCINO
🏨 Hotel dei Capitani $$
This well-converted hotel is in the heart of town. Many of the pretty rooms have lovely views, and there's a small pool.

KEY TO SYMBOLS

⊞	hotel
❚❚	restaurant
✉	address
☎	telephone number
⊘	days/times closed
⊜	nearest subway/mainline train station(s)
⊟	nearest bus/trolley-bus/tram route(s)
⛴	ferry
AX	American Express
CB	Carte Blanche
DC	Diners Club
MC	MasterCard
VI	VISA

Hotels

Price guide: double room with breakfast for two people

$	up to €115
$$	€115–€225
$$$	over €225

Restaurants

Price guide: dinner per person, excluding drinks

$	up to €30
$$	€30–€55
$$$	over €55

Agriturismo

Agriturismo is a term referring to accommodations on functioning farms or agricultural estates, giving guests the chance to enjoy local cooking at its place of origin. The concept began as a means of restoring old, unused rural properties and agricultural buildings, as well as encouraging traditional crafts and food production methods. Hundreds of lovely old structures have been converted into holiday accommodations – some on a room-only basis, others with simple rooms and dining facilities, and some as complete as a good hotel.

✉ Via Lapini 6 ☎ 0577 847 227
⊘ Closed mid-Jan. through Feb.
AX, CB, DC, MC, VI

❚❚ Taverna del Grappolo Blu $–$$

This friendly and informal little restaurant, tucked off the main streets, is a hit with diners who enjoy excellent cooking. Dishes might include *crostini* (toast with savory toppings), homemade pasta with truffle sauce, roast meat and delicious desserts.
✉ Scala di Via Moglio 1 ☎ 0577 847 150 ⊘ Closed 2 weeks Jan.–Dec.
AX, DC, MC, VI

MONTEPULCIANO

❚❚ La Grotta $$

A stroll downhill brings you to this pretty restaurant on the edge of town. There's an attractive garden for alfresco dining.
✉ Località San Biagio 16 ☎ 0578 757 607 ⊘ Closed Wed. and Jan. 6–end Feb. AX, CB, MC, VI

⊞ Hotel il Marzocco $

In a 16th-century building, this comfortable hotel off the main street has been run by members of the same family for more than 150 years.
✉ Piazza Savonarola 18 ☎ 0578 757 262 ⊘ Closed mid-Jan. to mid-Feb.
AX, CB, DC, MC, VI

NORCIA

❚❚ Granaro del Monte $$

Norcia's best restaurant is located in the Grotta Azzurra hotel, where you can eat truffle dishes, game in season and meat cooked over a huge open fire. Busy but friendly.
✉ Via Alfieri 12 ☎ 0743 816 513
AX, CB, DC, MC, VI

ORVIETO

⊞ Maitani $$

Less than 200 yards from the cathedral, this elegant and comfortable hotel in a historic building has good-size rooms.
✉ Via Maitani 5 ☎ 0763 342 011
⊘ Closed 3 weeks in Jan. AX, CB, MC, VI

❚❚ Tipica Trattoria Etrusca $$

This upscale restaurant in a medieval building is close to the cathedral. Truffles, game and traditional local dishes feature, and you can visit the wine vaults beneath the dining room.
✉ Via Maitani 10 ☎ 0763 344 016
⊘ Closed Mon. AX, CB, DC, MC, VI

PASSIGNANO

⊞ Kursaal $

The Kursaal stands amid trees beside the lake, and swimmers in the pool can look across the waters of Trasimeno. Public areas are spacious and tasteful and all the bedrooms are a good size; some with lake views.
✉ Viale Europa 24 ☎ 075 828 085
⊘ Closed Jan.–Feb. MC, VI

PERUGIA

❚❚ Osteria del Gambero $$

Among Perugia's best eateries, this restaurant serves good, creative Umbrian cuisine. Fish and seafood are featured and, in season, there is a tasting menu featuring Norcia's prized black truffles. The wine list is an encyclopedic romp through Italy and other countries.
✉ Via Baldeschi 8/a ⊘ Closed lunch Tue.– Sat., Nov.–Feb., Mon., Mar.– Oct. 2 weeks in Jan. and 2 weeks in Jul. ☎ 075 573 5461 MC, VI

⊞ San Gallo Palace $$

This big hotel is ideal for sightseeing. Modern rooms are large, and well-appointed, while the decor gives more than a nod to Renaissance style. There is an indoor pool and fitness center.
✉ Via Masi 9 ☎ 075 730 202
AX, DC, MC, VI

PIENZA

❚❚ Buca delle Fate $–$$

This big, buzzing restaurant is housed in a 16th-century palazzo and serves straightforward Tuscan cooking.
✉ Corso Rossellino 38/a ☎ 0578 748 448 ⊘ Closed Mon., 3 weeks in Jan. and Jun. AX, CB, DC, MC, VI

⊞ Relais il Chiostro di Pienza $$–$$$

Converted from a 15th-century convent, this is the only hotel in the old town. Frescoed rooms, vaulted ceilings, a garden with a view and a shady cloister.
✉ Corso Rossellino 26 ☎ 0578 748 400 ⊘ Closed Jan. 7 to mid-Mar.
AX, CB, DC, MC, VI

PISA

❚❚ Osteria del Porton Rosso $$

This rustic restaurant offers gastronomic menus at non-touristy prices. *Risotto al nero di seppia* (risotto with squid) is cooked to perfection, as is the *ravioli melanzane e pomodorini* (ravioli with eggplant

and baby tomatoes). For *secondi*, try the mixed seafood or one of the local variations of *baccalà* (salted cod).
✉ Via Porton Rosso 11 ☎ 050 580 566 ⊕ Closed Sun. and 3 weeks in Aug. AX, DC, MC, VI

⊞ Royal Victoria $$
This traditional 19th-century hotel beside the River Arno, has been run by the same family since 1837. You'll find spacious rooms with lofty ceilings, marble floors and discreet service. It is a good value and has a pleasant atmosphere.
✉ Lungarno Pacinotti 12 ☎ 050 940 111 AX, DC, MC, VI

RADDA IN CHIANTI
⊞ Relais Fattoria Vignale $$$
This 18th-century villa has been transformed into a luxury hotel. Frescoed ceilings and lovely stonework offset the antique furnishings. There's an excellent restaurant, pool and gardens.
✉ Via Pianigiani 8 ☎ 0577 730 300 ⊕ Closed Nov.–Mar. AX, CB, DC, MC, VI

⊞ Le Vigne $$
Set among vineyards, Le Vigne is a delightful spot with panoramic views – ideal for dining outside. The food combines traditional Tuscan dishes with creative flair. Great wine list.
✉ Podere le Vigne Est (just outside town) ☎ 0577 738 301 ⊕ Closed Dec.–Feb. AX, DC, MC, VI

SAN GIMIGNANO
⊞ Dorando $$
This Slow Food restaurant prides itself on impeccable sourcing of its seasonal ingredients. Dishes are truly Tuscan, and you'll find specialties such as rabbit cooked in white wine with herbs, rack of lamb and Tuscan fruit tarts. The cheeses are excellent and there is a good local wine list.
✉ Viccolo del'Oro 2 ☎ 0577 941 862 ⊕ Closed Mon., Dec.–Easter and mid-Jan. to mid-Feb. AX, DC, MC, VI

⊞ Leon Bianco $–$$
This tastefully converted, family-run hotel on the town's main square has spacious rooms, lofty vaulted ceilings and a pretty breakfast terrace.
✉ Piazza della Cisterna 13 ☎ 0577 941 294 ⊕ Closed Nov.–Dec., and second week in Jan. to second week in Feb. AX, CB, DC, MC, VI

SIENA
⊞ Al Marsili $$
Impeccable service, a wide-ranging wine list and interesting dishes all feature in the vaulted elegance of this upscale restaurant and wine bar.
✉ Via del Castoro 3 ☎ 0577 47 154 ⊕ Closed Mon. AX, CB, DC, MC, VI

⊞ Osteria Le Logge $$
This restaurant occupies a medieval apothecary's shop. The cooking is good, with plenty of Sienese dishes and *porcini* mushrooms in autumn.
✉ Via del Porrione 33 ☎ 0577 48 013 ⊕ Closed Sun. and Jan.–early Feb. AX, CB, DC, MC, VI

⊞ Palazzo Fani Mignanelli $–$$
Set on one of the main streets, this small hotel has a welcoming, family atmosphere. Rooms are a good size, there are antiques and traditional styling in bedrooms and public areas; all rooms have WiFi.
✉ Via Banchi di Sopra 15 ☎ 0577 283 566 AX, DC, MC, VI

SPELLO
⊞ Albergo Il Cacciatore $$
If you're looking for perfect terrace dining with a view, head for this hotel restaurant at the top end of town. Umbrian food and good local wines are served.
✉ Via Giulia 42 ☎ 0742 301 603 ⊕ Closed Sun. dinner, Mon. and 2 weeks in Jul. AX, CB, DC, MC, VI

⊞ Palazzo Bocci $$
This 17th-century palazzo was transformed in the mid-1990s into a luxury hotel. Vaulted ceilings, terraces and frescoes complete the stylish ambience.
✉ Via Cavour 17 ☎ 0742 301 021 464 AX, DC, MC, VI

SPOLETO
⊞ Gattapone $$
Every room has a view of the gorge and the Ponte delle Torri at this elegant hotel. Good public areas and pretty terraces complete the picture.
✉ Via del Ponte 6 ☎ 0743 223 447 AX, CB, DC, MC, VI

⊞ Il Tempio del Gusto $$
Chef Eros Patrizi is known in Italy for his passion for food. Beautifully presented plates of modern Italian cuisine might include goat's cheese tortellini with truffle sauce or rack of lamb with a pistachio crust.

✉ Via Arco di Druso 11 ☎ 0743 47121 ⊕ Closed Thu. and 2 weeks in Jan.–Feb. AX, CB, DC, MC, VI

TODI
⊞ Fonte Cesia $$
In the heart of the historic center, this 18th-century building still has original features, but the rooms are furnished in contemporary style.
✉ Via L. Leonj 3 ☎ 075 894 3737 AX, DC, MC, VI

⊞ Umbria $$
You will find a warm welcome and excellent cooking here. Enjoy such specialties as truffle dishes and wild boar. Reservations suggested.
✉ Via S. Bonaventura 13 ☎ 075 894 2737 ⊕ Closed Tue. AX, CB, DC, MC, VI

URBINO
⊞ Bonconte $–$$
Bonconte is just inside the city walls, close to the Palazzo Ducale. Avoid the smaller rooms on the top floor.
✉ Via delle Mura 28 ☎ 0722 2463 AX, CB, DC, MC, VI

⊞ Vecchia Urbino $$
Delicious food and an outstanding wine list pull in customers to this rustically elegant restaurant, run for years by the Monti family. Dishes include homemade *ravioloni* with truffles, tagliolini with artichokes and asparagus and roast pigeon. They serve a fine selection of olive oil, cheeses and local cured meat.
✉ Via dei Vasari 3/5 ☎ 0722 4447 ⊕ Closed Tue., 2 weeks in Jul. and 2 weeks Dec.–Jan. AX, DC, MC, VI

VOLTERRA
⊞ Ombra della Sera $–$$
This central restaurant serves local, seasonal dishes in three cozy rooms. Choices include local salami and *crostini* (toasted bread with Tuscan toppings), Volterra soup and pork with rosemary and white wine.
✉ Via Gramsci 70 ☎ 0588 86663 ⊕ Closed Mon., Nov.–Apr., mid-Nov. to mid-Dec. and 2 weeks in Feb. AX, DC, MC, VI

⊞ San Lino $
This comfortable hotel within the city's walls was once a convent. It has spacious rooms, and a terrace and pool behind the main building.
✉ Via S. Lino 26 ☎ 0588 85 250 ⊕ Closed Nov. AX, CB, DC, MC, VI

KEY TO SYMBOLS

⊞	hotel
❚❚	restaurant
✉	address
☎	telephone number
🕐	days/times closed
Ⓠ	nearest subway/mainline train station(s)
🚌	nearest bus/trolley-bus/tram route(s)
⛴	ferry
AX	American Express
CB	Carte Blanche
DC	Diners Club
MC	MasterCard
VI	VISA

Hotels
Price guide: double room with breakfast for two people
$	up to €115
$$	€115–€225
$$$	over €225

Restaurants
Price guide: dinner per person, excluding drinks
$	up to €30
$$	€30–€55
$$$	over €55

Bars

Brightly lit and sparklingly clean, bars are open from 6 a.m. until late at night and serve everything from soft drinks, coffee and tea to beer, wine and scotch. You'll usually find a good selection of snack foods and sandwiches, while many double up as *pasticcerie* (pastry shops) or *gelaterie* (ice-cream parlors). If you sit down for waiter service you will pay a premium, whether inside or out. The normal procedure is to pay for what you want first at the cash-desk *(la cassa)*, then take the receipt *(lo scontrino)* to the bar and repeat your order. All bars provide daily newspapers and have bathrooms – you may have to ask for the key from the bartender.

MONTECASSINO

⊞ Alba $–$$
This hotel in the town of Cassino is modern and comfortable. It's a good stopping point if you want to spend some time visiting the monastery.
✉ Via G. Di Biasio 53 ☎ 0776 270 000 AX, CB, DC, MC, VI

❚❚ Villa Grazia $$
Delightful renovated period villa in verdant grounds. The cuisine concentrates on local dishes.
✉ Via San Rocca 1 ☎ 0776 337 419 🕐 Closed Mon.–Tue. AX, DC, MC, VI

PESCASSEROLI

❚❚ Alle Vecchie Arcate $
In an old vaulted stone building, this is a good find in this remote area, offering fixed-price menus, all including quality, local produce. Roast lamb is good and the local cheeses are excellent.
✉ Via della Chiesa 41 ☎ 0863 910 781 🕐 Closed Mon., Nov.–Mar. and 2 weeks in Nov. MC, V1

⊞ Pagnani $–$$
Set in the heart of the Abruzzo countryside, this is a good base for touring the area. The hotel has an indoor pool, bar and restaurant.
✉ Via Collacchi 4 ☎ 0863 912 866 🕐 Closed some days in Apr. and Oct. AX, MC, VI

ROME

❚❚ Agata e Romeo $$$
This upscale restaurant offers Roman dishes in elegant surroundings and specializes in fish and seafood. Reservations required.
✉ Via Carlo Alberto 45 ☎ 06 446 6115 🕐 Closed Sat.–Sun., also 2 weeks in Jan. and 2 weeks in Aug. 🚌 71, 590, 649 AX, CB, DC, MC, VI

❚❚ Al 34 $$
This friendly restaurant offers traditional dishes with a modern twist. *Primi* include chickpea soup with cuttlefish or *maltagliata* (rough pasta) with green tomatoes and pecorino cheese. Main courses include roast suckling pig, steaks, skewers of swordfish or tuna with radicchio. Desserts are homemade.
✉ Via Mario de' Fiori 34 ☎ 06 679 5091 🕐 Closed Mon. Ⓠ Spagna 🚌 116, 117, 119 AX, DC, MC, VI

⊞ Casa Howard $$
This stylish boutique hotel is split into two houses with elegantly furnished rooms, opulent with silky fabrics, fresh flowers and a Turkish bath. Both establishments are near the Spanish Steps – one on Via Capo le Case, the other in Via Sistina. Breakfast is extra.
✉ Via Capo le Case 18 ☎ 06 6992 4555 Ⓠ Spagna MC, VI

❚❚ Checchino dal 1887 $$
A long-established restaurant specializing in traditional Roman dishes and delicate ricotta and fruit tarts. The long wine list is good.
✉ Via Monte Testaccio 30 ☎ 06 574 3816 🕐 Closed Sun.–Mon., Dec. 25–Jan. 1 Aug. 🚌 719 AX, CB, DC, MC, VI

❚❚ Life $$
A very popular contemporary eatery that sees a steady flow of clients. It combines a restaurant, pizzeria and wine bar.
✉ Via delle Vite ☎ 06 6938 0948 🕐 Daily noon–midnight Ⓠ Spagna 🚌 All routes down Via del Corso MC, VI

❚❚ Trattoria Morgana $$
This quintessentially Roman restaurant started in 1935, when a wine bar became a popular local eatery. It is packed with locals enjoying local specials such as snails, tripe and oxtail. You'll also find pasta, mozzarella from Campania, broiled meat and fresh fish. The wine list offers regional wines.
✉ Via Mecenate 19–21 ☎ 06 487 3122 🕐 Closed Mon. Ⓠ Vittorio Emanuele AX, MC, VI

⊞ Portoghesi $$
You'll be within a short walk of Piazza Navona at this old-fashioned hotel, tucked away on a cobbled street. The rooms have been refurbished, and there's a pretty roof terrace.
✉ Via dei Portoghesi 1 ☎ 06 686 4231 🚌 70, 116, 186, 492 CB, MC, VI

⊞ Westin Excelsior $$$
The opulent decor and high standard of service at this world-class luxury hotel make a few days here one of Rome's most sybaritic experiences.
✉ Via Vittorio Veneto 125 ☎ 06 47 081 Ⓠ Barbarini 🚌 52, 53, 95 AX, CB, DC, MC, VI

TARQUINIA

🍴 Arcadia $

Arcadia has a single, vaulted dining room near the cathedral. The couple who run it offer a warm welcome and a menu with a bias towards fish.

✉ Via Mazzini 6 ☎ 0766 855 501 🕑 Closed Jan. and Mon., except Aug. AX, DC, MC, VI

🏨 Tarconte $–$$

This hotel is good for visiting this historic Etruscan city. It has friendly, professional service and bright and comfortable rooms.

✉ Via della Tuscia 19 ☎ 0766 856 141 AX, CB, DC, MC, VI

TIVOLI

🍴 Sibilla $$–$$$

The surroundings are as memorable as the food at this elegant restaurant with a summer terrace. Service is discreet and professional and dishes include homemade cannelloni filled with three types of meat and artichokes, served in various ways.

✉ Via della Sibilla 50 ☎ 0774 335 281 🕑 Closed Mon., Oct–Mar. AC, DC, MC, VI

🏨 Torre Sant'Angelo $$

You'll find every modern comfort in this hotel. It's small enough for truly personal service, but also has the facilities of many larger hotels, including a restaurant and pool.

✉ Via Quintilio Varo ☎ 0774 332 533 AX, CB, DC, MC, VI

VITERBO

🍴 Al Vecchio Orologio $–$$

For good, straightforward and traditional cooking head here, where chef Antonella concentrates on local, seasonal food, with many vegetables from their own garden. There's *tagliata* (T-bone steak) sliced and served with arugula and parmesan, homemade pasta and good desserts. The wine list has interesting options.

✉ Via Orologio Vecchio 25 ☎ 335 337 754 🕑 Closed Mon., lunch Tue.–Fri. and 2 weeks in Jul. AX, MC, VI

🏨 Tuscia $–$$

This family-run hotel is near the medieval city center and within an easy stroll of the commercial area and shops. Rooms are pleasant and comfortable. Good value.

✉ Via Cairoli 41 ☎ 0761 344 400 AX, CB, DC, MC, VI

ALBEROBELLO

🏨 Colle dl Sole $

Functional, modern and a great value, the Colle del Sole lies a few hundred yards from the *trulli* zone. Rooms are immaculate and a good size, there's free WiFi and a pool. The hotel has its own restaurant.

✉ Via Indipendenza 63 ☎ 080 4321 814 AX, DC, MC, VI

AMALFI

🍴 Da Gemma $$

Enjoy traditional dishes on a terrace overlooking Amalfi's main square in one of the coast's most popular and best-known restaurants.

✉ Via Fra' Gerardo Sasso 11 ☎ 089 871 345 🕑 Closed Wed. (except Jul.–Aug.), mid-Nov. to mid-Dec. and Jan. AX, CB, MC, VI

🏨 Relais Villa Annalara $

This attractive villa is set in gardens with a courtyard and enchanting views. The air-conditioned rooms are individually designed in elegant style offering every comfort. Advanced reservations are recommended.

✉ Via delle Cartiere 1 ☎ 089 871 147 AX, DC, MC, VI

BARI

🍴 Ai 2 Ghiottoni $$–$$$

This modern restaurant puts the emphasis on local dishes. The wine list is weighted with Puglian wines.

✉ Via Putignani 11 ☎ 080 523 2240 🕑 Closed Sun. p.m., Mon. and 2 weeks in Aug. AX, CB, DC, MC, VI

🏨 Boston $$

A good midrange hotel within easy reach of both the historic center and the railroad station.

✉ Via Piccinni 155 ☎ 080 521 6633 AX, CB, DC, MC, VI

CAPRI

🏨 La Canasta $$

This intimate, good-value hotel is just five minutes' walk from the central square. Rooms are light and colorful with pretty furnishings; some have sea views. There's also a pool.

✉ Via Campo di Teste 6 ☎ 081 837 0561 AX, DC, MC, VI

🍴 Capannina $$

You can eat in the pretty dining room or on the green terrace of this well-known establishment, where specialties include imaginative fish and vegetable combinations.

✉ Via delle Botteghe 12 bis ☎ 081 837 0732 🕑 Closed Wed. (Mar. and Nov.) and mid-Nov. to Easter (except 1 week at New Year's) AX, CB, DC, MC, VI

🍴 Da Paolino $$$

Try the delicious *antipasto* buffet sitting outside in the shade of a lemon-tree pergola.

✉ Via Palazzo a Mare 11, Marina Grande ☎ 081 837 6102 🕑 Closed Nov.–Easter, and lunch Jun.–Oct., also Nov.–Dec. AX, CB, DC, MC, VI

LECCE

🏨 Patria Palace $$$

A superbly converted baroque palace is spread over three floors at the heart of town. The five-star rating is a guarantee of fine rooms with Liberty-style decor and modern facilities.

✉ Piazzetta Riccardi 13 ☎ 0832 245 111 AX, DC, MC, VI

🍴 Trattoria Casareccia $

Exceptional value for delicious home cooking in a homey atmosphere. Great welcome and some interesting Puglian cuisine.

✉ Via Costadura 19 ☎ 0832 245 178 🕑 Closed Mon., Sun. evening, Dec. 24–Jan. 6 and Aug. 30–Sep.15 DC, MC, VI

MARATEA

🏨 Hotel Spa Villa del Mare $$

Perched on a rocky headland, this hotel and spa has nice rooms, a pretty terrace and a private elevator down to the hotel's beach.

✉ Strada Statale Sud 18, Acquafredda ☎ 0973 878 007 🕑 Closed Nov. to mid-Mar. AX, CB, DC, MC, VI

🍴 Zà Mariuccia $$

A long-established restaurant in a pretty location, run by the same family for three generations. You can choose your fish from the tank.

✉ Via Grotte 2 ☎ 0973 876 163 🕑 Closed Thu. (except in Aug.) and Oct.–Feb.; also closed lunch Jun.– Aug. AX, CB, DC, MC, VI

MATERA

🍴 Baccanti $$

The famous *sassi* (caves) are home to this excellent restaurant, with tables beneath the hollowed-out vaults. The

KEY TO SYMBOLS

🏨	hotel
🍴	restaurant
✉	address
☎	telephone number
🚫	days/times closed
🚇	nearest subway/mainline train station(s)
🚌	nearest bus/trolley-bus/tram route(s)
⛴	ferry
AX	American Express
CB	Carte Blanche
DC	Diners Club
MC	MasterCard
VI	VISA

Hotels
Price guide: double room with breakfast for two people

$	up to €115
$$	€115–€225
$$$	over €225

Restaurants
Price guide: dinner per person, excluding drinks

$	up to €30
$$	€30–€55
$$$	over €55

Hotel Facilities
Outside resorts, mid-range Italian hotels are essentially places to sleep. Top-quality hotels have everything you'd expect, but smaller ones will not have every amenity. Many hotels have neither restaurant nor bar, and are unlikely to have lounge areas or other public rooms. Some do not offer breakfast. Rooms will be simple and functional, with tiled floors, limited closet space and no easy chairs. Satellite TV is increasing in the north, but is generally limited to hotels catering to business travelers. It is quite normal to ask to see the room before you accept it.

cuisine is seasonal, with many updated traditional dishes featuring wild herbs and field vegetables. A real dining experience.
✉ Via Sant'Angelo 58/61 ☎ 0835 333 704 🚫 Closed Sun. p.m. and Mon., 1 week in Jan.–Feb., and all Jul. AX, DC, MC, VI

🏨 Italia $
This comfortable hotel in a historic building has a good restaurant and views over the *sassi* quarter of town.
✉ Via Ridola 5 ☎ 0835 333 561 AX, CB, DC, MC, VI

NAPLES
🏨 Britannique $
This comfortable hotel in a 19th-century villa has lovely views over the Bay of Naples, a secluded garden and a restaurant.
✉ Corso Vittorio Emanuele II 133 ☎ 081 761 4145 🚌 V1 AX, CB, DC, MC, VI

🍴 La Cantinella $$$
This seafront restaurant specializes in creative fish preparations, which you can enjoy on the terrace.
✉ Via Cuma 42 ☎ 081 764 8684 🚫 Closed Sun. (except Nov.–May), Christmas and 2 weeks in Aug.
🚌 n3 AX, CD, DC, MC, VI

🍴 Ciro a Santa Brigida $$
This historic restaurant at the heart of the old city is a Neapolitan institution. It serves pizzas as well as seafood and fish, in a lively setting near the Galleria Umberto I.
✉ Via Santa Brigida 73 ☎ 081 552 4072 🚫 Closed Sun. and 3 weeks in Aug. AX, MC, VI

🍴 Don Salvatore $$
You'll find very good cooking using the freshest fish and other ingredients at this traditional restaurant, which also doubles as a pizzeria. Excellent desserts.
✉ Via Mergellina 4A ☎ 081 681 817 🚫 Closed Wed. 🚇 Mergellina 🚌 R3, C21 AX, CB, DC, MC, VI

🏨 Palazzo Decumani $$
In the heart of Spaccanapoli, this boutique hotel marries cutting-edge design and comfort with the baroque backdrop of this palazzo. Expect elegant and serene rooms, a contrast to the city outside.
✉ Piazza Giovanni Fortunato 8 ☎ 081 4201 379 AX, DC, MC, VI

🏨 Grand Hotel Parker's $$$
The 19th-century decor combines with 21st-century comforts at this elegant hotel, west of the center. The popular rooftop restaurant serves Neapolitan specialties.
✉ Corso Vittorio Emanuele II 135 ☎ 081 761 2474 🚌 V1 AX, CB, DC, MC, VI

🍴 Mimì alla Ferrovia $$
A typical Naples restaurant, buzzing and chaotic, where you can enjoy dishes using the freshest ingredients.
✉ Via Alfonso d'Aragona 21 ☎ 081 553 8525 🚫 Closed Sun. and 2 weeks in Aug. 🚌 42, 47, 110 AX, CB, DC, MC, VI

🏨 Villa Capodimonte $–$$
This lovely hotel is near the park surrounding Capodimonte. It offers modern comforts, traditional service and style, and peace and quiet.
✉ Via Moiariello 66 ☎ 081 459 000 🚌 R4, 24 AX, CB, DC, VI

POSITANO
🍴 La Cambusa $$
You can eat at a table on the terrace here at the main beach. The interior decor has a nautical theme.
✉ Piazza Vespucci 24 ☎ 089 812 051 🚫 Closed early Jan.–Feb., and Wed. in winter AX, CB, DC, MC, VI

🏨 Pupetto $$
A path leads from this hotel to the town center, but Pupetto offers peace and quiet in a lovely setting. Many of the functional but pretty rooms have sea views and the hotel restaurant has a dining terrace. There is a private beach area.
✉ Via Fornillo 37 ☎ 089 875 087 🚫 Closed mid-Nov. to Mar. AX, DC, MC, VI

REGGIO DI CALABRIA
🍴 Baylik $–$$
This friendly restaurant, near the harbor, offers imaginative seafood and vegetarian dishes. Also on the menu are items for celiacs (coeliacs).
✉ Vico Leone 3 ☎ 0965 48 624 🚫 Closed Mon. (except in Aug.) AX, CB, DC, MC, VI

🏨 Grand Hotel Excelsior $$$
Close to the Museo Nazionale and not far from the busy ferry port. The rooms here offer old-fashioned elegance, modern comforts and views across the Straits of Messina.

✉ Via Vittorio Veneto 66 ☎ 0965 812 211 AX, CB, DC, MC, VI

SORRENTO
🏨 Antiche Mura $$
This central hotel (near the old town walls) is surrounded by a garden. Rooms are a good size, but staff can put an extra bed in double rooms.
✉ Via Fuori Mura 7 ☎ 081 8073 523 AX, DC, MC, VI

🍴 Ristorante Museo Caruso $$$
This elegant, refined and award-winning restaurant has imaginative fish dishes and an extensive wine list.
✉ Via Sant'Antonino 12 ☎ 081 807 3156 AX, CB, DC, MC, VI

TROPEA
🍴 Pimm's $–$$
This friendly, good-value restaurant overlooking the sea serves Calabrian dishes and fish grills.
✉ Largo Migliarese 2 ☎ 0963 666 105 🚫 Closed Mon. (Sep.–Jun.) and 3 weeks in Jan. DC, MC, VI

🏨 Rocca Nettuno $$
Many rooms here are individual bungalows offering perfect privacy. An elevator runs down to the beach.
✉ Via Annunziata ☎ 0963 998 111 🚫 Closed Nov.–Mar. or Apr. AX, CB, DC, MC, VI

VIESTE
🍴 Al Dragone $$
Set in a natural cave, this friendly restaurant is in the heart of the old town. Excellent wine list and fish dishes of all sorts.
✉ Via Duomo 8 ☎ 0884 701 212 🚫 Closed late Oct.–Mar. or Apr. and Tue. from mid-Apr. through May and Oct. AX, CB, DC, VI

🏨 Seggio $$
A friendly family-run hotel in the heart of the old center, with an excellent restaurant, pool, terrace and steps down to a private beach.
✉ Via Veste 7 ☎ 0884 708 123 🚫 Closed Nov.–Mar. or Apr. MC, VI

SICILY

AGRIGENTO
🏨 Jolly Hotel della Valle $$
This modern hotel, overlooking the archeological zone, is close to the city center. It has comfortable rooms and a swimming pool.

✉ Via Ugo La Malfa 3 ☎ 0922 26 966 AX, CB, DC, MC, VI

🍴 Spizzulio $–$$
This *enoteca* (wine bar) with a good restaurant serves homemade dishes. There is an excellent wine list, and a professional sommelier. It specializes in traditional Sicilian and Italian foods. Reserve for the restaurant.
✉ Via Panoramica dei Templi 23 (just outside town) ☎ 0922 20 712 🚫 Closed 2 weeks in Nov. MC, VI

CEFALÙ
🏨 Alberi del Paradiso $$–$$$
Not far from the center and surrounded by ancient trees, this hotel has peaceful rooms, beautiful views and attentive and friendly service; the terrace restaurant makes good use of local produce, and the hotel has its own pool and private beach areas.
✉ Via di dei Mulini 18/20 ☎ 0921 423 900 🚫 Closed Jan. AX, DC, MC, VI

🍴 Ostaria del Duomo $$
You can eat outside in the piazza overlooking the cathedral at this restaurant, which specializes in Sicilian dishes. Good wine list.
✉ Via Seminario 5 ☎ 0921 421 838 🚫 Closed mid-Nov. to mid-Feb. or mid-Mar. AX, CB, DC, MC, VI

ENNA
🍴 Centrale $$
This family-run restaurant, in the old town, serves Sicilian specialties. Try the buffet-style vegetable *antipasto*.
✉ Piazza VI Dicembre 9 ☎ 0935 500 963 🚫 Closed Sat. lunch (except Jun.–Sep.) AX, CB, DC, MC, VI

🏨 Grand Albergo Sicilia $$
Enna's main hotel stands in the heart of the historic center. The interior belies its somewhat soulless appearance, with comfortable bedrooms and good reception and lounge areas. Friendly staff.
✉ Piazza Colaianni 7 ☎ 0935 500 850 AX, CB, DC, MC, VI

ERICE
🏨 Moderno $
On one of Erice's prettiest streets, this cozy hotel, in an 18th-century building, has an excellent restaurant and an attractive terrace.
✉ Via Vittorio Emanuele II 63 ☎ 0923 869 300 AX, CB, DC, MC, VI

🍴 Monte San Giuliano $$
The garden terrace provides a lovely setting for this typically Sicilian restaurant with traditional dishes on the menu. Reservations required.
✉ Vicolo San Rocco 7 ☎ 0923 869 595 🚫 Closed Mon., 3 weeks in Jan. and 3 weeks in Nov. AX, CB, DC, MC, VI

PALERMO
🍴 Osteria dei Vespri $$–$$$
This restaurant, in an old coach house, highlights the best of modern Sicilian cuisine, with new interpretations of local dishes. Try the tasting menu. There more than 350 wines on offer here.
✉ Piazza Croce dei Vespri 6 ☎ 091 6171 631 🚫 Closed Sun. and Jan.–Feb. AX, DC, MC, VI

🍴 'A Cuccagna $$
In the heart of the city, this friendly trattoria, with its cozy ambience, offers classic Sicilian cooking.
✉ Via Principe Granatelli 21/A ☎ 091 587 267 🚫 Closed 2 weeks in Aug. AX, CB, DC, MC, VI

🏨 Centrale Palace Hotel $$
A high quality hotel set in a former 18th-century palazzo, in the heart of the old city. Marble, antique furniture, frescoed walls, gilt mirrors and chandeliers predominate, but the rooms have modern facilities. There's a good restaurant and attractive roof terrace.
✉ Corso Vittorio Emanuele II 327 ☎ 091 336 666 AX, DC, MC, VI

🏨 Grand Hotel Piazza Borsa $$
The decor, style and quality of service in this stylish hotel belies its four-star rating and reasonable price range. The central part of the hotel was a 16th-century convent and the lobby is bordered by the original cloisters. There is also an attractive winter garden/conservatory.
✉ Via dei Cartari 18 ☎ 091 320 075 AX, CB, DC, MC, VI

🏨 Grand Hotel Villa Igiea $$$
This hotel, outside the center of Palermo, has an old-fashioned atmosphere and high standards of comfort and service. It stands in a beautiful seafront garden with tennis courts and swimming pool. Considered among Sicily's top hotels.
✉ Salita Belmonte 43 ☎ 091 631 2111 AX, DC, MC, VI

KEY TO SYMBOLS

🏨	hotel
🍴	restaurant
✉	address
☎	telephone number
🚫	days/times closed
🚇	nearest subway/mainline train station(s)
🚌	nearest bus/trolley-bus/tram route(s)
⛴	ferry
AX	American Express
CB	Carte Blanche
DC	Diners Club
MC	MasterCard
VI	VISA

Hotels
Price guide: double room with breakfast for two people
$ up to €115
$$ €115–€225
$$$ over €225

Restaurants
Price guide: dinner per person, excluding drinks
$ up to €30
$$ €30–€55
$$$ over €55

Types of Restaurants

There are many different types of restaurants in Italy, the distinctions between them subtle. A *trattoria*, *osteria* and *ristorante* are pretty similar in terms of price, atmosphere and cuisine, although originally *ristoranti* were far more fashionable than the humble *trattorie*. Less expensive choices might be a *pizzeria* (which often serves simple pasta and meat dishes as well as pizza) or a *birreria*. Other options include a *tavola calda* (hot table), a type of lunch bar, or a *rosticceria*, which is similar but also offers food to go.

🏨 Letizia $–$$
A friendly welcome awaits at this small, comfortable hotel in the heart of the artistic district and near the cultural attractions. Rooms are tastefully furnished. No elevator.
✉ Via Bottai 30 ☎ 091 589 110 AX, DC, MC, VI

🍴 Santandrea $–$$
Ingredients at this restaurant come from the nearby Vucciria market. There's no menu, but you can't go wrong from the list the server gives you. Reservations recommended.
✉ Piazza S. Andrea 4 ☎ 091 334 999 🚫 Closed lunch daily, Sun. and some weeks in Jan. AX, CB, DC, MC, V

🍴 Zafferano $$–$$$
In the vaults of an historic building in the center, this modern restaurant serves impeccable food using the best local produce. Try the linguine with sea urchin and dried cod's roe or macaroni with lobster sauce.
✉ Via XII Gennaio 8 ☎ 091 329 331 AX, MC, VI

SELINUNTE
🏨 Alceste $
This modern hotel is an ideal choice if you want to stay near the classical site; cool, airy rooms and a pretty terrace overlooking the sea.
✉ Via Alceste 21 ☎ 0924 46 184 AX, CB, DC, MC, VI

🍴 Pierrot $$
This Mediterranean-style restaurant has views of the sea and temples to enjoy while sampling fresh seafood.
✉ Via Marco Polo 108 ☎ 0924 46 205 🚫 Closed Tue. (Nov.–Feb.) and some days in Jan. AX, DC, MC, VI

SIRACUSA
🏨 Grand Hotel Ortigia $$$
This luxurious old hotel, on Ortigia in the heart of the old city, has been renovated to include contemporary design. Lovely sea views, excellent service and a rooftop restaurant.
✉ Viale Mazzini 12 ☎ 0931 464 600 AX, CB, DC, MC, VI

🍴 Don Camillo $$
The strength of this traditional Ortigia restaurant is the pasta; follow it with wonderfully fresh fish.
✉ Via Maestranza 96/100 ☎ 0931 67133 🚫 Closed Sun. AX, DC, MC, VI

TAORMINA
🍴 'A Zammara $$
This traditional and friendly restaurant serves a great range of Sicilian dishes.
✉ Via Fratelli Bandiera 15 ☎ 0942 22248 AX, MC, VI

🏨 San Domenico Palace $$$
A 15th-century convent houses Taormina's most luxurious hotel. Its elegant rooms, impeccable facilities and superb service perfectly complement the stunning views.
✉ Piazza S. Domenico 5 ☎ 0942 613 111 AX, CB, DC, MC, VI

🏨 Villa Carlotta $$–$$$
Rooms at this boutique hotel are elegantly furnished with spacious marble bathrooms and breakfast is served on the rooftop terrace. There is a shuttle to the beach.
✉ Via Pirandello 81 ☎ 0942 626 058 🚫 Closed mid-Jan. to mid-Feb. AX, CB, MC, VI

SARDINIA

CÁGLIARI
🍴 Dal Corsaro $$
This restaurant is an institution in Cágliari. It serves Sardinian dishes, and has an excellent wine list.
✉ Viale Regina Margherita 28 ☎ 070 664 318 🚫 Closed Sun., Dec. 23–Jan. 6 AX CB, MC, VI

🏨 Sardegna $$
The Sardegna is a quiet, comfortable hotel with good facilities and a restaurant.
✉ Via Lunigiana 50 ☎ 070 286 245 AX, CB, MC, VI

COSTA SMERALDA
🏨 Colonna San Marco $$–$$$
There are grander, more expensive hotels on the Costa Smeralda, but Colonna San Marco at the center of Porto Rotondo offers a good balance between comfort, facilities and price.
✉ Piazza San Marco, Porto Rotondo ☎ 0789 34 110 🚫 Closed Oct.–Mar. AX, DC, MC, VI

🍴 Gianni Pedrinelli $$$
This is a popular seafood restaurant so it is best to reserve.
✉ Strada provinciale bivio Pevero Sud, 1.5 km (0.9 miles) from Porto Cervo ☎ 0789 92 436 🚫 Closed Nov.–Feb. and for lunch Jun. 15–Sep. 15 AX, DC, MC, VI

Essential Information

U.S. CITIZENS

The information in this guide has been compiled for U.S. citizens traveling as tourists.

Travelers who are not U.S. citizens, or who are traveling on business, should check with their embassies and tourist offices for information on the countries they wish to visit.

Entry requirements are subject to change at short notice, and travelers are advised to check the current situation before they travel.

National Flag

Before You Go

Passports

Passport application forms can be obtained by contacting any federal or state court or post office authorized to accept passport applications. U.S. passport agencies have offices in most major cities. You can also request an application form by calling the National Passport Information Center at 1-877-487-2778. Comprehensive passport information and application forms are available on the U.S. State Department website at www.travel.state.gov.

Apply for your passport in good time as processing can take several months from the time of application until it arrives. Rush service is available for an extra charge. Before departure, make sure your passport is valid for at least six months after you are due to travel; some European countries require this.

You may have to leave your passport with the hotel when you check in; this is to satisfy regulations requiring the hotel to register all foreign visitors with local police authorities. You must show your passport whenever you cash a traveler's check and whenever national borders are crossed, although in practice border controls have been relaxed between many European Union (E.U.) member countries.

In addition to a passport, some countries require a visa. Travel visas are not necessary to visit Italy, but if you'll be traveling to other nations, check their entry requirements before you leave home.

Travel Insurance

Before departing, make sure you are covered by insurance that will reimburse travel expenses if you need to cancel or cut short your trip due to unforeseen circumstances. You'll also need coverage for property loss or theft, emergency health or dental treatment, and emergency evacuation if necessary. Before taking out extra insurance, check if your current homeowners or medical coverage covers you for travel abroad. If you make a claim, your insurance company will need proof of the incident or expenditure. Keep copies of police reports and documents, medical bills or statements, for your insurance claim.

Essential for Travelers

Required ● Recommended ● Not required ●

Passport	●
Visa	●
Travel, medical insurance	●
Round-trip or onward airline ticket	●
Local currency	●
Traveler's checks	●
Credit cards	●
First-aid kit and medicines	●
Health inoculations	●

Essential for Drivers

Required ● Recommended ● Not required ●

Driver's license	●
International Driving Permit	●
Car insurance (for private cars)	●
Car registration (for private cars)	●

*see also Driving section

When to Go

Despite its basically mild winters and warm summers, Italy has a varied and extreme climate. In winter, Venice, Turin and Milan can be quite chilly, and you can ski in parts of the country usually from December. The best months for sightseeing are April, May, June, September and October, although rain and cold linger in northern and mountain areas throughout spring and autumn. July and August are the hottest months. Winters can be severe, particularly in the Alps and fogbound plains of Lombardy and Emilia-Romagna. European school vacations are another factor in planning your trip. Schools in Italy are normally in session from September until early July. This makes May and June good months to visit, both from a weather standpoint and the fact that there are likely to be fewer crowds at major attractions.

Important Addresses

Italian Government Tourist Office
630 Fifth Avenue
Suite 1565 Rockefeller Center
New York, NY 10111
☎ (212) 245-5618; www.italiantourism.com
Italian State Tourist Board
Via Marghera 2–6
00185 Rome, Italy
☎ 06 49711; www.enit.it
American Embassy
Via Vittorio Veneto 121
00187 Rome, Italy
☎ 06 46741; www.italy.usembassy.gov
Open Mon.–Fri. 8:30–12:30 for U.S. citizen services
For non-emergency appointments apply online.

Customs

✔ **Goods brought into Italy from non-European Union countries limited to:**
200 cigarettes or 100 cigarillos or 50 cigars or 250 g. tobacco; 2 L. wine; 1 L. alcohol over 22% volume; 2 L. alcohol under 22% volume; 60 ml. perfume; 250 ml. toilet water; plus any other duty-free goods (including gifts) to the value of $300. There is no limit on the importation of tax-paid goods purchased within the European Union, provided they are for personal use. Visitors should declare cash over the value of €10,000. Returning to the U.S., you will be required to complete a customs declaration. You are allowed $400 worth of personal goods; keep sales slips and have them ready for inspection. Additional information at www.cbp.gov.

✘ No unlicensed drugs, weapons, ammunition, obscene material, pets or other animals, counterfeit money, copied goods, meat or poultry.

Money

Italy's currency is the euro (€), a currency shared by most other European Union countries. The euro is divided into 100 cents (¢). The denominations of euro bills are 5, 10, 20, 50, 100, 200 and 500. There are coins of 1, 2, 5, 10, 20 and 50¢ and €1 and €2. Exchange dollars or traveler's checks *(assegni turistici)* at a bank *(banca)* or exchange office *(ufficio di cambio)*. Hotels may exchange traveler's checks, but stores do not. ATMs *(sportello automatico)* are fairly common and accept major credit cards.

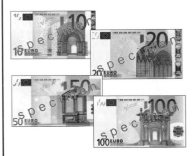

Tips and Gratuities

Restaurants (where service is not included)	10%–15%
Cafés/bars	small change
Taxis	15%
Porters	€2–3 per bag
Chambermaids	€2–3 per night
Restrooms	10¢ minimum
Cloakroom attendants	50¢

Communications

Post Office

✉ Buy stamps *(francobolli)* at a post office *(ufficio postale)* or at a tobacconist *(tabaccaio)*. Mailboxes often have two slots, one for local mail *(città)*, the other for out-of-town mail *(altre destinazione)*. Posta Prioritaria is a more expensive post service; or you can send mail *(espresso)* or registered *(raccomandata)*.

Telephones

☎ Pay phones are usually found in bars and other public places. Prepaid cards *(schede telefoniche)* for card-operated phones are available from tobacconists, bars, post offices, newsstands, railroad stations and dispensers showing a Telecom Italia (TI) logo. When making international calls use a prepaid card; tear the corner off before using it. Calls from hotel rooms always incur a surcharge.

Phoning Inside Italy

All telephone numbers in Italy include an area code that must always be dialed. To call the operator dial 10.

Phoning Italy from Abroad

The country code for Italy is 39. Note that Italian numbers in this book do not include the country code; you will need to prefix this number if you are phoning from another country. To call Italy from the United States or Canada dial the prefix 011 39. Include the first zero of the regional code. Example: 01 122 3344 becomes 011 39 01 122 3344. There is no standard number of digits in Italian numbers.

Phoning from Italy

To phone the United States or Canada from Italy, prefix the area code and number with 001. Example: (111) 222–3333 becomes 001 111 222–3333. To call international information dial 4176.

Emergency Numbers

☎ Police *(Polizia)* 113 (local), 112 (national)
Fire service *(Pompieri)*	112
Ambulance *(Ambulanza)*	112

Emergency calls are free from phone booths.
For all emergencies 113

Essential Information

Hours of Operation

- Stores Mon.–Sat.
- Offices Mon.–Fri.
- Banks Mon.–Fri.
- Post offices Mon.–Fri.
- Museums/Monuments
- Pharmacies

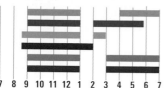

7 8 9 10 11 12 1 2 3 4 5 6 7

Department stores, some grocery stores and stores in tourist areas and main cities may not close at lunchtime, and sometimes stay open until later in the evening. Some stores close on Monday morning and may close on Saturday afternoon in summer; most stores close on Sunday.

Some banks close at 2 and do not reopen later in the afternoon.

Many museums are open into the early evening (usually 4–7); others are open all day, and a few stay open late into the evening. Many museums close early on Sunday (around 1), and most are closed Monday. Generally, the farther south, the longer the "siesta," usually until 4 or 4:30.

Post office times may vary slightly, and they may be open Sat. 8:30–noon.

National Holidays

Banks, businesses, and stores and museums close on these days. Most cities, towns and villages celebrate their patron saint's day, but generally most establishments remain open.

Jan. 1	New Year's Day
Jan. 6	Epiphany
Mar./Apr.	Easter Monday
Apr. 25	Liberation Day
May 1	Labor Day
Jun. 2	Anniversary of the Republic
Aug. 15	Assumption of the Virgin
Nov. 1	All Saints' Day
Dec. 8	Immaculate Conception
Dec. 25	Christmas Day
Dec. 26	St. Stephen's Day

Restrooms

Finding a restroom *(gabinetto/bagno)* can be difficult away from airports, rail and bus stations, highway service areas and museums. Leave a small tip (about 10¢) for the attendant. If using the facilities in a bar you will be expected to buy a drink. Some bars have separate restrooms for men *(signori)* and women *(signore)*.

Health Advice

Medical Services

Private medical insurance is strongly recommended. Visitors from non-European Union countries can receive treatment in a hospital accident and emergency room, but you will be charged if you are admitted to a bed. A general practitioner *(medico)* can deal with less urgent cases, but also will charge.

Dental Services

Emergency dental treatment is available from English-speaking dentists listed in the Yellow Pages *(pagine gialle)* online at www.paginegialle.it. A fee will be charged, so check that you are covered for treatment on your private medical insurance.

Sun Advice

In summer, particularly in July and August, it can be oppressively hot and humid in cities. On sunny days cover your head as well as your shoulders and use a sunscreen. Cathedrals and other stone buildings can be refreshingly cool. Take frequent breaks in the shade and drink plenty of fluids.

Drugs

A pharmacy *(farmacia)* displays a green cross symbol and has staff who can provide prescription medicines and offer advice on minor ailments. Information about the address of the nearest 24-hour facility is normally posted at every pharmacy.

Safe Water

In isolated rural areas it is not advisable to drink tap water. However, across most of the country tap water is perfectly safe, although most Italians prefer to drink bottled mineral water *(acqua minerale)*, which is inexpensive and widely available.

Personal Safety

Keep valuables hidden when you're on the move, and hold bags and cameras across your front – never hung over one shoulder. Put money in different places so if one bag is lost you have another source of funds. Tourist attractions and public transportation are prime territory for pickpockets. Avoid lingering alone after dark, particularly in parks or around railway stations. Contact a police officer if anyone becomes aggressive; police on city streets throughout Italy are usually very approachable.

National Transportation

Air *(Aeroplano)*

✖ Alitalia (www.alitalia.com) and several smaller national carriers, notably Meridiana (www.meridiana.it), offer frequent service between cities and islands. Fares are high, and you will often find it cheaper and more convenient to travel by rail. Students and passengers between 12 and 25 qualify for 25 percent discounts on certain Alitalia flights, and there are 30 percent reductions on some night flights, as well as 50 percent savings for family groups.

Train *(Treno)*

🚆 Italian State Railways, known as Trenitalia (www.trenitalia.it), but often referred to by its old name, Ferrovie dello Stato, or FS, provides an efficient range of services. Regionale or Inter-Regionali, Diretto and Espresso trains are slow for long journeys; InterCity, or InterCity Plus trains, which do not make stops at each station *(stazione)*, cost more but are faster; the Eurostar is the fastest and most expensive. One-way *(andata)* or round-trip *(andata e ritorno)* tickets *(biglietti)* are available in first *(prima)* or second *(seconda)* class. Fares, calculated on a kilometer basis, are some of the cheapest in Europe. Three-day, round-trip tickets are discounted 15 percent on distances up to 250 kilometers (155 miles) or 50 kilometers (31 miles) for a 1-day, round-trip ticket. Tickets are valid for 1 day from the day of issue for distances up to 250 kilometers (155 miles), plus an extra day of validity for each additional 200 kilometres (124 miles) up to a maximum of 6 days. The validity period takes effect from the moment you punch your ticket on the platform machines. Fines can be severe if you fail to validate (punch) your ticket. Tickets must be used within 2 months of purchase. Stations usually have separate ticket windows for reservations and sleepers *(cucetta)*. Reservations are worth considering for long trips in summer, when trains can be crowded. Trenitalia offers a wide range of reduced-price passes for both single and family travelers, offering savings of up to 50 percent. Log on to the Offers and Deals section in the English-language version of the website for more details; offers may vary from time to time. Tickets are available through the Trenitalia website (www.trenitalia.com) but some services cannot be booked more than seven days in advance.

Bus *(Autobus)*

🚍 There is no national bus company, but major cities have their own company for short-, medium- and some long-distance bus travel. International Eurolines run from the main Italian cities; ☎ 0861 199 1900 in Italy or 0039 0861 199 1900 from abroad; www.eurolines.it. Ask about

services at tourist offices or visit the local bus terminal *(autostazione)*. Tickets must usually be bought beforehand from *tabacchi* (tobacconists) or the bus terminal.

Ferry *(Traghetto)*

⛴ Genoa and Naples are the main Mediterranean ports, with regular service to Sicily and Sardinia. Naples also has a ferry to Capri and other islands.

Many services are reduced off-season, and some are cut. Car ferry bookings for summer travel to Sardinia and Elba should be made several months in advance.

Electricity

🔌 Italy has a 220-volt power supply (in some areas, 125 volts). Electrical sockets take plugs with two round pins, or sometimes three pins in a vertical row. American appliances will need a plug adapter and will require a transformer if they do not have a dual-voltage facility.

Photography

📷 Batteries and film can be easily purchased more or less anywhere. Memory chips for digital cameras, however, may be more difficult to come by, so it's advisable to make sure that you have adequate supplies before leaving home. If you don't have a digital camera, there are developing and printing facilities in most large towns, but these are generally expensive. It is safe to put your equipment or camera through security devices at the airport, but it's best carried in your hand luggage.

Media

⬤ Italy's national newspapers *(giornali)* include the authoritative Milan-based *Corriere della Sera*, the Turin-based *La Stampa* and the Rome-based *La Repubblica*.

The biggest-selling papers are sports papers. In larger cities, American newspapers (usually previous-day editions) and magazines are available; the most common are *USA Today*, the international edition of the *New York Times* and *Time* magazine. They can be purchased at airports and central train stations, as well as at newsstands and tobacconists.

Italian radio and television are deregulated and offer a vast range of national and local stations. Standards are low, with local networks geared mainly to advertising, pop music and old films. National stations are better, dividing equally between the three channels of the state RAI network and those founded by Silvio Berlusconi (Canale 5, Rete 4 and Italia Uno). On the radio you can pick up Voice of America, Radio Canada or BBC broadcasts, and larger hotels often have satellite or cable connections that broadcast BBC channels, the British Sky network or CNN.

Driving Regulations

Drive on the Right

 Driving is on the right, and you should yield at intersections to vehicles approaching from your right.

Seat Belts

 Must be worn in front seats at all times and in the rear seats where fitted.

Minimum Age

 The minimum age for driving a car in Italy is 18 (may be higher for some car rental firms).

Blood Alcohol

The legal blood alcohol limit is 0.05%. Random breath tests are carried out frequently, especially late at night.

Tolls

You will be issued a ticket on entering nearly every limited-access highway *(autostrada):* pay on leaving. You can buy prepaid cards at tollbooths, service areas, tourist offices or tobacco shops.

Additional Information

An International Driving Permit (IDP) is recommended when driving in Italy. It is a document containing your photograph and confirming that you hold a valid driver's license in your own country. It has a standard translation in several languages and is a useful document to carry; it can speed up formalities if you are involved in an accident.

A Green Card is advised if you are driving a private vehicle overseas to prove that you have liability insurance. For additional information contact your automobile insurer.

Dimmed headlights are required by law when driving even during the day.

Speed Limits

Regulations

Police can demand up to a quarter of an imposed fine to be paid on the spot.

 Limited-access highways *(autostrada)* 130 k.p.h. (80 m.p.h.)

 Main roads 90–110 k.p.h. (56–68 m.p.h.)

 Urban areas 50 k.p.h. (31 m.p.h.)

Car Rental

The leading rental firms have offices at airports, railroad stations and ferry terminals. Hertz offers discounted rates for AAA members. For reservations:

United States	Italy
Avis (800) 331 1212	199 100133
Budget (800) 527 0700	Book online in Italy
Hertz (800) 654 8226	Book online in Italy

To rent a car you will need a valid U.S. driver's license and preferably an International Driving Permit, and you will probably be asked to show your passport. You may be asked for an additional credit card or further proof of identity for renting premium or luxury cars. Most car rental companies will not rent to an individual under 21. If you intend to drive across national borders tell the company, as this will affect both the rate and the type of insurance documentation required. European cars are generally small and have manual transmissions, although most offer air-conditioning. Rates vary, but a AAA travel agent should be able to give an accurate estimate. Be sure to inquire about local taxes and find out what insurance coverage is included, and check whether you need a collision damage waiver. AAA Travel Agencies can reserve a car for you before you leave, provide payment arrangements, or reserve a car for you for specified dates and destinations. Rates are lower if reservations are made in the United States prior to departure, and guaranteed in U.S. dollars if you pay in advance.

Fuel

Gas in Italy is among the most expensive in Europe. It is unleaded *(senza piombo)* and sold in liters. Diesel *(gasolio)* is cheaper. Outside urban areas, stations are open daily 7–12:30 and 3–7:30. Gas stations on highways are open 24 hours. Credit cards are not widely accepted away from highways. Self-service and 24-hour pumps are becoming increasingly common.

Parking

Parking is often difficult in towns: Parking lots *(parcheggi)* are invariably full, and most historic centers are partially or fully closed to traffic. Check the signs in the vicinity of your car: Make certain there are no restrictions, that you pay for and display a parking sticker if necessary, and check closing times if you use a multistory parking garage. Cars may be towed if illegally parked; contact the local offices of the Vigili Urbani to reclaim your vehicle.

AAA

 **AAA Affiliated
Motoring Club**

Automobile Club D'Italia (ACI)
Via Marsala 8, 00185 Rome; www.aci.it
☎ 803 116 (24-hour emegency help line). If
you break down while driving, phone 116 or
800 000116 from a fixed phone (towing service).
Not all automobile clubs offer full services to
AAA members.

Breakdowns/Accidents

There are emergency phones at regular
intervals on all highways. If you are
involved in an accident, ☎ 118 for emergency
medical help, 112 or 113 for police help.
 Most car rental firms provide their own free
rescue service; if your car is rented, follow the
instructions given in the documentation.
 Use of a car repair service other than those
authorized by the rental company may violate
your rental agreement.

Road Signs

Driving in busy Italian cities can be a daunting pros-
pect if you're not used to the signs, driving habits
and local regulations. If you are renting a car, be
sure to get as much information from the rental
company as possible. They will usually provide a
chart of common road signs and an area road map.
Most road signs in Italy conform to the usual international standards; below is a glossary of terms that
may not be familiar to the foreign traveler:

entrada	entrance
incrocio	crossroads
lavori in corso	roadwork ahead
passaggio a livello	level crossing
rallentare	slow down
senso vietato	no entry
sosta vietata	no parking
svolta	curve
uscita	exit

Vehicles may pass
either side to reach
same destination

Ahead only

No entry for
vehicular traffic

No passing

Keep right

Steep hill

Traffic merges
from right

Double bend, first
to the right

Crossroads

Diverted highway ends

Other danger

Speech

Italian pronunciation is consistent with spelling, and vowels are always pronounced. The letter h is always silent, but can modify the sound of letters c and g. As a general rule, accentuate the next-to-last syllable.

c is hard before a, o, u, h   medico; Chianti
c is soft before i or e   ciao [chow]
g is hard before a, o, u, h
  Gucci, Lamborghini
g is soft before i or e   gelati [jel-ah-tee]
gl as in Amelia   figlia [fee-lyah]
gn as in union   gnocchi [nyee-ok-kee]
sc before i or e is soft   prosciutto
                                [pro-shoot-toh]
Where two consonants appear together, each belongs to a different syllable.

Airport

airport	*aeroporto*
airplane	*aeroplano*
arrivals	*arrivi*
departures	*partenze*
check-in	*accettazione*
information	*informazione*
ticket	*biglietto*
flight	*volo*
baggage	*bagagli*
passport	*passaporto*
window seat	*vicino al finestrino*
first class	*prima classe*
economy class	*classe turistica*
international	*internazionale*

Meeting People

good morning	*buon giorno*
excuse me	*scusi*
do you speak English?	*parla inglese?*
yes, no	*sì/no*
sorry	*scusami*
please	*per favore*
thank you	*grazie*
you're welcome	*prego*
I am American	*sono Americano/-a*
my name is…	*mi chiamo…*
I don't understand	*non capisco*
pleased to meet you	*piacevole per incontrilo*
how are you?	*com'è va*
okay	*va bene*
goodbye	*arrivederci*
goodnight	*buona notte*
see you later	*a presto*
have a good trip	*buon viaggio*

Hotel

the hotel	*l'albergo*
I have a reservation	*ho una prenotazione*
a room	*camera*
for one/ two nights	*per una/ due notte/-i*
one/ two people	*una/ due persone*
how much does it cost?	*quanto costa?*
key	*una chiave*
shower	*una doccia*
with in-room bathroom	*con bagno*
room service	*il servizio in camera*
porter	*il facchino*

Eating Out

a table for two	*un tavolo per due*
we've reserved	*abbiamo prenotato*
could we see the menu?	*ci porta il menù*
fixed-price menu	*il menù a prezzo fisso*
first course	*l'antipasto*
main course	*il secondo*
cheese	*formaggio*
dessert	*il dolci*
waiter/ waitress	*cameriere/ cameriera*
wine	*il vino*
mineral water	*acqua minerale*
what's this? (on menu)	*cosa è questo?*
I am a vegetarian	*sono vegetariano/a*
bread	*il pane*
beef	*il manzo*
chicken	*il pollo*
ham	*prosciutto*
lamb	*l'agnello*
pork	*il maiale*
seafood	*i frutti di mare*
mussels	*le cozze*
fish	*il pesce*
eggs	*uove*
salad	*insalata*
vegetables	*verdure*
soup	*minestra*
liqueur	*digestivo*
coffee	*il caffè*
hot	*caldo*
cold	*freddo*
good	*buono*
bad	*non è buono*
restroom	*bagno/toiletta*
the check	*il conto*

Directions

where is...?	*dov'è?*
turn left/right	*a sinistra/destra*
straight ahead	*sempre diritto*
how far is it?	*quanto è distante?*
near here	*qui vicino*
far	*lontano*
facing	*di fronte a*
opposite/in front of	*davanti a*
behind	*(in) dietro*

Post Office

post office	*l'ufficio postale*
stamp	*francobollo*
airmail	*posta aerea*
letter	*lettera*
postcard	*cartolina*
package	*pacchetto*
registered letter	*lettera raccomandata*
mailbox	*bucca delle lettere*
address	*indirizzo*

Telephone Calls

phone booth	*telefono pubblico*
phone card	*scheda telefonica*
operator	*il/la centralinista*
international access code	*il prefisso internazionale*
my number is...	*il mio numero è...*

Shopping

baker	*panificio*
delicatessen	*salumeria*
fish merchant	*pescheria*
market	*mercato*
grocery store	*supermercato*
bookstore	*la libreria*
fruit and vegetable	*frutta e verdura*
butcher	*macelleria*
do you have?	*avete?*
how much?	*quanto costa?*
store assistant	*commessa/o*

Pharmacy

pharmacy/a	*farmacia*
diarrhea tablets	*astringente*
bandage	*fascia*
tampons	*i tamponi*
razor blades	*le lamette*
suntan lotion	*olio solare*
aspirin	*aspirina*

Emergencies

police	*la polizia*
ambulance	*un' ambulanza*
fire department	*i pompieri*
doctor	*un medico*
accident	*incidente (m)*
first aid	*pronto soccorso*
where is the nearest hospital?	*dov'è l'ospedale più vicino?*
emergency number	*numero d'emergenza*
stop thief!	*al ladro!*
help!	*aiuto!*

Transportation

railroad station	*stazione*
subway	*metropolitana*
train	*treno*
platform	*binario*
ticket	*biglietto*
single or two-way	*andata o andata e ritorno*
bus station	*la stazione degli autobus*
bus	*autobus*
bus stop	*fermata dell'autobus*
timetable	*orario*
non-smoking	*vietato fumare*
taxi	*il taxi*

Money

credit card	*carta di credito*
traveler's checks	*assegni turistici*
exchange rate	*il cambio*
bank	*banca*

Numbers

1, 2, 3	*uno, due, tre*
4, 5, 6	*quattro, cinque, sei*
7, 8, 9	*sette, otto, nove*
10, 11, 12	*dieci, undici, dodici*
13, 14	*tredici, quattordici*
15, 16	*quindici, sedici*
17, 18	*diciassette, diciotto*
19, 20	*diciannove, venti*
30, 40	*trenta, quaranta*
50, 60	*cinquanta, sessanta*
70, 80	*settanta, ottanta*
90, 100	*novanta, cento*
500	*cinquecento*
1000	*mille*

Acknowledgments

The Automobile Association wishes to thank the following photographers and organisations for their assistance in the preparation of this book.
Abbreviations for the picture credits are as follows: (t) top; (b) bottom; (l) left; (r) right; (c) center; (AA) AA World Travel Library.

3 AA/C Sawyer; 4/5 AA/N Setchfield; 6 AA/N Setchfield; 8/9 AA/A Mockford & N Bonetti; 9 Ashley Cooper/Alamy; 10 AA/T Souter; 11 AA/J Tims; 12/13 AA/N Setchfield; 15t AA/J Tims; 14/15b AA/C Sawyer; 16/17 Terry Smith Images/ Alamy; 18/19 AA/A Mockford & N Bonetti; 19 AA/A Mockford & N Bonetti; 20 AA/A Mockford & N Bonetti; 23 AA/A Kouprianoff; 24 AA/J Tims; 26 AA/A Mockford & N Bonetti; 30 AA/A Mockford & N Bonetti; 31 AA/K Paterson; 34 AA/C Sawyer; 36 AA/C Sawyer; 37 AA/C Sawyer; 38 AA/A Mockford & N Bonetti; 39 AA/C Sawyer; 40 AA/C Sawyer; 42/43 AA/T Souter; 44 Jon Arnold Pictures/Alamy; 45 AA/A Mockford & N Bonetti; 47 AA/A Mockford & N Bonetti; 48/49 AA/A Mockford & N Bonetti; 51 AA/T Souter; 52 AA/T Souter; 53 AA/T Souter; 54 Bon Appetit/Alamy; 55 AA/T Souter; 56 AA/A Mockford & N Bonetti; 59 Beren Patterson/Alamy; 60/61 Dennis Hallinan/Alamy; 65 AA/A Mockford & N Bonetti; 66 AA/A Mockford & N Bonetti; 67 AA/A Mockford & N Bonetti; 69 AA/S McBride; 70 AA/A Mockford & N Bonetti; 71 AA/C Sawyer; 72 mauritius images GmbH/Alamy; 73 Hackenberg-Photo-Cologne/ Alamy; 75 Cubolmages srl/Alamy; 76 imagebroker/Alamy; 78 AA/A Mockford & N Bonetti; 81 Ian Dagnall/Alamy; 82 AA/J Tims; 84 AA/J Tims; 86/87 AA/C Sawyer; 87 AA/J Tims; 88 AA/J Tims; 91 AA/J Tims; 93 AA/J Tims; 94/95 AA/J Tims; 96/97 Keystone/Getty Images; 98 AA/J Tims; 100 AA/J Tims; 102/103 AA/J Tims; 104 AA/J Tims; 107 AA/J Tims; 108 AA/J Tims; 109 AA/J Tims; 110 AA/J Tims; 113 AA/T Souter; 115 Simeone Huber/Stone/Getty Images; 117 AA/J Tims; 118 AA/A Mockford & N Bonetti; 121 AA/P Wilson; 122/123 AA/A Mockford & N Bonetti; 123 AA/A Kouprianoff; 126 AA/A Mockford & N Bonetti; 127 AA/A Mockford & N Bonetti; 129 AA/A Mockford & N Bonetti; 131 AA/A Mockford & N Bonetti; 133 AA/A Mockford & N Bonetti; 134 AA/A Mockford & N Bonetti; 135 AA/A Mockford & N Bonetti; 136 AA/C Sawyer; 137 Taplight/Alamy; 138 AA/C Sawyer; 140 AA/A Mockford & N Bonetti; 141 AA/A Mockford & N Bonetti; 143 AA/A Mockford & N Bonetti; 144 AA/M Jourdan; 148/149 AA/M Jourdan; 153 AA/M Jourdan; 154 AA/M Jourdan; 155 AA/M Jourdan; 156 LOOK Die Bildagentur der Fotografen GmbH/ Alamy; 156/157 Stock Italia/Alamy; 158 AA/C Sawyer; 160 AA/C Sawyer; 162 Cubolmages srl/Alamy; 163 AA/C Sawyer; 165 AA/A Mockford & N Bonetti; 166 Imagestate Media Partners Limited - Impact Photos/Alamy; 167 AA/N Setchfield; 168 AA/N Setchfield; 172 AA/N Setchfield; 173 AA/M Jourdan; 176 AA/N Setchfield; 178 AA/C Sawyer; 179 AA/C Sawyer; 180 AA/N Setchfield; 182 AA/M Jourdan; 185 AA/N Setchfield; 186 AA/N Setchfield; 188 AA/N Setchfield; 189 Slim Aarons/Getty Images; 190 AA/C Sawyer; 191 AA/N Setchfield; 192 AA/C Sawyer; 193 AA/C Sawyer; 195 AA/C Sawyer; 196 AA/J Tims; 198 AA/J Tims; 214 Central Intelligence Agency; 215t AA/J Holmes; 215c AA/A Mockford & N Bonetti; 216 AA/C Sawyer.

Every effort has been made to trace the copyright holders, and we apologize in advance for any unintentional omissions or errors. We would be pleased to apply any corrections in a following edition of this publication.